Women of Sand and Myrrh

Women of Sand and Myrrh

Women of Sand and Myrrh

Hanan al-Shaykh

Translated by Catherine Cobham

Quartet Books

First published in English by Quartet Books Limited 1989
A member of a Namara Group
27/29 Goodge Street, London W1P 1FD

Paperback edition 1993

British Library Cataloguing in Publication Data
Al-Shaykh, Hanan, *1945*–
    Women of sand and myrrh.
    1. Title
    892′.736[F]
    ISBN 0-7043-2736-8 (cased)
          0-7043-0187-3 (paperback)

Typeset by MC Typeset Ltd, Gillingham, Kent
Printed and bound in Great Britain by
BPCC Hazell Books
Member of BPCC Ltd

Suha

1

I dropped on to the couch and the canary landed on my shoulder, chirping. I pushed him off: 'Leave me alone . . . not now!'

I looked at the pale curtains the colour of apricots, and at the glass tops of the little tables, and at the water-colours on the walls, and wished I could stay in this house all the time, just me and the canary. Everything in my house was soothing to look at, not like the furniture in the Institute or any of the other houses I went into, and such a change from the dusty streets, the colourless buildings, and the sand strewn with ruins.

When the men had come in I had been sitting in the rest-room, drinking the lemonade that I'd brought from home in a little thermos flask. I froze, then began to tremble. One of them said to me, 'Cover yourself up, woman.'

I saw a towel flying through the air towards me. I don't know who threw it, but I put it around my shoulders, looking down and seeing only the men's sandals and mules and long tobacco-stained nails. I didn't breathe again until I heard the sound of their receding footsteps as they vanished in response to the principal's protests from the next room; her voice raised in anger, she accused them of trespassing in an area reserved for women: 'Can't you read? This is an Institute of Learning and the notice on the door says "Entry forbidden to men".'

I had hoped that going to the Institute would be an escape for me, and perhaps a way of avoiding the anguish and fear which I'd suffered in the past year when I was working in the department store.

Every day there I used to hide in a big brown cardboard box, wondering whether the security man would suspect anything. I pictured to myself how the box looked from the outside, inscribed with the words 'FRAGILE – WITH CARE' and a picture of a glass tumbler. If ever I caught a faint whiff of my perfume I used to feel scared in case the man was blessed with an extraordinarily powerful sense of smell.

The fear that he would catch me was so intense that all other sensations – the sweat pouring from me like a sudden cold shower, the box's distinctive strong smell – were meaningless in comparison. When I had been concealed in the box for some time and could no longer hear the sound of footsteps I calmed down a little and found myself laughing in disbelief. I was hiding because I was a woman and I was working, and yet out in the world there were big cities and space stations; in a clean white room the product of a man's solitary ejaculation could be discharged into an infertile woman and you could see the foetus inside the mother's womb on television; there were concert-halls, applauding audiences, laughter, weeping, crowds of people moving around, hurricanes, schools, nightclubs, hermits in caves . . . I tried to stop working, but I couldn't: to go into the vast store with its white walls, and to see the coloured candles, the batteries, the greetings cards, the blue writing-paper, the aprons and towels with flowers and mushrooms on them, the children's toys, and the ballpoint pens with their sharp new smell, was to be reminded of the comforting trivia of a normal existence. Even the freezers on the far side of the store – white and clean and big, packed with soft drinks and ice-cream in cartons decorated with pictures of mangoes and strawberries, and the portions of frozen meat with veins running through them – looked beautiful to me, and I preferred it all to staying at home or going to visit the other women I knew. When the store's owner, Amer, began to entrust me with correspondence and making out orders, my feeling of importance knew no bounds; before that my work had been confined to arranging toys and displays of household goods on the second floor.

My job divided the day in two. It was as if I began again at four in the afternoon when I'd had lunch with my husband and my son Umar, who came home from school at two o'clock. I had ten minutes' sleep and then got up to help Umar with his Arabic before he went to Sitt Wafa for a private lesson.

In the beginning I was amazed that Amer's foreign wife should offer me this job, and then that I could be satisfied with it. I had a degree in Management Studies from the American University of Beirut, but nobody else had wanted to employ me. They were all scared of the law, the raids and reprisals. Even my husband had wriggled out of his promise to find me a job once he realized what things were like in this country. I kept on hiding in the box until the day I heard the sound of footsteps and then something which I took to be a hand or foot knocking against it. I held my breath, and found that I was praying for help and shaking all over, and I swore to myself there and then that if I got out of that box without being caught and made a fool of I'd give up the job.

On my first day at home after leaving the store I decided not to hang around the house for long. I didn't want to give myself the chance to be discontented and miserable like the time before. Even then I'd desperately resisted the torpor that enveloped this place, resisted being sucked down by the swamp whose waters never grew deeper but never completely dried up. Like the other women, I'd thrown myself into the life here so that I wouldn't feel sorry for myself. I'd given up following the news, local or international, and occupied myself with cake recipes, and with finding friends for Umar, and taking him to see a little ape although I knew it had bitten its owner ... I'd congratulated myself when I'd prepared dinner for five businessmen in an hour, or entertained Umar's friends with a puppet theatre I'd made myself, hammering in the nails and sewing and hanging the curtains. I'd sent for the puppets from Lebanon, and when they'd arrived I'd been more delighted with them than my son and his friends. But when the children's mothers had come and

...round unenthusiastically and not even applauded my attempts, I'd felt a great resentment towards them and kept back the sweetmeats that I'd made for them.

Should I go and see Suzanne, Maryam, Umm Kairouz? Suzanne, Hind, Reem, Stephanie, Laila? Suzanne, Umm Kairouz, Tahani? Suzanne, Amal or Maryam? Suzanne? Shahnaz? Khulud, Raja, Dalal, or Sabah? Suzanne? When I'd put Suzanne out of my mind, I pictured the other women's houses and imagined the sounds of their voices, and knew exactly what lay in wait for me.

Sabah: an analysis of marital relationships, her self-respect, the children. Shahnaz: the house and the furniture, the house and the furniture, her very, very successful son and her daughter who was only moderately successful, which of course was the teacher's fault. Raja: the best method of self-defence was black pepper which she put on a plate near the bed each time her husband went away. Then if somebody tried to rape her she'd throw the plate at him. Stephanie: it was the chance of a lifetime being here in the desert and there was no time to get depressed. She imported everything from her home country, Sweden, and sold it here. She pricked out seedlings and planted them in pots and when they grew into blossoming branches she sold them. She cut hair and coloured it, made clothes, baked pastries, all for a price. She'd roll up the banknotes in an aluminium container and put them in her fridge. Maryam: elegance, regardless of the surroundings. Leather boots in the heat of the desert. What annoyed her was the censors who spilt their black ink all over the pages of the magazines she read, and actually tore some of them out. Exercises to keep slim. The best way of exercising the stomach is to hold in your pee for as long as you can. Umm Kairouz: 'O Lord, may the ones who drove us out be driven out themselves one day. God damn the lot of them! Lebanon, Lebanon! Poor, poor Lebanon! Yesterday they were fighting again, but it's quiet today. I'm ready to go back, bombs and all. It's better than this hole.' Reem in the daytime: 'The housework doesn't leave me a minute to relax. That's what it's like with children to look after.' Reem at night, laughing: 'I can't change the way I laugh – my husband tells me off about it. When I asked a friend of his if his moustache was false he said, "See for yourself". I pulled it and it was real. He said, "So, don't I get a kiss? " and I said, "Why not? " and laughed.'

Tahani: 'I don't know! The telephone rings every second. And there's invitations to tea and coffee, starting from the early morning. Nothing but drinking, eating, telling silly stories, seeing who's got the nicest clothes. Even when we're playing ladies' bridge they come wearing rings with diamonds as big as eggs. For God's sake, aren't we meant to be modern women? We're educated, university graduates, but what can we do here? We're not allowed to work, not allowed to drive cars. There are no places to go on outings. Tell me what you want to drink. Tea, coffee, mint tea? Try these Umm Alis . . . You've never tasted them? God, is there really someone who doesn't know Umm Alis . . . See, you have the sheets of filo pastry ready, and the fruit and . . . Did you know the sheikha had a big dinner party and invited Ibtisam and Manal and they were sitting there and some woman said to them that the sheikha was having the party because her son the sheikh wanted to get married and it was a way of having a look at the likely candidates? And another woman said there's probably a camera hidden behind the curtains. Ibtisam and Manal kept on looking at the curtains until their eyes almost popped out. And afterwards the sheikha said to them that the curtains were made by Valentino. Can you imagine, Valentino makes their curtains for them!'

I got to know them the first year I arrived. Like every woman coming here I felt that this was time lost out of my life. I began to make friends with anyone just for something

... was living in a compound. The rooms were small and dark. The bathroom was like a bathroom in a cheap hotel. But the house was passable, compared to the grubby houses and twisting alleys and few primitive shops in the street where I'd lived before. I tried to make it look prettier. I changed the heavy gloomy curtains for lighter ones and threw the family's coloured sheets, which I'd packed with my clothes, over the couches. On the walls I stuck pictures of Swiss chalets and lakes. Umar was staying with my mother in Beirut until I'd finished getting the house ready.

I knew that life here was odd when I found that I had no garlic for my cooking and I couldn't go out to the shops and buy some. So I opened the door and stood on the step, looking about me at the other wooden houses painted white, the sparse trees, the water storage tanks, the sun burning down on the asphalt, and it made me imagine that I was somewhere in space. The houses stood at a distance from each other, the doors were closed, the air-conditioners hummed. Only when I could go in the car with my husband did I feel happy to leave the house. However hard I tried to buy everything I needed, I always forgot many things and the display on the shelves didn't help me. All the goods were mixed together: egg whisks, rolls of material, vegetables side by side with bars of soap, Arabic grammar books, bread, pocket knives and silver Maria Theresa dollars.

I found out that the inhabitants of the compound were Arabs and foreigners mixed. But I hadn't the courage to knock at their doors, perhaps because I had heard the adults swearing and the children shouting. I knew their quarrels by heart, even though their television sets were turned up so loud, and I knew the children's names, the mothers' feeble protests and the fathers' furious oaths.

It was only a matter of a few days before the women thronged to my house, reproaching me for not knocking on their doors. The one called Umm Kairouz said, 'Are you an angel or something? Is that why we didn't even know you

were here?' And another, downcast at her own lack of intelligence, commented, 'It's funny. I heard the toilet flushing and
thought it was working by itself, and I heard wood creaking
and said to my husband, "Stop eating. Every time you move
there's a creaking noise." '

I felt disillusioned: this wasn't the desert that I'd seen from
the aircraft, nor the one I'd read about or imagined to myself;
there was sand and wind but no old houses. I didn't want to
pass judgement on it from the few short weeks that I'd spent
in my wooden house and my neighbours' wooden houses.
But the first impression is the most important, because your
eye grows accustomed to its surroundings and no longer
connects with the mind and the heart in its responses.
Everyday-life existed in the desert, but it was the daily routine
of housewives and didn't go beyond the smell of coriander,
the neighbour who only half-opened her door because she
had wax on her thighs, fortune-telling in coffee grounds, food
on the stove, and gossip and knitting and babies' nappies. I
always felt that I was different from my neighbours, but still I
took comfort from their presence around me.

My husband, meanwhile, had gone further afield and
begun to discover what lay beyond our street and on the
other side of the shops and buildings we could see from our
house: he'd seen houses with good big rooms, and even
gardens, although these were made of gravel and sand. He
asked to be transferred to another house, and to my astonishment his request was granted. I rushed to tell my neighbours,
wanting to bring some joy to their hearts with the news that
there was to be a house they could visit outside the compound, for they talked at length about the difficulty of travelling outside the neighbourhood, and discussed the possibi-
lity of all the families sharing in the cost of a car and hiring a
driver so that they could visit the devils, as Umm Ghassan
put it. But instead of being glad at the news of my move they
showed signs of resentment. They all began to complain
about the companies that their husbands worked for and the

directors' wives with their houses and servants and drivers and strings of pearls. Their voices rose and they reminded me of women in a bathhouse when the water supply is cut off, and they sit around still covered in lather, noisily gossiping and arguing. One of them said antagonistically to me, 'You've been here two months and we've all been here for three years,' and added that there must be scorpions and snakes and big rats living in their hundreds underneath all these wooden houses raised up off the ground, and that every day she heard tapping and hissing. They began to vie with one another in telling stories about rats: one said a rat had dragged a chicken right out of the oven, and as they were all gasping in horror, Umm Ghassan interrupted, 'A kilo of meat disappeared from off my table when I went to open to door. They must have been watching me.'

At this Muna seized hold of her son and turned him upside down, inspecting his plump white foot. Then she said, as if reporting back to us, 'There *are* scorpions here. Perhaps it was a scorpion sting he had. I don't know which day it was he screamed and I lifted him out of his bed and he began to swell up. He was blue in the face, then his whole body turned as red as a pomegranate seed.'

They got up to go, and I looked at their empty coffee cups on the table. For a moment I felt a faint sadness, then I started to put all that had accumulated around me during these two months into boxes. When I finally sat down the house looked just as it had done when I entered it for the first time – the thick curtains, the line of dust shimmering in the bright air, the couches coarse to the touch. I couldn't help feeling sorry for my neighbours because they were staying on in these houses. I supposed that I would invite them to visit me in the new house, but as it turned out I never saw them again from that morning onwards, or even caught sight of them at a distance. I used to turn and look the other way every time I passed the compound. The sight of the yellow wooden roofs and walls and the dusty oleander plants reminded me of myself when I lived in there among those god—forsaken helpless women.

On the other hand, the thought that living in this country was only a temporary phase prevented me from feeling the same firmness of purpose as Sitt Wafa did towards her home: she planted basil and radishes and kept hens and a rooster in a coop that she built for them; the rooster had developed a nasty nature and when Sitt Wafa ran after him with a broom he turned round and chased her in turn. An odour of permanence emanated from her home and I saw jars of jam, dried yoghurt, thyme and cracked wheat stacked in the kitchen. I used to love going into her house and drinking mulberry juice, and made the excuse that I was coming with Umar to ask her about him so that I could see the children gathered around her while she instructed them one by one, or gave them dictation while shelling peas and shredding beans. The children loved her, although she shouted and pulled the ears of those who made mistakes, and called them 'Sir' and 'Madam' and continually threatened to take them off to the sheikh's school under the trees. They laughed at this because they'd seen the open-air school and the old man with his stick.

My life seemed to change after I moved to the new house. I no longer felt time stagnating as I had in the compound. I began to amuse myself making curtains and cushions, hanging pictures, tidying cupboards. I borrowed books about gardens and dug the garden and planted seeds, waiting from one day to the next for the green shoots to appear. I invited women to visit me, proud of my beautiful house, and offered them cake and tea in cups that matched the curtains. I decided to make my stay here useful, and joined an exercise class at Maryam's house, three times a week for an hour, another class for baking and decorating cakes, and a literary discussion group. I even became a pupil of Stephanie's learning embroidery and patchwork, and would have taken classes to learn how to arrange artificial flowers if the time had allowed. However I knew deep inside me that the way I was handling my life was doomed to failure; I was scared of the enormous disgust that I felt because I was leading such a sterile, unnatural existence, and to counter this I began to defend the way of life here, as a means of instilling into my mind what it ought to be thinking. In my discussions with women who hated it here, both Arabs and foreigners, I used to struggle to find objections to their arguments and take the discussions to absurd and trivial limits: I told them that the situation here was ideal in a way, and that they were lucky because they were seeing how cities were built, and witnessing the transformation of man from a bedouin into a city-dweller. This was a great opportunity for them, I added: nothing was laid on for them as it was in other countries, and they would have to fight for what they really wanted. Despite what I said, I myself thought that time was wasted in searching for and constructing what existed and was recognized as normal or obvious anywhere else in the world.

Things didn't progress as I'd convinced myself they would when I was forcing myself to attend classes. When the women at the exercise classes with me began to look like birds and animals, and when at the cake-decorating class I became involved in a vengeful struggle with the lid of the confectioner's cream instead of directing my energies to creating a rose on a cake, or when I began to drink coffee and eat biscuits instead of discussing books, and spent an age trying to make the thread go into the eye of the needle, or even just searching for the needle, I gave it all up and stayed at home. At this point, like most of the women here, I began to think in earnest about how fed up I was, how miserable I was, and how much I'd like to go away somewhere. The only solution was to get out of the house again, this time to work in the store.

I handled the paperwork, writing letters and demands and putting prices on everything. I used to flick through the shiny illustrated catalogues of goods and foodstuffs choosing what-ever took my fancy. When the things arrived I rushed to the crates, excitedly comparing the real thing with the picture I had of it and feeling that I had a link with the outside world as I turned a glass or a packet over in my hands. In spite of my knowledge and my zeal for my work, I made mistakes and these mistakes led to Amer's goods being censored by the port officials. They set fire to his crates to get rid of the pâté de foie gras which I'd ordered without noticing that pork fat was listed among its ingredients; I ordered games without realizing that they contained playing cards, and bay leaves and dried radishes and rosemary not knowing that they'd arrived saying on their packets that they added a delicious aroma and flavour to beef and chicken and pork. Amer had to make his employees cross out the word 'pork' on a thou-sand packets with their black pens. Although I grew more accurate with my orders there were still some boxes that had to be burnt.

The psychological tension that began to hang over the place became a bigger problem than hiding in the cardboard box. Amer and his wife were both extremely edgy, and the day he handed me the notification from the customs authori-ties to read, he was smoking like a doomed man having his last cigarette. He'd lost thousands: the boxes from the United States had been confiscated and their contents destroyed; I asked excitedly if someone had smuggled whisky or obscene videos in them. The soft toys and dolls had all been des-troyed, every one that was meant to be a human being or animal or bird, since it was not permissible to produce distor-tions of God's creatures. Although I was sorry, I laughed, and imagined those men turning over Barbie dolls and Snoopies and Woodstocks in their big hands and picking up china birds and crystal ashtrays in the shape of cats and thinking hostile thoughts about them, while they stared silently back.

I remembered how keen I used to be to watch the 'Muppet Show', how I'd laughed at Kermit the Frog and Miss Piggy: it had never occurred to me that these creatures singing and bobbing about giving amusement and pleasure to their audience were no more than dumb puppets. That was why when Umar asked me one day if they got new ones when the old ones wore out I felt sad, because I'd pictured them being real in spite of the strings attached to their arms and legs. I thought of them piled on top of one another in a box or cupboard in the studio when they weren't being used, their eyes dead, mouths closed and bodies lifeless.

I didn't actually leave my job until one morning I came face to face with the security man in the doorway of the store-room, whereupon I rushed in past him, up the stairs and made for the offices to hand in my resignation.

This time I knew that I wasn't going to visit anyone. My desert experience had to be related to the place, not just the people: I determined to try and communicate with my surroundings.

Claiming that I wanted to help my husband Basem with a study he had to do for the bank, I asked the driver Said to take me around the town, street by street, starting with the airport. He puffed out his chest proudly, although he had no idea what I meant, and touching his headcloth deferentially he answered, 'At your service.' As soon as we'd left the airport I began to take things in, making believe that I'd just arrived from a faraway country, and had never seen the desert before except in pictures. But it wasn't the desert that I saw, and I found myself in the middle of what amounted to a vast building site.

Trucks were unloading or loading up. Huge drums stood with electricity cables and telephone cables coiled around them. A crane that looked big enough to move mountains and cities grumbled and creaked as it lifted its load. A cement mixer turned constantly. There was a string of lorries and a petrol tanker, the sort that people stop and stare at in the street because of its size. It was like a giant that had eaten a lot of people; each of its four compartments was bigger than a car, and its driver hovered in the sky as if he was about to make a parachute drop somewhere in the desert.

I watched the men putting up a hoarding in the sand advertising the opening of a new supermarket that would sell tens of thousands of different brands, and I marvelled at the way that, while old hoardings look as if they've been built along with the city surroundings, these new ones here looked as if they had appeared by magic.

Some of the streets had no names, but there were buildings in them where a few weeks before there had only been steel girders, and they had filled up rapidly with occupants coming to work on other building sites. Interspersed between the real palms were plastic ones and green-painted metal ones planted in tubs down the middle of the streets in an attempt to beautify the place, and ornamental paving stones laid edge to edge around them as if conducting a dialogue with one another. Tools and pieces of machinery lay abandoned where they had been for the past three years, and a black-and-white goat was jumping around on them. After only a few moments she bounded off on to the dusty ground to escape the burning metal.

Then Said took me to the seashore where there were huge water-purifying plants, some already completed and some still being built. A white bird poised on a wire and fluttered its wings. There was a man wearing a white headcloth, his white robe flying out in the breeze as he supervised work at one of the plants. In the distance on top of that enormous steel building he looked like Superman.

The markets were a hive of building activity: they were knocking down the old buildings whose walls were riddled with the effects of heat and damp, buildings with little orna-mental stonework or wooden latticework considered lacking in artistic value. In their place rose buildings full of air-conditioners, neon lighting and garish, over-ornate tiles. Everything was unattractive except the calligraphic design of the expression 'What God wills' which was adorning one wall in a contrasting colour.

A strange smell wafted into the car and small murky black clouds swirled around me at street level. A vehicle drove slowly along spraying the people and the empty air with germicide.

Asian workmen swarmed everywhere, on foot, in cars, and up the high ladders, the Yemenis in their skirts and loose jackets and platform shoes, stumbling at every step. Periodically the sand was sprayed with oil to immobilize it but it renewed its attack with fresh vigour over the cultivated parts of the desert and the asphalted roads, against windows, and against the few trees trying to bloom and the luxurious cars jostling for place with the lorries and trucks.

I was a little disconcerted: the feeling I'd started out with of losing my sensitivity to the life going on around me was growing stronger, as was my awareness of the complete absence of women, at least from the world outside. Most of the houses seemed to be devoted to men and their affairs with the signs announcing offices and companies for this and that, and the one house built of red brick with Spanish windows had a sign stuck in the middle of it saying, 'Adli. Attorney at Law'. None of the houses had balconies, and everything was enclosed by high walls.

I found myself asking Said to take me to see Ingrid. Although I felt tired and nauseous from driving round and round in the car, I wanted to be with other people and get warmth and energy from hearing them talk and watching them move, so that I could breathe freely again and get back into the rhythm of life here.

I chose Ingrid because of her garden. The plants in it reminded me of Beirut: the blanket of lilac, the sunflowers, and a third flower, orange with a strong perfume. And apart from that, I had a weakness for her delicious cakes.

'The American? ' asked Said, and he pointed to his head making a circle with his finger.

I answered, half-laughing, 'No. Ingrid's the German, the

one with the garden.'

'Ah, the skinny one! Poor thing.'

Said remembered the women I visited even if he didn't remember their names, and he assessed their characters through their ways of talking and behaving since he didn't know any foreign languages. He could say 'good morning' to all the women I visited, smiling delightedly at his achievement so that his gold teeth, and the gaps in between them, were plainly visible. The first time he asked how to say 'good morning' in English and American and found they were the same, he exclaimed in surprise, 'Praise the Lord! They're the same as each other inside and out!'

Said had been sitting in the Adeni restaurant where he worked, when one of the customers read out in his hearing an advertisement for an accountant in the bank where Basem was manager. Said asked him what an accountant had to do and the man answered him sarcastically, 'Count money.' Said went off to the bank and asked to see the manager. Despite his persistence they wouldn't let him go in. He waited at the door and when Basem came out he reached for the notes in his pocket and counted them in front of him in a flash as if he were a professional gambler, not just an ordinary Yemeni in his skirt and sandals. Then he returned the cash to his belt and adjusted his coloured headcloth. Basem asked him where he worked and he answered in an Adeni restaurant, spiking the meat on skewers and roasting it. Could he read? Could he write? Said contented himself with a smile. He was employed in the bank as a cleaner and teaboy. After a while he asked Basem to teach him how to drive, and Basem explained the principles to him three times. In a few weeks Said begged Basem to let him drive his car and surprised Basem with his proficiency. When Basem questioned him, Said told him that he'd begun to practise every day, making use of every car that stopped at the bank after convincing its driver that he'd take it off and park it in a shady spot. Those who weren't willing had changed their minds when Said pretended to cry in front of them, muttering something about not being fit to be trusted.

When I arrived at Ingrid's I was sorry I'd come. The note of lethargy was still there in Ingrid's conversation. By the end of every sentence she spoke you were ready to fall asleep. I sat drowsily in front of her, angry at myself for coming and wishing I could sleep with my eyes open.

She was telling me about the man she'd found creeping into her house while I thought about the pastries or the table whose delicious aroma wafted across to me, and about the sunflowers as big as moons. Then she recounted news of her parents: how her mother had to lean on her father to walk, how her father had slipped and brought the old lady down with him and how they'd both stayed on the floor till the next day.

I immediately regretted the strong urge I had to laugh as I pictured the scene. I tried to be serious and concentrate on what Ingrid was saying, but failed and rose to my feet, making excuses. When Ingrid said, 'That was a short visit. You didn't even taste my pastries,' I hesitated, but the expression on Ingrid's face and the vision of renewed boredom made me hurry to the door and not even pause to look at the garden. It was very hot, and when I was in the car I saw the sunflowers peeping over the wall.

I sat in the car looking about me, uncertain where to go. The fierce glare penetrated the windows and the car body in spite of the air-conditioner, and the humidity in the outside air came through to me. Depressed by the concrete gardens I saw, I looked back inside the car.

On an impulse I asked Said to take me to Suzanne's house. To confirm what I'd said he raised his hand once more to his head making a circle with his forefinger: 'The American, Auntie?' I forced a laugh and nodded yes. Said appeared not to notice my curt response as he said, 'It's been a long time since you visited her, Auntie.'

As the car approached the Pepsi Cola works and I saw the

bottles moving along automatically and stopping to be filled behind the factory windows, I remembered how enthusiastic I'd been about my first visit to Suzanne's, mainly because of the Pepsi factory.

When Suzanne's servant, Ringo, opened the door I knew that I'd made the right choice this time. All at once I was in a world that had not the slightest connection with the desert, except for the brass tray hanging on the wall and the little brass coffee jugs arranged on the table. I loved the gloom created by the thickness of the curtains, and I loved the romantic music, the smell of coffee and the smiling photographs of Suzanne positioned carefully here and there.

Suzanne rushed from the kitchen shrieking excitedly, clasped me to her and kissed me, reproaching me for not coming to see her sooner and making me turn round in a circle so that she could look at what I was wearing: 'It's beautiful. Oh, how beautiful you look!'

She began to tell me her news, so full of enthusiasm that she didn't finish one topic before launching into the next, and repeated old news that I already knew. Each time I asked her about something she said, 'Okay . . . ' beginning to answer, then switched to another subject. She reminded me of the letter to her lover, and I found myself smiling as I recalled the day I'd met her in the store. She'd been talking in Arabic, murdering the letter *tha*, sticking out her tongue and swallowing the words like a fish swallowing her young in the face of danger. Now, just as I had been the very first time, I was astonished to go into her house and see the servant Ringo doing her platinum blond hair like a professional hairdresser. When Ringo went to the kitchen to make tea he moved like a girl who knows she's got a beautiful body. He poured the tea into cups in front of me, raising his little finger delicately like a hostess at a tea party and stirring it till the sugar was melted.

On my first visit Suzanne had asked me to write a letter in her name to her lover, a local man named Maaz. The words she told me to put were naïve, sentimental, cheap. Reading between the lines I could guess the sort of relationship they had. When she asked me if I liked her style, I nodded hypocritically. Then she asked Ringo to bring the box of tape cassettes, and from among the cassettes of *The Adventures of Dimbo*, Sri Lankan singers and even one of Muhammad Abdo, she pulled out one with her name on it and asked me to listen to it. For a moment I thought she was joking, but the expression on her face and Ringo's told me I was wrong, and I felt more and more embarrassed as Suzanne's voice sighed and whispered and called out that her Arab lover's face was as beautiful as the moon.

I'd stopped caring about the Pepsi bottles in the factory window and found myself looking forward to my visits to her just to hear her passionate stories about Maaz. Whenever I'd felt my interest in her flagging, her outlandish reports of violent scenes and fake suicide attempts had drawn me back. I only broke off my visits when Amer banned her temporarily from the store because she'd been joking with a salesman. The noise she was making had attracted attention, she was wearing bright red lipstick, and although her dress was long it showed the curve of her belly and buttocks as she moved. However, I continued to defend her and told them that her only fault was that she was too good-hearted. I watched her now as she talked for maybe an hour, and felt sorry for her when she started to cry. She'd got fatter, and the roots of her hair showed darker than the rest. As usual she showed me the traces on her forehead left by the bottle that Maaz had thrown at her, and she didn't stop begging me to go and see Maaz and talk to him and ask him to come back. I was noncommittal, and when pushed refused even to consider it. For a moment I regretted coming back, because I was getting involved once again in her tortuous entanglements. I reminded myself that I was an Arab and should be careful, but I found myself promising to get Maaz back for her another way. Although she begged me to tell her how, I wasn't going to: I was scared of her runaway tongue and her excitability, and I just said I'd see her the next day.

2

Suzanne and I went into Sita's house; Sita cured sickness and healed wounds with herbs and cauterization, and made amulets and ground lead to ward off the evil eye. It didn't seem like two years since my first visit. Sita was just as she had been then in her beautiful dress, whose rich colours had long faded. Her skin was coarse and wrinkled from the desert sun, and from her constant grimacing as she held the irons in the fire's glow. Her small yellow teeth looked like a child's milk teeth. Her room was just the same too, the stuffed peacock on the table and on the wall the inscription which I'd never been able to remember: 'Sita the famous, whose fame has spread near and far, makes jinn lie down, kindles the fires of love, and trust in God comes first of all.' Even the rooster sketched above these words hadn't stuck in my mind.

I'd wanted to go back to Sita's house once more and amuse myself by reading what was written on the wall. Said was always talking about her and would praise her highly whenever I took Umar to the doctor. If he heard that someone Basem knew was ill he'd try to persuade me to take him to Sita, and he swore to me that she'd cured a madman by making him bury his head in the sand for an hour every day, used a vulture's stomach to heal a festering wound, and strange plants for diabetes. When he noticed the surprise on my face he added, 'Even if she's no use she doesn't do any harm. Some people swear by the Almighty that she's cured them and brought back their loved onces from the gates of death, and others say only God can cure disease.'

Her house was half an hour's drive out of town. I remembered the first time, when Ingrid was with me, I'd become convinced that the herb doctor was a figment of Said's imagination. For the desert couldn't suddenly stop short, gather itself in and produce houses and palm trees. But his manner of driving and his continuous talk about her seemed to confirm that he knew the road already. 'We'll be at Sita's house in the twinkling of an eye,' he said. I thought that if it hadn't been for Ingrid's curiosity I wouldn't have come, and then in the distance houses and telegraph poles appeared, though as the car drew near it became clear that the houses were just huts with tin roofs and mud-brick walls, leaning against each other and sprouting television aerials. A couple of boys in vests and underpants were standing in a plastic washing-up bowl, scooping up water from it in an empty dried milk tin and a juice carton, and spraying it over themselves.

Said asked them where the doctor's house was and one of them said 'Sita?' pointing to a hut that was bigger than the ones around it. Said stayed outside, while Ingrid and I had to bend our heads to get through the open door into an unroofed yard. It was empty. I called, 'Sitt Sita,' and a voice answered. 'I'm in here.' We took a couple of steps forward and looked about us. There was another room, or enclosed area of some kind, because you couldn't really call it a room. We were astounded to see a man clad only in underpants stretched out there, his eyes fixed on the ceiling, while Sita bent over him massaging his body. We automatically turned our faces away and retreated a few steps. Before we'd had time to think what to do next we heard Sita's voice: 'Hallo. Just a minute until I've finished with this poor creature.' We laughed to start with, then Ingrid asked me in amazement how this could be happening here, and I answered her seriously, 'Why not? Sita's a doctor.'

We heard a series of shrieks that even seemed to startle the goat who'd been lying there chewing and twisting her head around from time to time to keep the flies off. A few minutes passed. Then the man came out with his clothes on, not looking in our direction. We went in to Sita. She was rubbing her hands in the ashes and explained, looking up at us, 'It sterilises the hands.' When I asked what was wrong with the man, she said, 'A cough and asthma.'

There was an odd smell. Sita put out the little stove, picked up the iron, and then dropped it because it was so hot; if she hadn't said, 'It's the old man's flesh burning,' we wouldn't have believed that she'd actually put the hot iron on his skin. She took hold of it again with the edge of her dress then picked up a rag from the ground and wiped it, repeating, 'It's the old man's flesh burning. Like when someone's burning the hair off sheep's trotters.' She added, elucidating, 'The man's chest is weak. It gurgles and rattles like the beads of a rosary. Creams and herbs don't work. I said to him I've worked on both your shoulder joints and I've cauterized you. I felt for all the joints in his body. There are people whose hip joints are hard to get hold of, and the joints in their calves. No two fingers are alike.' The strange smell persisted and Sita, still rubbing at the iron, remarked, 'The flesh is still sticking to it. It doesn't want to come off. The old fellow's skin must be like cured meat.'

Then it seemed to strike her that we hadn't yet mentioned why we'd come, although she didn't look at us. She threw the iron on to a brass tray covered in verdigris, smoothed down her black head shawl and adjusted the veil that she wore on the lower half of her face. Then she pulled it down slightly and wiped her nose and upper lip on the edge of her sleeve. She was wearing a dress so remarkable that I thought if the most famous designer in the world could have seen it he would have gasped in admiration and wished that he'd thought of it first: it was patterned with purple flowers the colour of indigo plants, and with the sun and grass on a white background; its shoulders and sleeves were embroidered in purple and fuschia-coloured thread, and the sleeves and the hem were trimmed with silver rings. Medicaments and dried herbs were all about the room and oils and creams in bottles and jars were arranged under sheets of old newspaper on the table, watched over by the stuffed peacock with gold-sequined feathers, who looked ready to weep.

Sita was manifestily irritated at our silence and she fidgeted and patted her dress, straightening it. When I said, 'Your dress is nice,' she gave a grudging smile and asked briskly, 'Which one of you is ill? '

'Neither of us, but my friend would like to write about you for a German magazine.'

Sita put her hand over her face: 'God forbid. No television.' I realized I ought not to have broached the subject directly, so quickly as if to cancel out the previous sentence, I said 'My head hurts.' And I wasn't really lying. I got a headache every afternoon. Sita reached out her two hands and grabbed hold of my head forcefully, asking, 'Where's the pain, daughter?' She scared me and I moved my head away abruptly: 'Not my head, I mean it could be anyone's head.' Frowning she replied, 'Have you come here to find out my secrets?' and she sat down, fiddling with the things that lay round about her and pretending to ignore us. In the end we withdrew silently.

This time, once we were sitting on Sita's cushions and she was sitting facing us, I relaxed because she hadn't recognized me and had welcomed us effusively and asked us, 'Tea or coffee?' But Suzanne's repeated urgings made me tell Sita straightaway the reason why we'd come. Sita seemed not to mind, for she rose up before I'd finished talking and lifted a curtain that hung down from one side of the table and took out a basket. Then she sat down again with the basket in her lap, turning over the little bottles in it and examining them, then giving me one uncertainly. I took it, trying to read the label. 'Coconut with jasmine'. Taking it back from me and peering at it she said, 'No, daughter. The writing's not important. They're bottles I get from the women's market and fill myself.'

Suzanne didn't know what was going on between me and Sita but she put her hand in the basket and saw the Indian women's faces, and asked me sarcastically if Sita was going to change her into one of them. I was busy reading the labels while Sita was still rummaging around among the bottles, occasionally picking one out to look at it more closely, then putting it back. In the end she selected a bottle, put the basket down and sat holding one of her toes.

'Perfumed Castor Oil for the Hair.' 'Oil containing forty-two herbs; an ancient remedy invented by the doctor at the Emperor Shah Alam's palace for falling hair.' 'Oil to make the hair grow longer, containing almond oil, lettuce and sandalwood.'

Sita was waiting for me to put the bottles back so that she could move the basket away. She smoothed down her dress and the shawl covering her hair, and looked at the bottle she'd picked out, then rested her hand on mine, saying, 'Here, daughter. Three drops. Only in tea, and best in scented tea. If you can, let him take it on an empty stomach and see what happens.' Then she laughed with gusto, leaning backwards from the force of it: 'See what happens. He'll come after you like a madman on his hands and knees, sniffing you out like a young pup.'

I tried to explain what she'd said to Suzanne and she asked me how she was supposed to give him three drops of the stuff when he'd stopped coming to visit her. I turned back to Sita: 'We might not see him. Perhaps an amulet would be better? ' She placed her hand on my shoulder: 'Daughter, didn't you say he was your husband?' and she didn't wait for me to reply as she knew there was nothing I could say. I tried to translate what had happened to Suzanne but Sita didn't like delay and argument. She was a practical person, and she seemed to be sure of what she was doing. She stood up, cut leather, got the fire going, assembled various preparations. Reciting prayers, she passed a piece of paper back and forth over the fire and took hold of my hand. With an involuntary movement I grasped Suzanne's hand and put it in Sita's, which made me think that I must believe in what Sita was doing.

Sita opened her eyes and wrote something on the piece of paper and laid it on the leather she'd cut. She opened a jar and dipped her finger in it then smeared it around the edges of the piece of leather, stuck them together, and handed it to me. 'The amulet has to be in the room that he's in. That's vital.' And I didn't say to her, 'How can it be when she doesn't see him?' She stood up smacking one palm against the other and saying, 'You're very welcome. Let's hope you don't need me again. Tea or coffee?' Then taking my hand and smiling she added, 'You're doing fine this time. You've made me feel that I can trust you, and you've asked for my advice. Last year you came to cheat me and steal my secrets.' I was amused and said, 'I thought you'd forgotten me.' She struck her chest: 'Forgotten you?' I asked her how much we owed her and she said, 'Whatever you want to pay me. I'm sure that when he comes crawling to you on his hands and knees you'll come back to reward me.' Then almost to herself, 'Lord above! Why are men so spineless? Tired and stale and uninterested in the pleasures of the flesh!' She pointed to the lower part of her stomach: 'A long time ago women used to come to me complaining about the blood and the pain. They'd say to me, "In the name of whoever called you Sita, give us a cure. Something so that our men are repelled by us and don't want to go to bed with us and leave us to sleep in peace." I said, "Shall I make up a charm for them so they'll marry a second time and a third time and spare you the degradation and the pain?" ' Laughing, she finished, 'Their voices reached the sky: "No, Sita. Any degradation rather than the pain of another wife." '

3

I went up to the roof of my house. The rabbits crouched under the motor of the air-conditioner and the pigeons' cage was empty. Grains of corn were scattered on the ground and on the roof tiles. The black-and-white pair had flown away after the female had laid one egg. Umar had asked me, 'Did the mother fly away because she didn't want her babies?' and I'd answered, 'Pigeons' minds don't work like that.'

I looked again over the parapet of the roof-terrace to the roofs of the other houses. Smoke was rising from distant factories. There was an oil blaze in one spot, and a layer of grey hung over it like dirty muslin. A smell of sewers and chemical waste rose up in the air. I thought to myself, 'Perhaps Umar was right.'

I wouldn't go to the Institute the next day: the atmosphere there now was like my last few weeks in the store before I left. And besides, what had happened to me the previous day had upset me a lot.

I'd been walking along the narrow street thinking that I was wrong to feel weighed down like this; I wanted to wipe away the imprint of misconceptions from my mind so that I could go back to being as I'd been when I first went to teach at the Institute, untroubled by reports and rumours of the men who came to inspect what was going on inside. This street was like another country. Little girls' dresses, mostly of cheap lace, hung on display together with more brightly-coloured dresses from mainland China. Veiled women spread themselves on the ground between the shops selling clothes made of nylon. I said to my student Tamr, 'If it hadn't been for you, I wouldn't have believed that there really were oases or springs in the desert like the ones in books.' Tamr laughed proudly; that morning she'd taken me from her father's house, which was in a different region from the one where I lived, to visit springs where mauve garlic flowers bloomed on the banks, and little girls stood enviously watching the boys plunging in and out of the water among the turtles and young frogs. When we were at her father's house she'd shown me the carvings on the walls and ceilings, and the roof still made of palm leaves. My attention had been attracted by the mud-brick dwellings among the new houses built of concrete and stainless steel. Tamr pointed to some glass-plated buildings and said, 'The camel market used to be here and the gold market still exists. In a month's time they're going to demolish it. There are still women selling henna and silver in it.'

I stopped when I saw some local embroidered material, and picked it up and felt it and decided to buy it in spite of Tamr's surprised reaction. Not long before, she'd bought some material imported from Europe. I counted out my money, thinking to myself that life was normal here in this district, perhaps because it hadn't yet lost the old ways. I heard a boy's voice saying, 'She's American,' and turned to him to correct him, afraid that they'd put up the prices. He winked at me and whispered, 'The old man.' Tamr explained, 'That old religious man. If he knew you were an Arab he'd be furious.' I glanced quickly behind me and saw an old man with a white beard and spectacles and a stick. 'Come on, let's go,' I said to Tamr in a low voice, and in English. I imagined that by talking English I'd become miraculously invisible but the man stood in our path and addressed himself to Tamr: 'Tell her to cover herself up. Our women don't walk about unveiled.' Tamr snapped, 'She's foreign, isn't she? They have their religion, we have ours.' I pretended to have no idea what was going on and said, 'Let's go to the car,' in English, as if I was talking to myself. I seemed to have provided an outlet for the old man's pent-up anger and he thrust out his stick, blocking my way, and screamed at me, 'Get out of here. You can't shop while you're unveiled.'

I felt besieged from every direction, as men and boys pushed forward from all over the market and stood in a circle round me and Tamr. Anger welled up in me, starting in my heart and rushing up into my head. When I confronted the man who was blocking my path, and was unable to push the stick out of the way or budge an inch, I knew that I didn't have control over my own life and was a prisoner of this stick and this group of people. I seethed with frustration and was sure I was going to cry. Although I could hear Tamr's voice raised in protest I felt completely isolated and she seemed just like all the other black-shrouded women.

Again a woman at a stall shouted at Tamr, 'Buy the lady an abaya and go to your homes. May Heaven's door be barred to her. And you're to blame too.'

Tamr rebuffed her: 'I didn't know you had the key to Heaven.' Then she turned to me quickly, pulling the bag out of my hand and unfolding the embroidered material. I took it and covered my head with it. And as I walked off, my shame and annoyance blocked out everything except a feeling of hatred towards Basem.

I didn't tell Said what had happened when we got back to the car, although Tamr burst out laughing and clapped her hands together crying, 'That old man! God help him!'

I rested my head in my hands and when I raised it the desert and the oasis of date palms were tinged orange by the evening sky. I was aware only of my helplessness. I had nothing, not even my eyes to stare and marvel. What had happened, I realized very well now, had been for the benefit of Tamr and others like her, to shackle the women's freedom of movement so that it wouldn't seem as easy and relaxed as we'd made it appear when we'd set out on our excursion. I took my head in my hands again.

I noticed that night had fallen while Umar and I had been up on the roof: the apartment blocks were silent; everywhere there were the concrete supports of buildings in the early stages of construction; stillness hung in the air above the hidden layer of noise, disturbed only by a hateful smell of food. The stars and the moon appeared meaningless. Did anything really exist? I tried to stretch up to see over the roof parapet and stared out as I always did, even though all I saw, day or night, summer or winter, were the houses and the oil fields.

Tomorrow Said would go to the Institute and hand in my resignation. The reason I would give: painful backaches that hindered my movement and took away my energy. From that day on I wouldn't see its door which every day had stood there like a portent, warning of tensions and unpleasant surprises to come, or the veiled women rushing through it, always waiting at the mercy of their husbands or brothers or drivers who might or might not remember the right time to come and take them back home.

On my first day at home I didn't rush out as I used to before to visit other women. I decided to live my life here in a different fashion and moreover to think precisely as I'd thought when looking from the aircraft window and seeing the desert for the first time. The stillness of the sands had drawn me to them; I wanted them to divulge their mystery to me so that I could become close to them and the history and geography books would come alive. The camel hair tents, the wide moon, the stars so near to earth, the oases, the mirages, the thirst and the pervasive fragrance of cardamon would all be a part of my life. But the huge airport had all the latest equipment and would have been like any other international airport but for the preponderance of Middle and Far Eastern faces. We drove along a broad motorway on our way to the hotel and I could see the town lit up, plenty of cars and even a few trees; and as we came closer, restaurants, hotels and stridently modern feats of architectural design.

Our hotel was luxurious although whoever designed it had been unsuccessful, obviously seeing things through foreign eyes and wanting to create his own idea of Arab architecture and furnishings, with the result that wealth superseded taste in every room. The picture windows looked out on to distant lights, and in the daytime I saw a big harbour and a sturdy bridge. Who'd said that we were in the desert here, when all the trappings and institutions of city life were to be found in abundance?

Not much time passed before I realized I'd been mistaken: I was neither in the desert nor in a city. The desert was only a place to be explored; even getting to know its natives was an experience like something out of a tourist brochure and they themselves were ill at ease with anything but hair tents and camels and sand. Those in the city, meanwhile, were in conflict with whatever came to them from beyond the desert. Every aircraft that landed on their sands brought something that frightened them and that they didn't want to know about because it didn't spring out of their own arid land. But these aircraft carried people and their different civilizations and they couldn't afford to reject them because the incomers were the ones who knew the secrets of the desert, almost as if they had been created in its belly and knew where the black liquid was and how to turn it into door handles and bathtaps made of gold.

That first day I went around the house, cleaned the canary's cage, sat down on the sofa, and thought to myself, 'Where are all the things that I wanted to do if I didn't go to teach?' I opened a drawer. There were coloured shells, silver rings, material. I closed it. The phone rang. I hurried to answer it. The canary flew from his open cage and perched on my shoulder as he always did when I picked up the receiver. My husband was telling me that he'd come and have coffee with me after lunch: 'I've got a few people from Beirut with me.' I found myself asking him, 'And when are we going to leave this country?' There was a silence, then he said laughing, 'You want to know this minute?' 'Yes. I have to know. I can't go on like this,' then I started to cry. I heard him hesitating on the other end of the line: 'We'll talk about it later. Come on. Bye bye.' Still crying, I shouted at him, 'I want to know how much longer we're staying in this bloody country.'

'What's all this about? Calm down, take it easy. What's happened? I don't understand. What's different since I left you this morning?' I repeated tearfully, 'Nothing's happened. I'm going to explode, that's all. I just want to know.'

And I knew that he didn't know. We were like all the Lebanese who'd transferred their businesses abroad and had been luckier than they expected. I tried to make myself get up but I couldn't and stayed where I was, my head in my hands, the canary on my shoulder, thinking about my family and Basem's family and my friends. None of them were happy in Beirut now, all wavering between staying and leaving. My sister wrote to me from Brazil, the sad letters of an exile. The phone again. Maryam on the line. I found myself gradually growing calmer as if I was getting back into daily life here once more. I took the material from the drawer and began to make a bedouin puppet. I drew in the eyes, the eyebrows, the lips and remained absorbed, unaware of the time until my son Umar came home from school, calling out and shouting at me to take him down to see the baby camel near our house. I was still thinking about the colour of the puppet's lips as he pulled me along with him, the camera in his other hand. Down in the street I saw to my surprise that there was a dog nosing around the camel and it was responding playfully to the dog's interest. I clicked the shutter and we approached the two of them with Said shouting to us, 'Go gently. The camel's afraid and he's a cunning beast.'

Basem and his three friends arrived. I gave them coffee while the canary flew about the house and approached the glass-topped table, and landed on the plate of biscuits. He pecked desultorily at a piece of biscuit but perhaps he found it too dry. He flew off again then landed on my shoulder and moved up close to my face, trying to take some biscuit out of my mouth. 'See that son of a bitch!' remarked one of the guests in surprise. When I stood up with the canary on my shoulder another of them asked, 'How's life? You look as if you're enjoying it here.' I thought it's the canary on my shoulder that's given him that idea, and not only the canary, perhaps the furniture and the nice house as well. I returned, 'I'm all right. But if only I could walk about the place.' Basem chipped in, 'By the way, I've brought you a walking-machine. Don't exaggerate, Suha, you can walk about any compound.' I busied myself putting the canary back into his cage. If this conversation had taken place in our first year here I would have answered him that walking wasn't just an activity of the feet: eyes needed a change of scenery too and in the compound you went along on a green carpet which resembled grass, or on real grass threatened every instant by sand. I always used to discuss the place with him and ask him if the smell of damp bothered him and if he noticed how time stagnated, and he would answer, 'I don't have time to scratch my head.' Fighting off my despair, I would ask curtly, 'Don't you have the feeling that life here isn't normal?'

When the conversation between Basem and the other men turned as usual to money and business, I thought even people who aren't living here have been caught up in this obsession with money and can no longer talk about anything unconnected with money, chances for good deals, petrol. Slyly I interrupted them: 'Do you know, a committee of doctors did ECGs on a large sample of the men around here and thought the machinery had broken down. They all came out blank.' My smart remark was lost on the three men and when one of them asked what I meant Basem replied, 'Suha always likes to philosophize about things. She means we don't feel anything and we're always chasing after money. An instructive summing-up!'

That night I broached the subject of our staying here again. I tried to be realistic, positive, decisive. I told Basem that I wanted the truth, wanted to know how long we were going to spend here so that I could prepare myself psychologically, and impressed upon him that I wouldn't by angry whatever the answer might be. When he answered hesitantly, 'A year. Two years. Maybe three,' I screamed at him. I thumped my hand against the door as I went to open it and echoed Umm Kairouz's words: 'I'll go mad. I could accept life in the fighting, but not this.' I went out but as I reached the door of the overgrown garden I turned back and found Basem standing on the doorstep. I went in with him and said, 'It's good that I found out.'

The next day I decided to do what I'd done the day after I arrived when I was acclimatizing myself to the place: go down to the hotel swimming-pool and jump in off the boards, put oil on my legs, smile at the waiter who brought me orange juice and stretch out contentedly. But the spirit of that day was never recaptured. Then I'd looked at the mosaic in the swimming-pool and thought to myself that it was like the green of the sea, admired the sturdy blue sunshades and the clean comfortable chaises-longues and marvelled at the coolness of the juice in the stifling atmosphere. But the veneer of newness had worn off and I'd stopped going to the swimming-pool after a man had come in and banged on the tables, separating the male swimmers from the females. Most of the women took refuge in the changing-rooms trembling, and the few foreigners among them didn't understand what was going on. In his attempts not to look at the semi-naked bodies in the pool the man had begun to thump his stick looking in the opposite direction, and had slipped and fallen in the water. His head rose to the surface and went under again a number of times, and he swallowed large amounts of water and almost drowned.

Today as I paid the entry fee I made up my mind to speak English. Despite the burning sun I lay back in a chaise-longue by the pool, lifted my hair off my neck and wiped away the sweat: 'God, do I have to stay? I can't take another hour in this country.' Nobody heard me but the flies and the clammy air. I took my face cream and had barely opened the lid before it poured out like a stream of hot water. 'Even cosmetics melt.' I threw it down, opened a magazine, laid it aside. I looked around me. Foreign women. Arab women. Children.

Two days a week for women and the rest of the time for men. No music. Only the racket of motors and a bulldozer working nearby. I closed my eyes, opened them and closed them again when I saw a woman approaching. I didn't want to talk to any woman. I'd stopped visiting and receiving visitors and hadn't even opened the door to Suzanne in spite of being curious to know what had happened to Maaz since our visit to Sita.

I'd been years in this desert and a quarter of an hour stretched out on the chaise-longue. There was no music playing. Music's the work of the devil: it infiltrates the mind and whispers seductively to it. I looked at my magazine for a few moments but saw the signs of normal life in it and felt depressed and threw it down. I thought nostalgically of the first year here and closed my eyes again recalling the shapes and colours of the goats that were new to me then; I'd gone into the shops, few in those days, examining all the Indian merchandise, turning over the daggers and bracelets, the real coral and the fake, and passing my hand over the smooth aged wood of the doors which had been ripped out of the mud brick houses. I even got to know about the foodstuffs in the freezers and the prices of everything. I was enthusiastic about the local people: I'd come here to find out what there was in the women's wooden chests and imagined green and blue and red and white cashmere shawls and rubies and diamonds, one for every finger, but I'd been wrong. The people of the desert had changed and were still changing: they were throwing out their carved sofas, and stainless steel and jewels from Bangkok had become important in their lives.

I no longer felt inspired by the puppets' costumes that I used to enjoy making. Books began to frustrate me because they took me off into surroundings so remote from where I was. In spite of my boredom I wasn't interested in witnessing the building of cities stone by stone, or their expansion, and I could no longer stand the sound of the loudspeakers on the cars that roved around the narrow sandy or asphalted streets enumerating the different kinds of tree they were planting. I did not want to be somewhere that was just starting up. Even the first landings on the moon seemed like ancient history to me now. The newspapers arrived late and the news was already out of date and that was why what went on in the world no longer touched me. Everything seemed as if it was happening on another planet.

The Indian waiter was coming towards me now devouring me with his eyes. I put the towel around me before I asked him if one of the men had come to stop the women swimming. No, they all had to go into the restaurant because the swimming pool had been reserved for a family who were of some importance by the look of them. I just nodded for by now I could see the other women getting into arguments with their children about leaving the pool.

The place emptied although waves still ruffled the blue water where people had been jumping and swimming. I didn't want to rise from my seat for two reasons: I'd have had to get fully dressed to go into the restaurant, and I was curious to see the important family. I expected a woman in a veil and abaya who'd sit on the edge of the pool, like the ones I'd seen at the seaside sitting with children in over-large bathing costumes while their father enjoyed himself in the water. I saw a young girl followed by a pretty woman in a long dress whose hair reached below her waist. Before she took off her dress at the side of the pool she looked around her and saw me, or perhaps she didn't, because she didn't protest, but gathered up her hair, lifted if off her back and went down into the pool. She stood holding on to the steps, then after a while she floated still holding the steps. Her daughter, who was an excellent swimmer, threw water at her and she turned her face away with her free hand on her hair, saying 'Stop it,' in a coquettish voice.

I stood up and jumped into the water, thinking that I now knew why people built private swimming-pools for them-

selves. The water without lots of bodies in it looked much
more refreshing. The woman was still holding on to the steps
when I got there. We exchanged smiles and before I moved
away I heard her asking me in English if I'd teach her to
swim. When I answered yes in Arabic she said, 'I told myself
that's an Arab face. Are you from Lebanon?'

I stood with her in the water and told her to blow into the
water as a first step, but she didn't know how to. I told her to
breathe in and hold her breath, then plunge her head into the
water and stop holding on and take her feet off the bottom.
She did as I said but she couldn't stop herself clinging on to
the steps. She tried once again and still couldn't . When she
asked me if I'd come to her house and give her swimming
lessons I laughed awkwardly. Seeing the reluctance on my
face she pressed me with good-natured charm: 'Please. The
car will come for you and take you back afterwards. And the
pool at our house is big.' I couldn't conceal my surprise and
wondered how to reply to the woman whose name was Nur,
who clearly realized what I was thinking. 'I was fed up,' she
explained. 'and I said to my daughter Ghada that we should
have a change and go the the hotel pool.' Then she sat down
beside me and began telling me about her time at school in
Cairo and how much she liked Lebanon, and every time I
stood up to go she insisted that I stayed and I realized that she
was bored.

I regretted my capitulation the next day when Nur's driver
appeared at the door. I was sleepy. The car drew to a halt
with me outside a house that I'd often seen before. It wasn't
far from where we lived and Umar called it the spaceship
while I had privately named it the moon house. Its walls were
built of beautiful stone. 'They must be mad,' I thought,
'spending all that cash as if they were in Switzerland.' Inside
the house it was hard to believe in the existence of the dust
from the desert and the ugly dilapidated houses, all alike, and
the pot-holed narrow streets with piles of rubbish at every
corner. I could see trees and green grass in Nur's garden

although some of the foliage had withered. How quickly the plants died even in the gardens of the rich houses because of sand storms, or goats that got in and ate everything that was green.

Nur was waiting for me in the swimming-pool. As I dived into the clean water I thought no one looking from outside would be able to guess what lay behind those walls. At first I was annoyed, then increasingly indifferent, in the face of Nur's fear and her failure to listen to what she ought to do in order to stay afloat. But I continued to encourage her, while she apologized and played the part of the embarrassed pupil.

My visits to her became more frequent although I gave up hope of ever teaching her to swim, especially when she confessed to me that this was the fourth time she'd tried to learn. Before me she'd joined a swimming club somewhere in Europe, and her husband Saleh had tried to teach her too. But Nur's personality and the atmosphere of her house, so different from the other houses I knew, attracted me back there.

4

It was difficult for us to become friends, for I had effectively sealed off the channels of communication to every living creature and every inanimate object in this country. I left my house rarely and didn't give myself the chance to get to know people who would transport me to other worlds. I wasn't suffering from the depression of the desert which attacked every woman from time to time, even the ones who were content with this restricted way of life: for a woman never knows why she suddenly withdraws from everyday life for a time any more than she knows why the cloud of depression suddenly lifts from her.

But I wanted peace once I began to grasp the contradictions which existed between my house and the outside world. Every time I walked into my house I felt that I was entering a different world far removed from the other: all the variations and details of life inside appeared reasonable and sensible; the international news on the radio and television appeared important; listening to it, you felt that it was talking about people and events that you understood. While if you heard the same news on the car radio, driving along the sand or the newly-improved roads, it seemed remote from reality, transmitted in an indolent tongue understood by no one, because it didn't consist of endless talk about money and business. Even the news which concerned everyday economic life gave the impression that it didn't change from one day to the next as it did in the rest of the world. After all, the gold market here was a few little shops around an unroofed courtyard with the goldsmiths sitting on the ground in front of low tables covered with gold articles and substances for melting them down and polishing them. Black beetles ran over its sandy floor and women stood around, the gold on their arms jingling as they fingered necklaces and gold belts, or bought gilded Qur'ans and ear-rings and bracelets for their children, while their husbands reluctantly counted out vast amounts of money and gave it to the goldsmith who sorted the notes into neat bundles of a hundred and snapped elastic bands round them.

Nur reawakened my curiosity, but only for a short time. Her house was like a peep-show where servants and nannies of different races milled around with children, gazelles and saluki dogs. A delicate perfume floated to meet me whenever I went through the door, and Arab and foreign music reverberated through the spacious rooms. Beautiful clothes, high fashion, the latest of everything - including the furniture and the chocolates she offered me, like Godiva from Belgium and

Chantilly from Lebanon - mangoes and pineapples from the Philippines. It was a large house with white marble everywhere and the trees in the garden visible through the windows, acting as a buffer between the house and the desert. The noise that filled it reminded me of Sitt Wafa's house, and in both of them I found some semblance of normality.

In Nur's house I used to sit and wonder where to look next. There were two video machines in the huge sitting-room. The furniture was used to divide the room into three sections. Her daughter and Umar and some other children were shouting and screaming as they fought satellites on the video screen. Female friends and relations of Nur watched stars like Dalida and the Egyptian Nellie on television, and the Filipino men-servants sang and called to each other with loud whistles. Dogs wandered in, wrestled with the children, and wandered out. Budgerigars and canaries and green and white parrots hopped around their aviaries talking to one another. There was a big aquarium alive with different sea creatures. When the friends and relations got bored they would come over to Nur and me and then I wondered which of them to talk to or look at. Some of them were enveloped in abayas and veils and had henna patterns on their hands, while others wore clothes in the latest styles and colours; their jewellery was either embossed bedouin gold or modern international designer style. Which magazine should I flick through? It seemed as if all the world's magazines, and the magazines produced by all the big international stores, were there on the table. When Said came to take me home I was always surprised how quickly the time had passed.

But Nur's house was no longer so exciting after I'd seen the show over and over again, and swimming in the pool was no longer a novelty, and I didn't pay proper attention to what Nur was saying. The times I did listen to her complaints which were always on the same theme — how bored she was and how much she wanted to go abroad — I used to soothe her in exactly the same way that Basem soothed me: 'Never mind. Be patient,' without meaning what I said. Because I was turned in on myself to such an extent, I couldn't establish a real friendship with any woman here. 'My friends are in Beirut and I don't feel in tune with anyone else.' But I also used to say to Basem that I couldn't break off relations with Nur as I'd done with the rest because she found an answer to every excuse I gave; whether I said Said wasn't around, Umar was ill, I wasn't feeling well or I was busy. When I didn't answer the telephone Nur came in person and knocked on my door asking if the telephone was out of order. I began to feel annoyed by her and her persistence, and complained about it to Basem. He suggested that I should benefit from her and get to know the desert region here. Despite my lack of enthusiasm, I welcomed the idea and thought it sounded better than sitting on my sofa or Nur's hour after hour. So one day we went together right into the desert to an oasis community and visited some of Nur's relations in brand-new tents with sitting-rooms, dining-rooms, showers and toilets and a water pump outside. We sat on Persian and Pakistani rugs. The women seemed more real in these huge tents, although they'd only come to spend a few days in the desert. One of them asked Nur about her husband Saleh; 'May God guide him,' she remarked as she started to speak about him, which I presumed was because he was always travelling: whenever I asked Nur about her husband he was away on business. She took me to watch a bride-to-be being bathed and beautified and decorated with henna, and I saw how different the women looked without their veils and black abayas. They were laughing and shouting to one another and exchanging frank comments and gestures as they watched the bride. At night we went to the wedding ceremony and I was happy just to watch, while Nur danced, chewing gum. I didn't eat anything. Nur ate, while I looked at the women and at the stars that seemed almost within reach.

When the phone rang early one morning I picked up the receiver although I was sure that it would be Nur, and I agreed to visit her because I wanted to get out of the house that day, particularly as I hadn't left if for days. When I entered the house I found the opposite of what I had expected. Nur looked as if she'd spent the night in a cold bath, immersed in icy loneliness. At her side was her bottle of tranquillizers. When Nur took one of these she slept peacefully for hours but when she woke up she moved slowly as if the ground wasn't to be trodden on but just brushed with the soles of her feet. There was a mound of cigarette butts in the ashtray. The pallor of her face made her a part of the sugar-coloured sofa, except for the two points of blackness that flickered there from time to time. Her hands too blended in with the sofa and she held the ashtray listlessly. In front of her on the table was a bowl with pomegranate grains in it, and another of peeled cucumber and carrot. The Filipino maid picked up the two bowls and glanced at Nur before disappearing with them. I was about to ask her what had happened when the maid came back with a bowl of peeled oranges and apples and grapes.

Nur was beside herself. She bent her head and said, 'I want to die. Every day I can feel myself beginning to explode. I want to travel and I can't. Saleh's got my passport. I can't live another moment in this house, I'm going to run away.' I sat beside her and said, feigning concern, 'Calm down, Nur. It's not so bad. Send a telegram asking him to send you the passport. Saleh'll be back soon. It's not such a disaster.' I thought to myself how spoilt she was. Then I looked around me. For the first time I thought about the cost of everything: the ceiling, the floor tiles, sofas, tables, chandeliers, display cabinets; it was as if every piece had been chosen to give an aura of rock-solidness and life as it should be lived. And yet the house was steeped in loneliness, perhaps because of the absence of visitors and their children at this hour. The doors and windows were hidden by curtains as if they didn't exist, as if there were no aperture in this house for the plants to breathe through and everything was crouching under a solid glass cover. Again I pretended to be concerned: 'What's wrong, Nur? Calm down. Don't worry. You'll be able to go abroad soon.'

Nur wept, and the tears brought the spirit back into her face: 'I can't stand any more. I've had enough. He's got to divorce me, or come back to me. I can't live like a date hanging off a branch, neither firmly attached to the branch nor lying comfortably on the ground.' Half interested now, I found myself saying, 'All right. Why haven't you either got divorced or come back together before now?' The only reply I could hear was her bitter weeping. Her long black hair was in a mess from the fury of her fit of crying and she lifted her head and twisted up her hair and threw it to the side: 'I just don't know what to do. I want to die. I've had enough. I want to die.'

I didn't know what to say to her, but I acknowledged to myself that I was hard and self-centred because I wasn't moved by her tears now, and because I was thinking about Umar coming home and wondering whether Said had understood that he was supposed to come for me in an hour. Then I justified this by imagining that my reaction would have been different if I'd seen one of my friends in Lebanon crying.

Nur was sobbing hysterically now. I got up and found a box of tissues and brought it over and stood awkwardly before her, not knowing how to make her take one. I tried again in a low voice: 'Nur. Calm down a bit.' I hated myself because these were the only words I could think of to say but for the first time I found myself taking Nur's situation seriously. I had assumed that Saleh, like all the husbands here, was just away a lot or had another wife somewhere. The feeling that the house was without a man was clear although Nur was always threatening her daughter: 'I'm telling you, your father's going to beat you. He'll be back soon and then you'll see.'

I thought, 'Nur must trust me and my feelings for her, otherwise she wouldn't choose to seek help from me in preference to all her other friends and relations. Perhaps it's because I'm a stranger? But she's got lots of friends like me, who aren't from the desert.'

I rested my hand on Nur's hair, then patted her shoulder and said to her, 'There's a solution to everything, Nur.' Nur mumbled some words that I didn't understand. She looked up and reached for some tissues and wiped her eyes, then said, 'It's a huge catastrophe.'

I was surprised and pleased that my words had evoked some response in her, and for the first time she appeared ready to look at her situation without crying. I said, 'Ask him for a divorce. It'd be better than living like this.'

It was as if I'd reminded her of something worse. She bowed her head again and repeated, 'It's a huge catastrophe. If I get divorced, who do I marry?' I was taken aback by Nur's question but instead of saying jokingly to her, 'How can you think about marriage when you haven't thought about divorce yet?' I asked reasonably, 'Did you quarrel? What about? Let somebody try and bring you back together.' Dabbing at the tears and sweat on her face, Nur answered, 'He won't budge. He's got a heart of stone, and his head's not much different.' Then leading me back to the main issue she repeated, 'I want to go away. I can't bear living here. If only I could go on a trip for a week or two . . . '

I let Nur cry and I couldn't help looking at my face in the tissue packet holder as I took a tissue from it, to see how I looked; Nur had even thought of getting a metal cover for the tissue box. I thought I looked beautiful. What was the use? I handed some more tissues to Nur who sat up and said, 'How lucky you are, how fortunate to be Lebanese.' I was about to answer, 'But I'm stuck here, like you' but no – the perfume that I smelt whenever I came into Nur's house now coursed suddenly and powerfully through the corridors of my blood, into the blue veins in my head, massaging them. I relaxed as if I was floating on a surface that was like water but without the wetness or the tension. I was suddenly conscious that I wasn't from here, that I could travel, and go where I pleased, by myself, for a year, two years, three, or leave for good. But Nur would return however often she went away and however long she stayed away. I felt invigorated by these sensations and I returned to the box of tissues, pretending to take one while I was really stealing glances at my reflection, assuring it again of the reality which I'd grown oblivious to and which had confronted me in the midst of Nur's passionate outburst. Only now did I appreciate that this outburst was less violent than it might have been, given the situation she was in. So I tried to return to Saleh, to the root of the problem, but Nur was only interested in retrieving her passport and going abroad and a disquisition on the subject of her husband bored her. She was already trying to think of alternative ways of getting out and urged me to help with practical suggestions. I offered: 'You're ill and need a specialist?' 'No. They wouldn't believe it.' 'Your mother's very ill and you have to travel to look for a cure?' 'Possible. But who'd persuade my mother to go?' I was running out of patience: 'Get another passport.' 'No. These days you have to have a photograph. Before it was easy. No photos for women. Just the name.' At this I said with relief, 'If only I looked like you. I could have given you my passport.' Nur answered, 'Thank you, my sweet. And thank you for helping me.' What help could she mean? I'd only handed her some tissues, and in exchange she'd given me a crystal ball where I'd seen my face and my life.

Nur began coming to my house and going to my room, closely followed by a man who slipped in after her like a thief while I sat in the sitting-room or in the kitchen waiting for the outer door to open and close and for the sound of Nur's footsteps, her kiss on my cheek and her words, always the same, 'I don't know how I'd live without you, my sweet.' An hour and she was gone, leaving me to go into my room looking for traces of Nur's meeting with the man so that I could get rid of them, and thinking why does she get in between the sheets? Why isn't she more sensitive to such things? I would open the window and change the sheets, to chase away the smell of Nur, then go over to the table to see if she'd forgotten a ring or a necklace or a bracelet. It was plain that these clandestine meetings were dispelling all the grief and confusion that she'd been suffering from, leaving her calm and in control of the rest of her day. They were like food and drink to her, so that when Basem had the painters in to the house for several days and when even after it was painted she couldn't resume her meetings for several more days, she pleaded with me to come instead to her house at eleven in the morning and let in a man who would be carrying a black briefcase. I received him pretending to the world that he was the doctor and let him into her room after asking the servant girl nicely to shut the door behind her. I went into the bathroom and turned on the tap as hard as it would go looking at myself in the mirror, asking my reflection how long I would be in Nur's life. I opened the cupboards and saw rusty razors and razor blades and bottles with remnants of men's cologne in them in among the face creams and bags of henna. The water was still running and the sound of it drowned out any movement in the bedroom. I opened the curtain at the window and a cloud of dust flew up. I could see a little bit of the swimming-pool and some patches of green grass and trees with pale, sickly leaves. Over the wall came the noise of the water pumps, and I could see the colourless houses with their metallic doors and window frames glinting in the sun. Would anyone passing by this house believe that in one of its rooms there was a woman in bed with a man who wasn't her husband? This man she'd met in a store, and there had been many others like him; one she'd met at a street crossing, another on a visit to the hospital; she'd slept with the man who'd come selling jewels and material to her in her house and the landscape gardener who advised her on the design of her garden when she was considering planting it with Japanese trees. I thought to myself how human beings

continually manage to overcome their circumstances, thinking up the strangest ways to give substance to their desires.
Before I'd always doubted if sex existed in houses like these
and here I was listening to Nur laughing behind the locked
door. I turned off the tap to hear better and then turned it on
again.

These meetings weren't Nur's lifesavers for long. She began
to dream about going abroad again saying that she didn't like
daytime encounters, although she didn't stop doing it until I
asked her to; one of the men whom she'd seen in my house
came to the door one day to ask me if he could bring his
foreign girlfriend there. He handed me a bottle of whisky and
a big piece of pork. Trembling, I gave them back to him and
didn't answer. I wanted to shut the door in his face or to
scream at him to make him understand me and Nur and the
risks we had taken. But it seemed complicated to explain, and
I couldn't look him in the eye and say to him straight out that
Nur and I were playing with fire.

5

I didn't hesitate for a moment when Nur asked me to come to
her house early one morning, and it wasn't because her voice
sounded weak on the line. She was in bed enveloped in a light
cloud of steam rising from a vaporiser. It seemed to have
opened up her features so that she looked like a fruit that had
ripened prematurely in a greenhouse. I said jollily to her,
'Well? What's the fairy princess doing today?' and she wept
silently. I didn't take any notice. I wasn't in the mood to listen
to her complaining. This was the first time I'd been out after

three days cooped up in the house because of the rain. The dark clouds, the pools of water on the road and in the garden had filled me with happiness.

Rain had come to the desert this year. The sun and the moon had disappeared and the voices praying from the mosque sounded dry and echoless, competing with each other in volume and number. I found myself taking Umar in my arms in the night, calming him because he couldn't sleep. He said to me, 'You're a liar. That's not a prayer.' He was used to hearing the prayer regularly at dawn and this was eight in the evening. I answered him gently, 'They're praying for rain. It has to rain for the dates and the crops to ripen, and to wash away the germs.'

During the night he woke up screaming and came to my bed several times. Lightning and thunder chased each other around the sky and the rain poured down. I went back to bed hoping that I'd reassured him and listened to the rain hammering on the bathroom roof. I smiled contentedly. When Basem opened the door in the morning he gave a shout of wonder and I rushed to see the flooded garden. The water in the street was several inches deep and had begun to come in under the garden door.

Even the rain here was different: it didn't stay on the buildings, and they didn't soak it up. They remained pale, the colour of the dust, like the trees, while the rushing waters swept the building materials out into the street, the wood floating along on the surface. In some places the sand turned to mud. Most of the traffic came to a halt and the drivers got out hitching up their robes to just below their knees and wading through the water showing their skinny legs. Jeeps were the only vehicles that could get through despite the muddy spray that stuck to their windscreens. The shops closed and some women went in cars laughing across the street to visit their neighbours but most of them stayed indoors. When the rain stopped and the sun came out, instead of a rainbow hundreds of mosquitoes hovered in the air like ballet dancers with their long legs.

I didn't ask Nur what was wrong but said enthusiastically, 'I meant to tell you, I saw Saleh on television the other day. You so-and-so. I didn't know he was so attractive and so young. He spoke well. I liked him. He's intelligent, and you know, he looks like Ghada.' Nur shouted back, 'He's not worth an onion skin. I didn't even want to see him face to face this time. I just sent Ghada off without making any trouble.' Then she asked what I wanted to drink, to change the subject.

Before I answered she suddenly began to beat her head and her face with the palms of her hands so violently that I jumped up from my seat and took hold of her arms. Her paroxysm showed no signs of abating and she screamed, 'I'm fed up. I've tried and I can't go on any longer. When I'm depressed I say, "Never mind, Nur", but then I get desperate and I feel ready to explode again. Sometimes I hope he doesn't come to take Ghada or that I don't know he's in the country. Then I pray that when he comes I'll be away somewhere. If only I could be!' And she started striking her head and sobbing again, while I grabbed her arms and tried to soothe her. I hadn't realized that Nur was so strong up till now.

I'd grown used to her gentle voice with its soft desert accent and the affectionate words she spoke to her salukis as she patted them on the head; I'd watched her often cuddling the little gazelle, and sticking her finger in the cream and licking it to make sure it was fresh, and lifting her face to be kissed by her veiled visitors. When she put her head in her hands again and I tried to pull them away she pressed my hand with one of her hot hands then cast her head on to my shoulder like a sad child. She hadn't stopped crying all the time but I couldn't bring myself to pat her shoulder or hold her to comfort her. I felt embarrassed and wished Nur would control herself, while she stayed where she was like a child safe in her mother's arms at last. I didn't move but I said,

'Nur. Let's think of a way,' trying to get her off me. Nur's face was no longer on my shoulder but against my neck. I ignored the butterfly fluttering and stayed quite still. I felt a moist warmth, then a light-headedness that made me tremble and still I didn't move. Nur's face was still pressed against me. Suddenly the warmth of her breathing made my heart pound and a feeling surged through me that scared me. I trembled again but I didn't want to pull away. I sat forcing myself to remain immobile, staring at the upholstery. Nur realized what was happening to me and as if she was taking me by the hand and advancing step by step, she paused for a little while before nuzzling her face against my neck, then encircling me with her arms and drawing me to her. The warmth spread over my neck, dropping down into my body at the same time. Shutting out everything else, I said to myself, 'Nur's kissing me,' and I didn't think as I did in real life 'A kiss is between a man and a woman', but just wanted more. Every point in my body that Nur reached she aroused and left in a state of agitation.

My muscles didn't stay tensed up and as they relaxed I found myself lying back on the bed then a rhythmic movement started up which made me dizzy from the different sensation of pleasure it produced in me. It was a beautiful purely instinctual rhythm, which seemed to take off and fly like the wisps of steam still floating about the room.

Reality returned to me as soon as I became aware of Nur's weight smothering me. I pulled my eyes away and fixed them on the ceiling. Then I felt a sudden nausea, then disgust, and wished I could disappear through the cracks in the ceiling. I didn't want to stay lying there and give Nur the impression that I was happy at what had happened, and at the same time I wanted to be separate from my body and give it orders: tell it to stand up and go away just as I wanted to do, open the door and chase it out. But as it was I got up and stood there, not daring to look at Nur, or around the room, or down at my skirt. I'd pulled my skirt over my legs while I was still lying on the bed, knowing that I would never feel quite the same liking for them as I had done before, or look after them so carefully or bother so much about what tights I wore.

My skirt looked as if one of Nur's dogs had chewed it and spat it out. I wanted to turn to her and tell her that I had no connection with the woman who'd been panting with her a little while before. But I just went on standing there, quivering slightly, not daring to move, while Nur sat at her dressing table and reached for her hairbrush, loosened her plaits, brushed her hair, replaited it and pulled down her nightdress. She didn't look at me but smiled in the mirror as she saw me leaving, and said goodbye. I couldn't distance myself from what had happened. I went to the car and sat in it, my face almost touching the window, and saw nothing until I reached my own front door. I heard Basem and Umar talking together and longed to be sitting between them feeling bored, or lying in my bed ill, instead of having to go in to them now. I had a terrible desire to throw myself into their arms and cry. I wished I could rush into my room without seeing them. But I stood rooted to the spot when I heard Umar saying, 'She's here.' I got as far as the dining-room when Basem intercepted me: 'What's happened?' Trying to sound casual I replied, 'Nur's ill and I got the doctor to her.' Jokingly he remarked, 'If she's ill why's your face so pale? ' and I said quickly, 'Her driver hit another car and I had a fright.'

I swallowed. It was as if I had a big stone in my gullet which hurt me every time I breathed. I didn't wait for Umar in the bathroom while he cleaned his teeth, as he asked me to. 'I'll come and see you in a little while, darling,' I said apologetically.

I went into my room and I knew how risky it would be to cry now but I couldn't help it. I looked at the photo of me with Umar and Basem on my dressing table and turned it face down in case their eyes bored through me and saw the recent scene with Nur. Then I turned it back again and stared at Basem with his spectacles and pale eyes and smooth hair, and his big nose that was out of proportion to the rest of his features. The sight of his striped shirt whose collar I always sprayed with some special cleaner for collars and cuffs made him appear familiar, like a brother or friend or someone who had sat next to me at school.

I went about the house like someone immunized against hearing and seeing until Umar's bedtime. Then I went to bed the same as I did every other night, while Basem sat watching a film on the video until late. I closed my eyes and I felt as if I were emerging from a dark cave on to a blue sea glowing with light. I opened a window in my head and looked through it and saw a motor working soundlessly in a room lined with velvety wallpaper just as I'd pictured it before, with red and blue wires around it. I opened a window looking on to my heart and saw a motor boiling and thudding there. I asked my noisy heart, and my mind, which went silently back and forth in its room, what was on the pages which I hadn't yet read. What was passing along those red and blue wires? What were the subjects of the paintings hanging on the velvet walls? What was the significance of a heart being heart-shaped when I didn't even know who was beginning and who was reaching an end, who growing, who diminishing?

I am Suha. I am twenty-five-years old. My mother is Sitt Widad and my father is Dr Adnan. I'm not bent like Sahar, although I've laughed and joked and exchanged comments and gestures about men with other girls like me. I'm normal. I saw myself on a bed in the cold of the mountain with Suhail, Aida's friend, in the middle. All the guests had gone, carrying bags of grapes under their arms. I'd held a party to pick our grapes at the end of the summer. I'd had the idea because my parents were in Europe and I liked having my friends to visit me in my house. The three of us were drunk and I wanted some coffee to sober up. I got it ready but when I took it to the others I found Aida stretched out on my bed facing the wall with Suhail lying beside her, and without thinking I crept on to the bed behind Suhail. It was the smell of him perhaps, or the cold and being drunk, that made me squeeze up against him. He turned and reached his hand out to the back of my neck then moved it down my back and rested it there. I felt confused, comprehending all at once the sort of relationship which Aida and Suhail must have, but I let his hand reach under my skirt. 'How are you feeling, Aida?' 'Fine,' replied Aida, with her eyes closed. His hands were on my flesh, moving up the slope of my body, pulsating. Then he said, 'Chopin,' and Aida asked him, 'Do you like Chopin?' 'I think he's fantastic,' answered Suhail, 'and I like Ravel's *Bolero*.' I knew that Aida wouldn't believe what I was doing now even if she turned over and saw it. She said, 'I tried to make Suha like classical music.' Suhail had begun breathing more heavily. He answered, 'Suha likes rock,' and lifted himself over me so he was at the edge and I was in the middle. I wanted to stay where I was but at the same time I wanted to get up. I wondered whether to let myself go and disregard Aida, but I felt sorry for her whichever I did. She said, 'Suha likes blues as well,' and Suhail said, 'Really?' as he opened his flies. 'My head's heavy,' I said. I began to talk wildly about anything and gathered my hair up off my head while Suhail moved faster and faster then suddenly got up and asked, 'Where's the coffee?'

The heart and the mind opened their two chambers, allowing me to steal a glance into them. I'm indifferent now to Suhail, Maurice, Adnan, Adil, and I understand that time takes a huge eraser and rubs out names and then writes others in and renews feelings and emotions. I'd got to know Basem and fallen in love with him, and my heart had leapt for joy when he asked me to marry him. Now I didn't want to look into either chamber. I chased away all the images and questions and misgivings and convinced myself that I'd forgotten what had happened in Nur's room. But the heart and mind were faithful and searched virtuously through their records, unearthing causes and explanations which might supply them with adequate justification for eradicating the event. They made me see myself a month before, when I'd escaped to my bed and listened to a child crying above the sound of the air-conditioner, and music – Western, Arab and Indian – floating out over the rooftops. I'd put my hand under the pillow to pull it nearer to me and smelt Nur's smell and heard her laughter and seen her thick black hair.

I imagined her with a man, warm and at the same time powerless, pliant and bending like a doll made of dough, wanting what was forbidden. The severity with which it was forbidden reminded people of it at every moment, and it wormed its way into their minds and bodies. Even when you were buying tampons and sanitary towels and perfumes and spray deodorants, the man behind the cash desk changed colour and you knew what he was thinking about as he smiled or assumed an air of indifference. There was a campaign being conducted in the press against the display of women's underwear, and its leader was a girl in her twenties who had already raised the subject of bracelets and other jewellery; according to her they were symbols of slavery reminiscent of the age of harems and slave boys and girls, and make-up and jewellery on a woman was a provocation to adultery and fornication even if it was made from behind veils and black drapes.

Although these thoughts of mine drew things together and had some substance, I couldn't help feeling miserable. I began reminding myself how I'd thought of Nur as having a kind of illness as I stared at the pillows and the cover that day, and said to myself this is where Nur rolled around and breathed fast and slow with a man, separated from him only by their fine body hairs. However, I couldn't see it like that now, much as I wanted to.

A week passed and I drifted in and out of reality, staring out of the window at the dusty desert and the mechanical waste. The telephone rang and I didn't answer. I didn't want to hear Nur's voice. But she came to see me early one morning. She sat down on the sofa, then stood up and seemed to be examining my house for the first time. She grasped hold of the coral and shells, the puppets hanging from the ceiling, the old silver necklaces and bracelets and anklets, and smiled and sat down again in front of me, her limbs loose and relaxed. I was still only half there, trying to make normal conversation and not succeeding. Every question or statement I wanted to utter seemed to have a connection with us, either directly or indirectly, and I only breathed again when Nur left.

When another day or two had gone by I began to feel a yearning. I missed the particular atmosphere that comes into being only if a person is alone, has spare time on her hands and is waiting for something to happen. For recently we had no longer sat chatting like visitors, each telling the other what she'd been doing. We'd begun to live our lives together, going to the department store, visiting Suzanne, entering the hotel in fear and trembling and ordering tea and cake only to rise up together after hastily swallowing the tea, because the looks of the other guests were almost beginning to be directed towards us, almost becoming a reproach. We went deep into the desert and saw a mirage of many colours. Instead of receding into the distance, it had come closer to us as we approached it in the car, and then it wasn't a mirage after all.

I couldn't help exclaiming in wonder at the carpet of yellow and white daisies, other flowers whose names I didn't know, and thick-stemmed ones standing straight as pegs: 'Those are called snake poison,' I said. It wasn't the colours that made my heart beat faster, but the smell, fragrant and powerful and new and strange to my nose. I picked a daisy and brought it close to my mouth and chewed its petals, trying to bring together the taste and the smell. As we went further among the flowers the smell grew and changed, from jasmine, to white iris, to narcissus. We sat down on the grass and sand and Nur pulled the petals off the daisy one by one: 'He loves me, he loves me not.' I stretched out and smiled as a sudden realization dawned on me. My relationship with Basem only existed inside the four walls of the house now; it didn't even extend to the garden or the car or the street. I rarely sat next to him in the front seat of the car. I didn't walk along with him in the street or go to the shops with him. We didn't lie together beside the pool and I didn't sit with him even on the back seat on the way to the airport; he sat in front next to Said. He'd never met Nur yet, or Tamr, and our conversations were brief, restricted to matters connected with everyday life, holidays, the news from Lebanon and family and friends.

Through the rooms of my mind and heart passed images of how I'd gone to bed early, trying to read against the noise of the television and the laughter and talking of Basem's friends. I'd stopped inviting men and women together because I'd become convinced that such gatherings were futile. The women furtively examined each other's clothes, working out the financial situation of each other's husbands so that they could feel either proud or jealous, while the men talked about money and business openly. I was glad that I wasn't obliged to sit with them but it made me realize how lonely I was.

Sometimes I used to refuse Basem when he came unusually early to the bedroom. It would depend on how fed up I'd felt during the day and how resentful that I was still in the desert. Sometimes I convinced myself that he had no alternative but to stay here, and that he was happy in his work. On these occasions I let him take me in his arms and cover me with kisses and I held him to me in memory of the past and the days of normality. However much I tried to relax I felt conscious of every noise outside and every movement in the bed, and the climax of our lovemaking was lost to me like a piece of paper blown near me by the wind, and blown away again every time I caught up with it. Then I felt angry because I'd shown a desire to participate and not come. Throughout the night I tossed and turned unable to sleep, as if I'd committed a sin, and as if I'd found out for the first time that I wasn't in control of my body and that only my feelings could make it move, but they wouldn't forget their dissatisfaction and were rebelling.

Still breaking the petals off the daisy, Nur had said, 'When they brought me back here and I saw the desert from the plane I screamed. In the car I threw up three or four times and when I got to the house I banged my head against the walls. I couldn't sleep or eat and I wouldn't greet my relatives without letting them see how angry I was. I sat for hours and days as dumb as that table. I locked the door of my room and got a mirror and stared at my face; I counted the hairs of my eyebrows and eyelashes, twisted my hair round my fingers, just like mad people do. All my life I never liked seeing the desert. My mother says that before I was old enough to understand, I used to cry and they didn't know the reason. When I became conscious of my surroundings, I closed my eyes in the car. I was the opposite of my sisters and brothers. They loved looking out of the windows. I never did. It's always made me depressed.'

Our relationship wove itself together from day to day. I was like a fisherman who casts his line into water where he knows there are no fish, or even weeds, but feels a sense of calm and a release from the boredom of his routine every time he does it, and prefers it at least to doing nothing, although every day when he comes back to fish again he feels a little restless and disgruntled.

In the days that followed, I plucked up enough courage to kiss Nur, when I'd shut my eyes and opened them fifty times. My limbs went numb before I reached that nameless, otherworldly region with her. I couldn't open my eyes again easily; it was as if I was standing beside a large firework that might go off at any minute, or was dazzled in the presence of Nur the imperious queen bee. This was no longer an experiment; I'd tried a new fruit which I'd thought would be inedible and instead I'd found it intoxicatingly sweet; I couldn't just spit out the stone and go on my way.

Our secret relationship began to complement our relationship outside the house. I sensed a transformation: whatever plant it was I'd tasted had drugged me and made me lose my memory. I no longer noticed how slowly the time crawled by in the desert, or the pervasive smell of chemicals which used to irritate me so much, or the colours of the new buildings which I had once named Instant Ruins, or the wires hanging down from the outside walls, or the lack of trees. Feelings of agitation and rage no longer crept up on me as they had done before: now when I saw the women's tailor poking his head out of his tiny window to receive material and a pattern from one of his customers, I shrugged my shoulders indifferently: and I laughed when I heard one of Nur's mother's visitors forbidding her daughter to go alone in Nur's car. 'If you leave a man alone with a woman, the Devil makes it three,' she pronounced adamantly, despite Nur's protestations that the driver's morals were unimpeachable and he'd been with her for years.

But I felt irritated when one day Nur came to me in my house; only then did our relationship seem a reality. Instead of the smell of incense and furniture and food which filled my senses when I was in her room, and her bed which was like the cockpit of a plane and was studded with buttons on either side and had a chamois leather bedhead to match her wardrobe and mirror and seat, there were Umar's drawings blowing about in the draught from the air-conditioner and my yellow case on top of the wardrobe, and this time I couldn't feel that I was a visitor or an onlooker. Previously I'd gone back home and it seemed as if I'd never left: Basem's freshly-ironed clothes hung on the door knob; his clean shirts were still spread out on the bed to finish drying. I was aware of myself getting Umar's things ready and answering the telephone and acting so normally that I began to question if I'd really only returned from Nur's house a few minutes before, and if me stretching out on her bed and us kissing and clinging to each other and squirming about had really happened.

My room was still as it had always been except for the traces of Nur and her perfume. Bedrooms all over the world are always private and special. I used to love going into my parents' room to see the cut-glass moon mounted into the wood of their bed, although I never once saw it lit up. And I could still remember my European teacher's bedroom when I went to visit her with the rest of the class after she'd had her appendix out. To my surprise I saw toys of every shape and size scattered about the room. My teacher was about fifty years old and she didn't smile easily.

Before I was married I used to love my friends to see my room; I'd leave my tennis racquet lying on the table on purpose and the classical records and thick books on art and literature in obvious places, and foreign dictionaries, and the photograph of me receiving my school certificate. When I was married I chose the colours in the bedroom and took care that my night-dresses and even the tissues all matched each other. Now in the desert I'd come to think of the bedroom simply as somewhere to sleep.

6

I was surprised when I saw the hall packed with women from the desert: I couldn't think where they'd been hiding all the time because the town always seemed forlorn and half-empty. They were like a strange and wondrous kind of bird with their beaks and gay plumage, or female magicians gathered to see the colour of the air that night. They dressed in magnificent colours and styles: Marie Antoinette was there,

Cleopatra, Madame de Pompadour, Scarlett O'Hara and Raqiya Ibrahim.

Their hairstyles too were out of keeping with this hall, which had been built especially for wedding parties after a private house had collapsed because of the great number of guests crammed into it. Even the ceiling of this place had fallen in on some women one night, and with that in mind I sat at the back near the door, although Nur protested angrily. The women looked heartless tonight. Was it because of their clothes, or because their veils hung down to their noses or their hair reached their waists? Nur had gathered up her hair under a white cap fringed with seed pearls on the ends of fine threads, and she wore a long dress by Valentino, who'd designed the same dress in a shorter length for European women.

The concert this evening was being given by a singer named Ghusun. Her fame had spread after she'd met Abd Al-Halim Hafez and he'd heard her bedouin voice and asked her to sing in Cairo. She took along her sisters and female relations to back her on drums and tambourines, but they were terrified by the lights and the audience and refused to sit up on the stage, even with their veils on. So Ghusun was left singing to the microphone alone with her lute.

When Ghusun appeared she looked like a heroic female warrior from an African tribe. Her hair was like a wig she'd found among the bric-à-brac left behind by some Western mission, but her features were African. She wore a dress that was half black, half red, with big gathers at the shoulders that extended down the sleeves. Gold chains and coloured necklaces hung round her neck and rings sparkled on her fingers. She aimed to dazzle the crowd, knowing that her place in society was precarious and her reputation unsavoury, because since she was little she'd sung and played the lute at weddings to earn her living.

Applause rang out but it was harsh and quickly over. The noise level rose. A boy of about four stayed close to the rustle of his mother's dress as she passed between the rows of women. I stared at their dresses and their faces, as they chewed gum with their mouths open, most of them still veiled. Their abayas were bundled up on their laps and it looked as if their dresses had big black stains in the middle. A fat girl, her head still covered, climbed up on the boards where Ghusun was singing and began to dance. She was followed by another, perhaps her sister; a thick gold chain bounced and jingled against her gold belt.

I supposed they were from the singer's band of dancers and musicians but I was wrong, for many more girls and women climbed up on the stage. The rhythms of their dancing, not Arab, and not a rapid European beat, but African, was mostly in the feet, with one hand held up in the air like someone calling out for help. It was as if they forgot themselves on the stage, even the thin girl who'd caught my eye because she was so thin and had such a pretty face. She'd greeted Nur warmly, talking in a low voice which trembled slightly with embarrassment, but there she was now dancing boldly to the beat. Nur chewed her gum and moved in time to the music, almost jumping up and down on the chair. For fun I said, 'You look as if you think you're dancing with them!' She leapt out of her chair and up on to the stage, the seed pearls flying around her head, her dress clinging to her. She stood out from the other dancers like a Hollywood star performing a jazz number.

I felt embarrassed suddenly, and amazed that this music and the naïve words – 'I'm in love, and I've got Indian hair' – could prompt Nur to dance with such spontaneous exuberance.

Ghusun stopped singing to announce jokingly, 'No one who's pregnant should be dancing.' One of them must have asked her, 'What if you're married?' because she went on laughingly, 'Then it's the opposite; it you're married you have to dance so you get pregnant quickly.' She moved her hands and waggled her chest in a gesture of confirmation.

Nur came back to her place and grabbed my hands and pulled me up saying, 'I'll introduce you to Ghusun. She's good fun. And you can see more from up there.' I felt ashamed of my clothes which seemed odd because they were so simple, and my flat sandles. Suddenly I was made uncomfortable by Nur's hand in mine, even though the women here rarely went about without holding hands. As Nur climbed back on the stage I hesitated for a moment despite the dozens of women already there. Nur went up and kissed Ghusun, who didn't get up but proffered a cheek and a hand to me and said with a wink, 'Are you the one from Beirut? I'll sing a song especially for you.' Then she turned to Nur as if she were finishing a story: 'Later on her poor mother shook her to wake her up for school and she was dead.' I interrupted, studying Ghusun's face: 'Who was?' 'Someone Nur knew. She choked to death in her sleep.'

I sat down next to Nur in the middle of all the others sitting there looking at me. Some of them were unveiled and stared at me, chewing gum and sipping tea. I noticed some of their expressions in particular and it seemed as if they were pleading with me. I brushed aside the thought that perhaps they knew about my relationship with Nur. They were passing a narghile round. One of them held it and took a long drag as if it was the elixir of life, and didn't let go of it until she was bending almost double where she sat. Another, older than the rest, drew on it with her eyes closed, not speaking or moving, as if it would give her back her youth. They looked pleadingly still, but as if constrained, into the faces and at the bodies of the dancers dancing to arouse.

> ' "Do you want to come out?"
> "Just try me," I said.
> "But don't be jealous," she said,
> "You won't be alone."
> So I said, "Forget it.
> You can leave me at home." '

Ghusun sang this smiling and the women sang along with her through their teeth, resting their gum on their tongues. How could the throat and tongue sing and the ear enjoy hearing words so much at odds with reality? They were like old women trying to darn enormous holes in socks. If they really thought about what the words said they might wish the tea and chewing gum would turn to deadly poison. 'I must be wrong,' I told myself, for they looked happy, clapped enthusiastically, and one of them lifted her veil a little so she could let out a wild trill of joy and appreciation. The henna was black around the fingers of the hands that were clapping. Ghusun stood up; her body was beautiful with her taffeta dress tight across her chest, showing off the slenderness of her waist. Was she leaving? About to dance? With the air of one who has no intention of exerting herself she gave her body a little shake making her breasts quiver, smiled and approached the edge of the stage like a feather fluttering in a current of air. All at once the shouting and laughter rose to a crescendo.

Nur drew my attention to a woman in the first row of the audience. Her hair was tied up in a black kerchief and she was twisting her neck around with enormous strength, as if detaching her head from the rest of her body. The women pushed her towards the stage. I had no idea what was going on. She stood facing Ghusun and both women were trembling slightly. Ghusun couldn't detach her neck from her body in the way that the other woman could. The woman began rocking her stomach and thighs as if she were receiving something with them, then thrusting it away. Ghusun tried to twist and bend in the same way, but she couldn't. The woman facing her bent backwards until she touched the floor and her stomach and thighs began to shudder. The singer didn't try to imitate her this time, but stood there laughing. 'What are they doing?' I asked Nur in embarrassment. 'Dancing,' answered Nur. The woman had got up and stood facing the singer again. She put her right shoulder against the singer's left, and they moved their thighs and stomachs rhyth-mically, then paused. One of the women in the audience rushed up and whispered in Ghusun's ear then went back to her place. Ghusun's expression changed but she didn't stop dancing. The woman bowed close to the singer's shoulder then to her neck and then touched her face. The singer backed away and the audience laughed and clapped. The tambourines and drums played louder. The woman moved in again, a quiet fire burning in her eyes in spite of the lack of air and oxygen. She was tall and slim and brown-skinned with gentle features, and her ear-rings were two broad circles of gold which gave an added sharpness to her large ears. Her neck was long and slender and carried on it a network of hundreds of blue, mauve, red and flesh-coloured veins.

I turned to ask Nur who this woman was and she ans-wered, applauding delightedly, 'She's Jaleela, the nanny of the Sidassi girls. She raised their mother before them and when the mother died and the father married again she stayed in the house with the daughters. They take her with them wherever they go and whoever invites the daughters has to invite Jaleela first.'

Jaleela was still challenging the singer with brazen move-ments of her hands, her tongue and every part of her body, leaving it to transmit its own signals. But the rhythmic nature of her movement made it into a dance: she didn't sway or rock her body; she ordered it or shook in response to it, disregarding the shouting around her; her ear was centred on the music and her other senses on the full-lipped singer. Jaleela's eyes were in an agony of passion, her mouth a stubborn line. She tried to touch the singer's face, to kiss her on the lips in the midst of the clapping and laughter, the crashing of tambourines and shouts of encouragement. But the singer drew back, laughed, put her hand up to her mouth and seemed to take something from between her teeth which she held in her fingers, gesticulating to the audience. 'What's going on? ' I asked Nur, my nerves all on edge. Nur answered simply, 'They're doing a local dance. One of the dancers grips a ring or a gold sovereign between her teeth and the other has to pull it out with her teeth.'

As if I were Umar I asked, 'Why don't they finish off the dance then? ' 'Ghusun doesn't want to. This woman Jaleela's awful. She must be gay.'

Ghusun's voice rang out singing about beauty, beauty's eye, beauty's form. The women and girls were all dancing although Ghusun cautioned them: 'Just two at a time. Two at a time, please.' But their enthusiasm, the music and the feeling of freedom away from the house and children, and the evening which still promised surprises made them fall over one another to get to the stage and jump around in a primitive dance, more than satisfied with the occasion although it was brief compared to many local weddings and evening parties. I took no pleasure in the songs or the happy dancing atmosphere; indeed I felt angry at the joy which filled the hall, although I tried to imagine how these women felt. A quite different feeling began to creep over me until I could no longer bring my face close to Nur's or turn when she spoke to me. When the singer and the woman danced with the ring between them, one trying to pull it from between the other's teeth, I couldn't bear to meet her eyes, or brush against her sleeve inadvertently, or hear the sound of her voice.

I was weary of the smell of chewing gum and incense, and their shouted conversations to one another from different parts of the hall. Their applause, even their dancing, seemed unacceptable; the music and the songs about love and imaginary love affairs had no connection with these dresses, these perfumes; their emotions that night were out of keeping with their veils. They were six hundred women, their ages ranging from the twenties to the forties, who knew that they were prisoners even in this hall because they couldn't leave it until their drivers or their husbands came to pick them up.

What did the night have to offer beyond the recalling of familiar tunes and the two women's dance? And I knew this was why Nur asked me if I'd go back home with her even just for an hour. My anger, which had died down of its own accord, flared up again at this and I didn't answer her. I was suddenly gripped again by the feeling I'd had when Nur had come into my bedroom and sprawled on my bed, as if the objects around the place which belonged to Umar and Basem had begun to grow sad reproachful eyes. With each day that passed the relationship appeared more furtive and unwholesome because it was inconceivable that it should either go away or be exposed. I began to fight against myself, as if there were two distinct parts of me. Every time Basem made love to me I clung to him trying to drive out Nur's image, angry at my sense of shame in the face of Basem's tenderness. Afterwards I would stand under the shower, and clutch my head in my hands and say out loud that what was happening to me wasn't real, that I wasn't real, my breathing, my head, my voice, my son himself were all illusions.

I found myself getting increasingly impatient as Nur spoke to me like a lover, then moved on to the details of her day, telling me what she was wearing then, what she was doing, who was at her house, what she was going to eat, using pet names and endearments that I wasn't accustomed to hearing even between a man and a woman. Only Nur's desert accent which I loved to hear stopped me making fun of her. I knew that my need to meet her, no longer to exchange conversation or to complain to each other or have fun, was aroused by the thought of one specific aspect, and our muscular spasms increased in intensity whenever circumstances threatened to intervene to impede our activity: a visitor, Nur's mother, Nur's daughter. Every time I stood up, straightening my skirt, I felt a surge of anger and vowed not to see Nur again, and forced my brain to recall the image of a gay bar in Berlin which I'd gone to out of curiosity with Basem and a group of friends.

I sat where I was like a cat watching a mouse, waiting for the right moment to pounce. I thought of the atmosphere in

my house; there was a feeling of the past, a sense of order and
stability emanating from the furniture, from Basem's talk and
from Umar's shouting and laughter; he'd be asleep now
between his Superman sheets. Anxiously, Nur asked again,
'Are you coming to my place for an hour?'

I drew back, took a hold on myself, and dared no more
than a shake of the head. I decided to get up from my seat, go
home and never see Nur again. I understood that it was the
dance of the two women and the excitement accompanying
each of their movements which lay behind Nur's invitation to
me on this occasion. But still I marched off past rows of
women to the door of the hall. I turned to look back and saw
them dancing under the fluorescent lights as if they were
drugged. Outside there was a dust storm, and dozens of men
stood at the entrance waiting, appearing to be guarding the
women inside.

I saw Basem waiting with Said in the car. He spoke first:
'You're late. I was worried about you. Said told me they
might not allow women to go home alone with their chauf-
feurs at night. Tell me, how did you enjoy yourself? ' I smiled
and replied, 'It was great.'

In my mind's eye drifted images of Ghusun, and the lust-
crazed old woman urging the girls to dance, pulling them up
on to the floor, embracing them and clasping them to her.
She sat with desire in her eyes, which descended to her tongue
as she complimented the women on their beauty and said
other more obscure things in short, jabbing phrases.

7

The canary hadn't sung since a female companion entered his life. She'd bewitched him while he was showing her the secrets of the house. Whenever he smelt the rice and came to the table as usual to peck a grain or two, or flew and landed on my shoulder, she called him to her. She had taken possession of his throat and he no longer sang or made a sound except when she was lost somewhere in the house and called out for help. Then, turning his little head from side to side, he would tell her that he was coming and fly through the rooms searching for her. When they were both in the cage at night he twittered lovingly to her with a sincerity which was plain to see, and touched her beak with his own. I'd realized that he needed a female when he stained his mirror perching and looking in it constantly, bending his head to peck at his reflection and singing loudly. When this female came into his life in flesh and blood he no longer sang of his loneliness and longing.

I stretched my hand inside the cage, trying to get him to hop on to my finger, then on to my shoulder as he usually did. This made the female more scared then ever and her anxious twitterings rose to a shrill cry. When he wouldn't come to me I banged the cage door shut, then smiled bitterly and sang to him:

'I had a little bird
So charming and fine
He woke early, before me
And warbled and sang
And hopped gaily about
And bathed his bright feathers.
But then he got married
And like a balloon

He began to deflate.
O, little bird
O, my canary.'

The garden-door bell rang. I wondered who it was who
didn't know how to open it. It was Kawkab, Nur's mother.
My heart beat fast. I tried to keep my voice normal and asked
how Nur was and why she hadn't come too, as if the mother
knew what was between us. She pulled off her dusty abaya
and rolled it up in her lap, then swivelled her eyes around,
looking piercingly from above her face veil. 'It's nice here.
Did you get the material from Lebanon?' She gestured with
her hand to the curtains then waved towards the sofa.

She didn't wait for a reply and asked about the bearskin on
the floor: 'What's that?' Then she added, fanning her face
with her hand, 'It's hot. What did you say it was called? A
bear. And you didn't get rid of its head? Look at its mouth
and its tongue hanging out, all ready to eat someone. God
forbid!' I didn't like the bear; Basem had come home with it
one day, and because Umar was so attached to it I'd grown
used to it. I hated Kawkab, hated her face, even though it was
withered with tiredness and the harshness of her life. Suddenly she embarked on the subject which she'd come to
discuss. Putting on a sympathetic voice, she said, 'Nur's not
very well.' I hated the look of her face still more. 'She's like a
stick of incense. She's coughing her lungs up. Yesterday I fed
her a kilo of bananas but her cough's still bothering her and
her chest hurts. You and Nur are sisters, best friends, and yet
you don't come and see her any more.' Her tone changed and
scolding now she said harshly, 'She told me that you're
heartless. You leave the phone off the hook and when she
comes to see you, you don't open the door to her. And your
driver tells lies and says you're not in. You ought to be
ashamed! Ashamed!'

I looked down at my fingers, trying to stop myself shaking.
I hadn't known that I could be so weak. I excused myself and

went into the kitchen and rested my head against the fridge for a few seconds. I clasped my hands round my neck and pressed. When it started to hurt I stopped and opened the fridge and took out a jug, fetched two glasses and put them on a tray. How I didn't drop them I don't know; my hands were trembling and I walked slowly, my eyes on the tray, pretending that I was concentrating on balancing the glasses: two empty glasses, since I'd left the jug in the kitchen. I smiled at Nur's mother: 'How stupid of me. I've forgotten the lemonade.' I came back with the jug and poured some lemonade nervously into her glass. She raised her veil and swallowed it in one go and put down the empty glass, then said as if rounding off the conversation or replying to a question, 'No, daughter, it won't do. A child's soul is precious to its mother's heart. You're a mother, you should know. Come and see Nur and you can talk to each other and make it up.' As if I didn't want her to hear me, I mumbled, 'I'll try and come this afternoon.'

Nur's mother stood up, laid her hand on mine and baring her yellow teeth attempted a lighter note: 'Come on. Come back with me now for a few minutes. Let me see you telling each other off and making up.' And she pressed my hand and squeezed my fingers tightly.

In spite of her show of affection I could only feel repelled by her. Still, I went with her to the door, opened it and went out with her. I didn't even take my purse and walked with one hand tightly clasping the other. My annoyance had turned into sadness and I wanted to cry. As I entered Nur's sitting-room I realized that we'd made the journey there at high speed; Nur's mother hadn't spoken to me on the way, as if she felt no need to cajole me any longer.

It was ten days or more since I'd been in that house, two days after Ghusun's concert. That day I'd woken up in the early afternoon, morose and discontented. I'd phoned Suzanne, Tamr and Ingrid, but none of them was at home. It was Nur's daughter's birthday party and I'd already decided not to send Umar. I'd promised myself that I'd read or iron my blouse, wash a dress, tidy my room, make a puppet, clean the birdcage, write some letters, repair a broken shell necklace, make a jelly, but I did none of these thngs; I got dressed and decided to go to Sitt Wafa, the Arabic teacher, but when I went out Said wasn't around.

I felt irritated with him, then I remembered that I'd finally given him permission to go to the mosque for the afternoon prayer. In the past I'd forbidden him because he stayed away for so long and he'd always given me the same answer: 'It's the company, Auntie. Every day somebody from home turns up and the news is fresh, fresh.' He didn't like praying in his room and for a week he wouldn't speak to me. Then one day I heard a sharp cry from the garden and when I rushed out I found him there weeping and he said to me, 'A snake, Auntie; it was huge. It saw me doing my ablutions and shot out its tongue to bite me but it knew I was getting ready to pray and it was afraid.' He realized that this trick hadn't worked so a bit later he came crying again and said that the sheikh of the mosque had seen him and threatened him and said, 'You heathen! You don't come to the mosque any more. Have you stopped praying?'

I went back into the house and was thinking about taking off my old nail varnish and putting on some new, when the phone rang. It was Nur, reminding me about Ghada's party and saying, 'Everyone's waiting for Umar.' Trying to sound normal, I said, 'Umar's at Sitt Wafa's and Said's not here,' but as usual Nur insisted on sending her car. When she'd hung up I looked around for a present to take and saw the female canary at the door of the cage, frightened to come out and fly. I shut the door on her and picked up the cage, annoyed with myself that I hadn't thought of getting rid of her before now.

The party was for the mothers as well, and they sat talking and eating while the children played between the sitting-room and the garden, chasing the dogs and the gazelles.

When it was over I stood up, reassured and happy because Nur too seemed to have decided that our relationship should become an ordinary friendship; even my initial embarrassment had disappeared within moments of entering. But now Nur clasped my hand and gulped, 'It's still early.' I answered her untruthfully, 'No, really. Basem's coming home early today.' But Umar protested, drumming his feet on the floor, which gave Nur the opportunity to interrupt and say ingratiatingly, 'Would you like to sleep at our house, Umar, and play with the gazelles?' He was silent, gathering himself up to answer, then said, 'Me and mama.' Feeling as if my breathing was being constricted, I said sharply, 'No, darling. Come on. Baba'll be all by himself in the house.'

Umar ran off after one of the gazelles while Nur said beseechingly, 'Me and Umar agree. Please, Suha, stay with me for the night. I'm scared and fed up.' But I walked towards the door, feeling my patience running out. 'That's enough of this rubbish, Nur. I can't possibly stay with you for the night. Grow up! You've got a child and so have I. And I love my husband and you love yours.' I didn't regret bringing our husbands into the conversation but Nur sprang over to the door and stood barring the way with a stubborn expression on her face. I went over and pulled back the curtain and then tried the other door but it was locked. I thought of Umar. What if he wanted to come in and couldn't or if he saw me through the glass door and called to me and I stood there without moving, unable to answer him or open the door?

I looked around me and my eyes rested on the telephone; I pleaded with it to ring. Suddenly I said, 'Now I understand why Saleh left you. You're spoilt and thoughtless.' Nur didn't answer me, but continued to brace herself against the door with all the strength she possessed. Her great house had dwindled to nothing and it was as if her life was all concentrated in that door. She said, 'I don't understand. You're the one I want and yet you behave so coldly. I'm ready to live with you and leave Saleh and my family for you, and you're even worried that the dogs and the gazelles might come in and see us! I really don't understand your nature. If somebody loves you, you run away from them and torture yourself about it . . .'

Things didn't go as I'd planned. Nur fought and protested, but she was like a moth that knows it will get burnt if it comes too close to the lamp. When I reached home after flatly refusing to spend the night with her, I don't know how I got into the house or what I said to Basem or how I looked as I sat waiting. I knew that she would chase me. The phone rang: Nur was crying, saying she was sorry, asking me to forgive her. Afraid that Basem might notice, I said quickly, 'I'll talk to you tomorrow.' A few seconds later she phoned again and I repeated, 'Tomorrow', put the receiver down and unplugged the telephone, to Basem's astonishment. 'Nur's bored, and she's too demanding,' I said carelessly. 'More bored than you?' asked Basem teasingly. 'I don't believe it. And anyway you always have friends who are bored and discontented.'

I stared at my reflection in the mirror and thought, is this really happening to me with a woman? I'd asked myself this question hundreds of times and rediscovered each time that this experience with Nur was deeply shocking to me.

Next day I couldn't see Nur anywhere. Her mother took me by the hand and opened the door of Nur's bedroom, saying, 'Come along, my daughter. Human beings shouldn't abandon one another.' She turned away and then I saw Nur lying full length on the bed. I'd promised myself that I would talk calmly and settle the matter once and for all, and this was what I wanted to do, but instead I shouted, 'So, Nur? You sent your mother, did you?' I knew as soon as I heard myself speak that I'd made a mistake. I'd imagined handling Nur in a completely different way so that we'd be like two friends exchanging confidences and I'd say that Basem had found out about us and threatened to divorce me and take

Umar away from me. But all I could do was say with a sort of malicious delight, 'So, Nur? You sent your mother after me, did you?'

Nur's scream reverberated around the room and made the dust rise from the curtains. Kawkab suddenly reappeared, her eyes transformed into black stones with sparks flying from them; because the rest of her face was covered by a face veil all her anger shot out of her eyes. 'Be patient, my daughter,' she said, lifting Nur's hair off her neck and face to soothe her. 'Be patient. I want to talk to this . . . this woman without a conscience, and find out what's going on in her mind.' What was she talking about? She walked up to me, her eyes ablaze, and shouted, 'Only God Almighty can make my daughter suffer!' Nur shouted at her mother who paid no attention and continued to blaze with anger. She thrust her face right up next to mine and said, 'If anyone harms as much as a fingernail of Nur's, I'll brand her until there's no light left in her eyes.' Then she dragged me out of the room by the arm, although Nur shouted at her and jumped up off the bed and caught hold of her mother's hand. Nur and her mother are vampires, I thought, and I'm their prey. I've got to escape fast. Her mother pushed Nur back inside her room, banged the door shut, and finished, 'Now d'you realize what Nur means to me? So one word from me to Saleh, and you and your husband and family are out. Deported.'

Was it possible? What would happen to Basem? But instead of crying or shouting back at her, I thought she doesn't know what's between me and her daughter. I found courage again and as if they were the only words I knew how to speak I said calmly and slowly, trying to control a trembling in my voice, 'What Nur and I do together is forbidden. We have an illicit relationship.'

The mother cleared her throat and moved her fiery eyes off me for a moment and I thought, quickly now I can get out of the door and forget this house, tear it out of my memory, whatever it takes. I'd actually gone a few steps when I heard a small noise behind me; it was the woman's dress trailing along the floor and when she grabbed my hand I screamed, frightened by the suddenness of the movement. Leaning forward she whispered almost in my ear, 'That's wrong, my daughter. Wrong. But adultery with a man is worse. And you know what things are like between Nur and her husband.' I didn't tell her that I didn't know him, nor did I say, 'Who is this man who can manage to live with your daughter?' I just wanted to get out of the door, and out of the country. The woman reached a hand into her bosom and took out a small cloth bag. Horrified, I thought she was about to try and drug me or poison me but she took out an English gold pound and pressed it into my hand.

The gold between my fingers made my heart race again until it hurt me. The feel of it seemed to bring me to an abrupt decision: I could only resolve the situation by talking to Nur. Going on talking to her mother was like banging my head against a brick wall: she was a creature from another world.

I went back in to Nur and let the gold coin clatter on to the table. She was turned to the wall. 'A gold pound from your mother,' I said, looking into her face, hating it. I let my eyes roam around the room trying not to look at Nur again, trying to ignore her presence and focus my thoughts far away from there for a few moments. I had to get away, to imagine myself in an aeroplane, and ignore Nur's sobs and the smell of food and the bed with studs on either side and the shaded lamps and the curtains drawn to blot out the existence of what lay behind. I remembered the first time I'd come to Nur's house, and the time that Nur had thrown herself on me and held me to her. I saw myself exchanging the impossible with her. It was as if it had happened, but to somebody else, and hadn't left its mark on me. But I cried because what was happening now wasn't what I'd wanted to happen nor what I'd promised myself would happen; because Nur was crying and we ought to have been rushing off together on a wild ride like before; and because it was impossible to get out of this house.

Only this time, like a singer with a beautiful voice who can't help bursting into song, or like a bee compelled to plunge its head into a flower, I stood up and it was as if all the power in the world was spreading along my veins and arriving in my brain. I could do nothing to control it; I just knew how lucky I was because I would never live in this house, and I wasn't lonely and didn't suffer from emotional impoverishment, and because I knew what I wanted and I was about to go through the door and out of the house and garden and I would never see them again even if every hair of my head was pulled out one by one and they tried to drag me back in by force. I saw the mother sitting on the floor; she was leaning back against the sofa, which was covered in material patterned with lemons and strawberries, and she beckoned to me to come over to her. But I walked on like a sleepwalker, a big smile on my lips, past her, out of the door, through the garden and into the fresh air.

I entered my house like a whirlwind. I didn't let Umar watch the end of his TV programme. 'Into the bathroom this minute,' I shouted, rushing ahead of him to wash my face. I piled my hair up under a plastic shower cap, undressed, and finding the hooks on the back of the door empty, I bent and took a shirt of my husband's out of the clothes basket, smelt it, threw it back in the basket, looked around me, then picked it out again and put it on. I turned on the showed and the water came out looking murky. I exclaimed in disgust, 'Ouf! They say the sea water's been desalinated and look at it, it's still sandy!' When the water was warm I called Umar at the top of my voice, and called again. He ambled along and took off his clothes holding on to the door handle, then got into the bath. He approached the spray of water from the shower then backed away again. 'What? Is it too hot or too cold?' I asked irritably. He said, 'From here it seems cold. When I get used to it, it's nice,' and stayed where he was. Again I asked irritably, 'And when are you going to get used to it? Next year?' And again he tried to stand under it, keeping at a distance until I took his hand and pulled him right under. When I started rubbing his hair he wriggled about and said, 'The shampoo's stinging my eyes.'

'This is Johnson's Baby Shampoo. It doesn't sting.' He didn't stop fidgeting and moving away from under my hand, until I slapped his hand hard. Then he realized I wasn't playing, and even when the water got hotter he just said quietly, 'This water's getting really hot,' and squirmed. I dried him quickly and knew that I was rubbing him too hard. Handing him his underwear and pyjamas, I said, 'Put them on in your room, darling. I want to have a bath.' Then I unhooked the shower and washed away the few remaining traces of soap, hung it up again and filled the bath. I threw Basem's shirt back in the dirty clothes basket and stood close to the mirror, examining my face. I was struck by the way it hadn't changed; my turbulent emotions, my confusion, my resolve didn't show on it. I felt happier at the thought that Umar hadn't seen a different face. The water gradually covered me. It was very hot but I withstood the temptation to add some cold to it and lay there sweating. This seemed to strengthen my resolve and I said to myself, 'That's it. I'm leaving this country, whatever happens. I'm no better off than the people still living in Lebanon.'

I would let Basem know of my decision, which I felt was irrevocable. I pictured him coming home from the office, tired and hungry. He'd ask me the reason and I didn't know what I should reply, even though the reasons were flying around in the air, indoors and out, evident and tangible. I was like a prisoner who couldn't give convincing reasons why he should be released.

'I can't tell myself this is just an experience which I have to go through. I'm an Arab. I'm supposed to feel that I have some connection with the culture here, but I feel none at all. I'm completely detached from it. I'm getting older. I'm wasting my time.'

My words were unconvincing. They were words that the

heroine had learnt by heart. I tried again: 'Let me go. I want to live a normal life. I want to walk about, not go in the car all the time, and I want to dress how I like. Yes, I've got a small mind. I don't want to feel afraid when I send a film to be developed if my arms aren't covered in the photos. I don't have any reasons. I can't tell any more lies. I don't want to be afraid. I don't want to tell lies.'

I was overflowing with emotion. I felt as if I was trembling and I lifted my hand up out of the water then let it sink back in. I didn't want him to say, 'It's just one of these fits you have every now and then. It'll pass like it always does then you'll calm down again.' I had to convince him that this time I was serious and there was no room for discussion.

I wavered before Basem, who was sitting with his papers from work spread out in front of him, his pipe cupped in his fingers and traces of sweat on his shirt. Life seemed normal and ordinary and my decision irrelevant. But because of the tone of voice I used and my general coldness I made it sound firm.

Knowing the answer in advance, I said, 'You mean you wouldn't think of leaving and going back with me?'

He interrupted me, stuffing tobacco into his pipe: 'Me? Now? You're mad! Not for at least two years.'

I sat in front of him mentally blocking my ears so that his words wouldn't get through to me. It was as if I'd smeared my body in anaesthetizing fluid to deaden my senses, although I hardly needed anaesthetizing: for months now I'd been getting gradually more impervious to external stimuli. He said, 'You haven't got enough to do, that's the trouble. Go and look for some kind of work again and do it at home.'

'I swear, I've never been properly employed here,' I burst out vehemently. 'I was just killing time.' Suddenly I felt angry and depressed and I shouted, 'Do you think my job in the supermarket was a real job? Or my teaching at the Institute? A woman who'd only been to primary school could have taught there.'

This outburst seemed to give me some comfort. Things appeared to be straightforward. I found myself staring at him as he fiddled with his pipe, and I sensed his uneasiness. All of a sudden I wasn't interested in hearing what he had to say. I began to remember the day he and I had decided to get married.

We were in the terrace café of a Beirut hotel. All the other tables were empty even though the sea was only a few metres away. We'd never thought of coming to this café before but that day we'd met early to apply for British visas so that we could go to Wimbledon, and they'd told us to come back for our passports in two hours.

The ice creams were melting although the heat was pleasant. I looked at the rust on the metal canopy, the potted plants on the tables. 'Maybe this is the first time anybody's sat here,' I said.

Basem replied abstractedly, 'Did you notice the questions in the embassy? What's your relationship to each other? Are you engaged? It must have been to find out if we were fedayeen, or perhaps just because we were a young man and a young woman travelling together. Of course he would have been surprised. He wasn't a European.'

Embarrassed, I remarked, 'Even Mata Hari and Philby wouldn't have been interrogated in so much depth. But it's good we convinced him and he's going to give us visas.'

Basem spoke first: 'Let's get married in London.'

I was taken aback. Although we'd spoken of it before, the sudden mention of marriage now confused me. The beating of my heart seemed to take over my whole body, but I said lightly, 'Why the sudden decision?'

'Because I love you,' he said, taking hold of my hand.

I wanted a house of my own. I would go back to it, open the fridge, take out a bottle of beer, listen to music turned up as loud as I wanted, sit alone or talk with friends in an atmosphere which would be quite different from my parents' house, although that was comfortable enough: people couldn't help relaxing in the atmosphere created by my mother. They all loved visiting our house, eating there and spending the evening with us. The food was always delicious, the drink flowed liberally, and my mother was a talker; she wanted to be the focal point of any gathering and without meaning to, she was always waiting for approval: of the food, the furniture, the pistachio nuts, or of her hairstyle, her lipstick, her outfit, her high heels, the way she'd preserved her youth and had so few wrinkles in spite of her fifty years; then of her liveliness, her original conversation, and the way she kept up with politics and world affairs.

I went on sitting in front of Basem, deliberately blocking off all the ways into my mind and heart. He sat with his head in his hands. I asked him if he was hungry. He raised his head and said, 'Does that mean you care about me?' I didn't answer and decided that I wouldn't enter into any more discussion with him and that it would be better if I left the room. As I stood up he said, 'What about Umar's school? Or doesn't that make any difference to you either?' I answered, 'I'll wait till his term's finished, of course.' When he sensed my stubborness he played his last card: 'I'm sure you'll change your mind after one week there. Life with your mother isn't easy; you'll probably quarrel with each other the day after you arrive. And I'm not prepared to come back with you to sort out the house or buy a flat at the moment. And renting's impossible . . .' I shrugged my shoulders and said, 'Too bad. I'll have to put up with it for now.'

It seemed the canary sensed my determination to leave. He dropped the piece of biscuit which he was pecking at and flew on to my shoulder.

Tamr

1

I sat in the car alone, queen of all I surveyed, and breathed
deeply, inhaling the air through my nose and into my lungs;
although my face was swathed in black I looked at the other
cars out of the corner of my eye. Riding in a car was no
longer a wish or a dream: I was bowling along the streets at
great speed and rejoicing; I hadn't reckoned on the distances
being so short and all the places so close. I thought, now I can
do anything I want.

When I'd first caught sight of the gleam of the car, which
was waiting for me at the battered wooden door, my heart
beat faster, and I felt the same as when I had a sudden vision
of a luscious fruit or cold water on a hot day.

Now I was passing tall buildings with glass fronts and
others with façades of marble and gleaming tiles; handsome
villas surrounded by trees; foreign restaurants – Filipino,
Korean, Sri Lankan, Indian, Pakistani, Yemeni and Lebanese;
numerous little plots of green grass and half-finished hotels
and apartment buildings.

I shook my head, muttering to myself in admiration, 'It's
what God has willed,' although I knew I'd never enter them.
Once I'd been on the point of entering the white hotel: I'd
bought tickets for a fashion show for me and Batul but it was
prohibited. Anyhow all that kind of thing was for men, and
for foreigners, who lived a different life. I saw a high wall
with patterned tiles. Two marble columns framed the
gateway, inlaid with fragments of copper and crowned with
copper urns. Said must have heard me gasp. 'That's a new
mansion,' he said. The wall stretched away endlessly in front
of my eyes. Perhaps this was the place which the Institute had
thought of for the Heritage Revival Festival. The woman
director had exhorted us to go back to eating local dishes in
the open under palm trees, preparing them in big cooking

pots over open coal and wood fires in the bedouin manner. The message was clear: we should return to the food of the people, rely on the produce of the area, stop imitating foreigners and be proud of our desert land. I reached out to touch the car's blue upholstery and found myself thinking with faint sadness how it was this which had stood for a long time between me and so many things: shopping, flying visits, celebrating when a relation or friend had a baby, sharing in the sorrow when someone died. The car made me think about the constant apprehensive planning required to gain access to it. It wasn't there for the taking, and was bound up with long waiting, standing firm in the face of despair until either my aunt visited us or my brother Rashid was in the mood to take us on a short excursion. Days here passed like months or years except when there were wedding celebrations and for these I was allowed to stay up till dawn, and they were the only times I felt free.

The car was one of the reasons why at first I hadn't been allowed to go to the Institute to learn how to read and write. The roar Rashid let out when my aunt tried to persuade him to let me go there is still ringing in my ears: 'I didn't like the idea of your going to London in the first place. I know you. You're a rebel. All your life you've played with boys. You ran away from Ibrahim, and you told me that the sheikh got so drunk he divorced you. And now you're asking me to hire a car for you and Batul so that you can go off to weddings unchaperoned with any driver you can find.' My aunt interrupted him: 'I don't know what she's done wrong. The sheikh divorced her after a month of marriage and married someone older, who wasn't as beautiful as Tamr and didn't come from such a good family.' Quickly I replied, 'Really, I'm quite happy. If the sheikh hadn't divorced me, I'd have divorced him. I'm happy now.'

Rashid was silent. Then he spoke again: 'No, Aunt. I have boundless affection for you, and Tamr won't interfere with it. But who gave her a roof over her head and supported her and her son? And who snatched Muhammad away from his father? It was me, no one else. No, Aunt. Tamr's not going to the Institute. I swear that it doesn't bother me having her to live with me. But she must think of her future.'

I went off into my room crying. After a bit I got up off the bed, wiped my eyes and went back to my aunt and Rashid. Struggling to control my voice and slow down my breathing I said: 'What's wrong with me going to study? The Anaiz girls, the Mabruk girls, all of them go, even the old women. And Qumasha and Mawda. Rashid paused on his way out and replied, 'You're not going. I haven't time to take you there anyway. And you're not going in their cars. You'd do better to think about getting married.'

'I'm not marrying for a third time!' I looked first at my aunt, who was sitting with her head bent and her hand resting on her crippled leg, then at my mother who had her hand up to her mouth. I rose and went to bed, but I didn't sleep at all that night. So transport was the problem? He could take me then; he'd occasionally given us lifts when Batul had asked him to. Perhaps Batul would have to enrol at the Institute, but what was to be done about her five children?

The next morning I measured out rice from the sack, picked it over, and cooked it along with the broth, the meat and the vegetables, then had a bath and put on my dress, and my abaya and veil. My throat muscles tightened as they did whenever I rebelled and did what I wanted to do. As I shut the door behind me I called out, 'The food's ready and I'm off to the Institute.' I walked along determinedly in my thick abaya, my throat growing tighter and my palms sweating. Only once I looked back towards the house and saw that its iron door was closed. I didn't notice the heat, or my sweat, or the distance. Instead I concentrated on the obstacles in my path which forced me to cross from one side of the street to the other – heaps of stone and steel beams and mounds of sand left lying about the streets. I couldn't see the Institute

building, but it didn't matter. I heard a car horn and stopped
myself turning round, drawing my abaya more closely round
me and wrapping the black head cover twice round my face.
A car horn, and Rashid's voice calling to me. I turned then;
he'd opened the back door for me. I stood where I was for a
moment but my thoughts were a jumble. I climbed into the
back seat and Rashid didn't speak the entire way home.
Gradually my throat muscles relaxed, and as I sat in silence I
decided to go on hunger strike. When my mother and Batul
pleaded with me for the sake of my son Muhammad, I agreed
to drink a little tea without sugar, but I ate nothing for three
days.

On the fourth day I felt weak and tired. As I lay in bed, I
heard my mother saying, 'Are the Institute and books worth
getting yourself in this state for?' Batul persuaded Rashid to
come in and see me just before the evening prayer and I was
confident that my fast must soon be over. In a voice which
sounded as if he was making an effort to be kind he said,
'What are you doing to yourself, Tamr?' 'I want to go to the
Institute and get educated,' I answered tearfully. His reply
was quite unexpected, and I didn't believe it until he repeated
it: 'You're not going to the Institute.' 'Then I won't eat,' I
said firmly. He went out of the room and I thought I heard
him saying, 'As you wish.' I no longer thought about anything. From time to time I opened my eyes. I could hear my
mother crying, Batul screaming, and I seemed to see my
mother striking her face with the palms of her hands. Batul's
children kept asking questions and one of her daughters said,
'Auntie Tamr's going to die!'

Batul appeared annoyed at the strength of my resistance.
She came in and made me sit up and tried to force a piece of
apple between my teeth without success. I needed all my
strength to move my face away and I began turning my head
rapidly from one side to the other. My mother eased me back
on to the pillow and laid her hand on my forehead reciting
prayers. Raised voices echoed off the walls and ceilings.

Batul's voice called out, 'Listen to me, Rashid. I swear to God you won't come near me and you're not my lawful husband unless you personally take Tamr to the Institute. Can you hear me, everybody?' My mother walked around with the incense burner in her hand, wailing and crying. She came towards my bed: 'Batul and your brother are fighting and who knows, they might divorce, all because you won't give up the idea of the Institute. Those English have had an effect on you. They must have put a spell on you and poisoned your mind. Tamr, my daughter, get up and ask God's pardon. Batul and your brother are going to get a divorce.'

My muscles went limp and I no longer seemed to have any interest in what the voices were saying. Batul and my mother came to sit me up, so that I'd be able to face in the right direction and say my prayers, but I couldn't. They stayed with me all night long, pleading with me in the name of the Almighty, kissing me then screaming at me, trying to force my jaws open. They managed to get a spoon in but half the soup dribbled down my chin and on to my neck. I shouted at them but my voice came out strangely weak: 'If anybody makes me eat I'll never forgive them and God won't either.' Batul shouted back, 'My God, you don't love anyone except yourself. I thought you and I were like sisters.'

I opened my eyes and I was frightened. The room was in silence. They must have all wearied of trying to convince me. I don't know how much time had gone by but suddenly Batul rushed in kissing me and crying 'Congratulations,' followed by my mother who was trilling for joy and singing, 'O Tamr, O Tamr, you're going to the Institute by car and you'll come back reading and writing.' I was tired, but even so I struggled into a sitting position, propping myself up with pillows. I opened my mouth to eat without the faintest desire, as if I'd lost my taste for food. Batul reported to me that Rashid had begun to sleep in the sitting-room, took no notice of her, and had stopped speaking to her. Her annoyance had prompted her to march into the sitting-room full of men that afternoon and fling herself at his feet kissing them and weeping. 'Forgive your sister, Rashid; God is forgiving. Knowledge is light. Fatima the Prophet's daughter could express herself eloquently and read and write.'

Rashid had been deeply discomfited. His face became the colour of blood. There and then he found the courage to agree. Everyone in the room knew about his refusal and his sister's fast. In front of them all Batul had knelt at his feet and invoked the Prophet's daughter. He raised her face from his feet and said, 'Be happy, Umm Ashraf. You can tell my sister to stop fasting.'

I said good morning to Said as I climbed confidently into the car, and thank you when I got out. I stood pressing Suha's doorbell with a smile on my face, marvelling at her ideas, as I looked at the ancient door which she'd bought from the herdswoman living nearby; in its place she'd had an iron door installed for the woman. Whenever I went into Suha's house, I felt as if I were boarding a plane and flying away, a similar feeling to the one I'd had the day I went to the Institute and met Suha for the first time.

Inside and out, the Institute building was the same as the other houses round about. High walls surrounded it and its garden was no more than a clearing of sand. The women teaching there made me feel as if I was abroad: they seemed to have no connection with the buildings, or the sign on its door – Gulf Institute for Women and Girls – or the brightly-patterned couches in the sitting-room, and the pictures on the walls torn from books and tourist brochures.

I sat at a table near some old women wearing face veils, and younger women, some of whom had left their headwraps on but bundled their abayas up in their laps.

I was astonished to find that there existed in my country women like the women in London and Lebanon and Egypt, the kind of women I'd seen on videos. Even Mary, my English neighbour, wasn't like that; in fact I'd never seen her in anything but a full length caftan.

I didn't hear a single word of the lesson. I was looking at the teacher Suha so intently that I was staring into her face, at her hair, her clothes, her shoes and her hands. I thought about where she was living and couldn't imagine that a woman like her would be able to go about the streets in her tight-waisted, low-cut dress, wearing that broad gold belt, long purple ear-rings and purple shoes with open toes which revealed her long toenails painted purple. And the hair. I couldn't find words to describe its colour and style: it fell in tousled disarray over her forehead and ears and neck.

During the break I saw the other teachers. They weren't beautiful like Suha. I thought about them too: where do they live? How do they live? Do they walk about the streets? Do they go down to the shops? What are their houses like? Are they like my neighbour Mary's house, ordinary, except for the electric mixer and the tumble dryer? Do they have children? Where do their children play – out among the sand and stones? Even the young girls from the desert were different under their abayas: they'd taken trouble over their hairstyles, their dresses didn't hang down to the floor, and they greeted one another with one kiss on each cheek, not with a third in the customary way.

I went back home and told my mother and Batul what I'd seen at the Institute. My mother clasped her hands together and insisted that I take her with me the next day to see the teacher Suha and the others, especially the American who went around smoking a cigarette in a holder. I laughed and held out my hands: 'No. No, no. I'd be too embarrassed.'

I was scared of the remarks my mother would make and the stories she'd tell. I went into my room and stuck my tongue out in the mirror, examining it closely to see if one of the arteries in it had contracted and that was why it was so difficult for me to speak English; or was it just that English didn't go with a woman who wore an abaya and whose hair reeked of incense?

Every evening I waited for the television to become silent, the children's crying to die down, waited till the door to the garden was shut and the black sheep had stopped bleating, till the women visitors had left and the relations set off back to their homes. Even when I'd excused myself someone would always follow me to my room, jokingly pulling the books away from me, or Batul or my mother would come in with almost the same phrase, the same sigh, on their lips: 'It's not right, Tamr. Really it's not.' When my aunt came to visit us she called to me all the time to come and squat at her side and entertain her.

After some weeks my relations with Suha went beyond those of a teacher and student. She invited me to her house and I made excuses several times before I was frank with her and said that Rashid would lay down the condition that she must visit us first. Suha was delighted and said that she'd rarely been invited into the local people's houses and had always wanted to see them. The first time she came, I was glad to have the chance to ride in the back of the car next to her but I felt embarrassed to see my teacher chatting uninhibitedly with the Yemini driver.

I kissed Suha on both cheeks as usual and asked her if we could sit in the garden. I noticed boxes and cases against the wall but it didn't occur to me to ask who was going away because her house was always changing its appearance and she was always receiving things from abroad. 'In this heat?' she expostulated. 'We can sit on the green grass,' I smiled. 'D'you call that grass, and green?' she asked in a disgruntled way. 'Even though the wind and sand have left nothing, green or otherwise?' But she stood up and handed me a glass of tea and went ahead of me into the garden carrying a glass for herself, and we sat down. Suha's eyes roamed over her garden and she remarked that she could see nothing in it that she wouldn't be able to see on the other side of the garden wall, but I sat benevolently studying the tomato plant with the green fruit hanging from it, the water in the round plastic basin and the mauve and white bougainvillea on the wall. I didn't like the scented tea she served but I sipped it all the same. I preferred it well stewed, and Suha had added a Lipton's tea bag to my glass and left it until the tea became a deep brown colour. I sipped my tea feeling thoroughly happy. I loved foreigners' houses. They were new and spacious. I began as usual to recount my problems with my brother and the bank, not noticing the listless expression on Suha's face nor her distracted manner, until she interrupted me: 'Did you get the paper from the sheikh?' 'Tomorrow,' I replied excitedly. Our eyes met and we both began to laugh, remembering the day not long before when I'd asked to borrow Said and the car and she'd immediately begged to be allowed to come too. 'I'd love you to,' I'd replied, and she'd looked as blissfully happy as if I'd opened the door of Paradise to her. I was amazed because I hadn't come across a person who asked permission like this before. Whenever we had the chance to leave the house we swarmed out like locusts, big and little, young and old. In the car she never stopped asking me if I was upset and if I felt any shame or anxiety. 'Why should I?' I asked. 'Why?' she shouted back in surprise, 'When you're on your way to ask your ex-husband for a divorce certificate after fifteen years?'

I laughed: 'What about it?' I replied. I started to remember the way to the big house; it was the largest one in our area. A sentence escaped from my lips: 'I hope the garden'll be like it was before, Suha. It had an oleander and a prickly pear and yellow roses.'

Suha slapped my hand lightly: 'You're impossible, Tamr. Thinking of the garden at a time like this!'

I began giving directions to Said and we ended up in a dead end street. 'Obviously you've forgotten the way,' Suha remarked laughing.

I looked all around me. 'I don't know what they've done with the road, sister. It's higher, lower, bigger, as far as I can see.' Said asked who was the owner of the house and when I mentioned the name, he said, 'I know him. One of my group of friends is a driver for them.' Not until we drove in through the open gate did I spy it. We got out of the car. Said went forward and hailed the doorman. There were numerous doors in the tall building which was built around an open courtyard. A woman appeared, crying, 'Welcome, welcome,' and kissed us. We followed her up a staircase with a scarlet fitted carpet. As she climbed she talked: 'The sheikha has lots of nice stories to tell. She's just arrived from down south. It was some wedding, there was enough food for a whole valley. Welcome to you. The people who couldn't be there are forgiven.'

Suha asked me what she was talking about. 'They had a wedding,' I replied, then correcting myself I said it again using the Lebanese word for wedding and imitating a Lebanese accent. We followed the woman into the large salon. I went up to the sheikha who wore a dress of gold silk and on her wrist lots of gold bangles set with precious stones which outshone all the gold gleaming around the room. She kissed me on both cheeks and then did the same to Suha. 'Welcome,' she said. 'How are you? Are you well? ' 'Thanks be to God. How are you?' I replied. The sheikha leant forward to move the lump of incense in the burner and Suha looked about her. I too took the opportunity to snatch a glance around while the sheikha wasn't looking. The furniture was new and there was crystal ware and objects made of what looked like silver, a verse from the Qur'an worked in gold, a Ramadan calendar, a stuffed falcon and beside it on a glass table, an arrangement of roses made of semiprecious stones. All this was new to me. Before the room had been no more than a humble sitting-room. Vast sofas stood against the wall. Gesturing towards Suha, the sheikha said, 'Would the lady prefer to sit on the sofa instead?' I smiled. 'It's all right. My friend's Lebanese. She was a teacher at the Institute.' Then I introduced myself: 'I'm Tamr, Tawi's daughter.' The sheikha gasped, her eyes bright. 'I'm sorry, I didn't know who you were. When you got married I was in the south. I was very upset when I heard that you were divorced. I remember, I said to the sheikh, "You divorced Tawi's daughter? The girl whose forefathers' blood is one with the desert sand?" How are you? Are you married again? What's your son's name?' 'Muhammad.' 'Ah – Muhammad. And what is he doing? I see, studying. My son Abd al–Rahman married Nimr's daughter the day before yesterday. You should have seen the bride: she was dressed like they were in the old days and she weighed as much as a camel, God bless her. Couldn't you have been with us?'

'Congratulations,' I said. 'I hope they'll be happy and give you grandsons and granddaughters. But what I came for, sheikha, was a certificate of my divorce from the sheikh. I want to open a workshop and they asked me for it.'

'Fine,' she answered simply, 'Ask for anything you want. There's no problem, Tamr. But tell me, your son Muhammad, was he the one whom Ibrahim's family kidnapped and then your brother chased after them and snatched him back?'

'That's right, sheikha,' I replied smiling. 'So you've remembered.'

The sheikha sipped her coffee and Suha and I did the same. 'I know everything,' she said. 'When I visit here the women in the house tell me all the gossip.' Then she turned to the other women and told them the story of my son's abduction. After some hesitation, because the sheikha wasn't old in spite of her gold teeth and the streaks of white in her black hair, Suha interrupted, 'Is the sheikh your son?'

The sheikha reached out playfully to Suha and gently smacked her hand. 'No, my daughter. I'm his first wife. And then the oil and the money came and the sheikh wanted more wives.' Probably realizing that Suha wouldn't know the Qur'an, she added, 'The Almighty said, "Marry of such women that please you: two, or three, or four. But if you fear that you cannot treat so many justly, then marry one only

. . ." So he married a second wife.' There was silence for a few moments, then the sheikha transferred her attention to the other women. I didn't rise to leave until I'd drunk some cold fruit juice, followed by tea, then coffee, and eaten some cake. I stood up and kissed the sheikha and asked, 'Shall I come tomorrow to get the certificate?' 'Will it be all right when the sheikh comes back?' she said. 'He's gone into the desert for two or three days with a group of his friends to hunt gazelles, but write the year of your marriage and your divorce for me on a piece of paper.' I wrote the two dates on some paper from Suha's handbag. As the sheikha took it from me Suha nudged me, and when we got outside she said, 'What d'you bet that'll never reach the sheikh?' I laughed but answered reassuringly, 'It'll be all right, God willing.' I said goodbye to her and, my cheeks flushed, thanked her for coming with me and lending me Said and the car. Suha couldn't help conveying her misgivings to me once more, and I reassured her again, saying confidently, 'She promised and it's my right.' Then she asked me, 'What do you feel, seeing the house after fifteen years?' 'Nothing,' I answered laughing. 'It wasn't my home. I was like a guest in it.'

I noticed that Suha still looked distracted and had stopped talking. 'You look as if you've got a headache,' I said. 'Perhaps it's the heat. Let's go inside where it's air-conditioned.' I told her what had happened between me and Rashid and how he'd turned down my new plan. Without waiting until I'd finished speaking she burst out, 'Maybe Rashid's right. Maybe you'll lose out, putting everything you've got into a dressmaking business, and sewing machines and hair dryers and Filipino women.'

'What else can I do? The schools don't accept qualifications from the Institute. You have to have a university degree. Besides, everyone complains about the shortage of dressmakers. Women aren't allowed to be measured. There isn't even any consultation between a dressmaker and his customer – the little window that he opens between you and him isn't enough – and nobody buys the ready-made dresses in the shops. How can a woman buy a dress without trying it on? Then there's nobody to do hair and colour it. Honestly, Rashid's not thinking about me making a loss. He just wants me to get married. He thinks I'll bring shame on him. It's Batul's fault. She told him about my quarrel with Ibrahim: Ibrahim said to me on the phone, "I don't want people to say that the mother of my son's like a woman from one of those Far Eastern expatriate families, doing people's sewing, and washing their hair. On top of that there'll be women coming and going. How will my son be able to show his face in public when the authorities come and close the place down?" When I'd heard what he had to say, I lost control of myself completely. The blood rushed into my face and I buried my head in my hands and screamed out loud. Then I took my hands away to see the blood which I thought I could feel pouring from my head and face, and clutched my heart and imagined my hands covered in bruises from its wild beating. I rushed off into my room and tore my nightdress and banged my head against the chest and the wall, and struck my face. Poor Batul couldn't get hold of me. I took off all my clothes, screaming, "Come and look, everyone. See for yourselves if I'm a slut." '

I took a sip from my glass waiting to hear Suha's irritated comments and her expressions of sorrow at my situation. But instead of sympathizing she stood up to pour more tea, then as if the words had been on the tip of her tongue for a long time and came tumbling out all at once, she asked, 'Why don't you go abroad to live and be free of all this?'

'How can I?'

With renewed enthusiasm Suha said, 'Your English friend Mary could put you up for a bit and afterwards something would come along.' I laughed and patted Suha's shoulder. 'Come on, Suha. What are you thinking of? Do you want me to go away and never come back? Leave my country and live in London? What would I do in London? A person away from his country and his nearest and dearest isn't worth a stick of incense. It's true I was happy abroad. But how I missed it here! I even missed the humidity and the dust and the heat, believe me. And what would they say about me? That I'd run away. For what reason?'

Suha said, 'I'm running away. Look, everything's packed.' She pointed towards the wall. I laughed, not bothering to look over at the case and the trunks. 'Impossible. I don't believe you. You must just be going on holiday.' 'I promise you,' she replied, 'I'm leaving in two days and not coming back.'

Still amused by what I thought was her exaggerating, I said confidently, 'That's what you say, but as soon as you find out what it's like to be away from here you'll be back.'

Suha was plainly annoyed at my implying that she had no alternative but to live here, and answered sarcastically, 'God forbid. I hope I never even see it in my dreams.'

'What's the reason?' I asked her. 'You go to restaurants. You've got a car. You go to the pool.' Then looking about me, 'You've got a big house, air-conditioning even in the bathroom, a garden. No, you've nothing to complain about.'

She sighed, and then almost screamed, 'For goodness sake, Tamr! Where do you live? Out by the date palms. Of course. You're well named, aren't you!* I can't breathe. There's no freedom here. You can't play tennis, go to the cinema, go for walks. There's no entertainment – didn't you hear how a crowd of them went to the hotel, dragged the men in the band off the stage, broke their guitars and threw them out? And they told the women to wait in another room.'

'God forbid,' I interrupted her, 'Those are just rumours.'

'What do you mean, Tamr? ' she cried. 'A friend of mine was there. And the trouble was that her husband was away. Imagine if they'd known that she'd come out in the evening

*Tamr means 'dates' in Arabic.

without her husband! Thank God she escaped. All the women got out through the window.'

'Why should they keep their mouths shut?' I retorted sharply. 'Once when Batul and I were settling up with a supplier a quarter of an hour before prayer time, an old man came into the shop and banged on the table. I shouted at him and asked him what he wanted, but you have to excuse them – there are so many foreigners here.'

Suha changed the subject; forcing a weak smile she asked me, 'So what are you going to do?' 'You'll see tomorrow,' I answered with enthusiasm. 'I'm going to get a licence to open my own workshop, in my name, that's if Said can take me and bring me back.' 'Said and I are at your service,' answered Suha. I rose to kiss her on both cheeks. 'I don't know what I would have done without you. Thank you from the bottom of my heart, darling.' Suha thought I meant the car and Said, but what I was really grateful to her for was introducing me to another way of life in the desert which I'd known nothing of, starting with colours and furnishings and ending up with civilization. I thanked God that I'd gone to the Institute, had Suha as my teacher, eaten a slice of cake on that white plate with flowers on it, drunk tea with honey in it instead of sugar, which according to Suha was "white poison", and seen Suha's canary chirping, flying freely about the house, from her shoulder to the telephone receiver to the chair. It was all new and my mind had picked it up and recorded it.

2

'Tamr. Not another word! Listen! Don't turn me into an infidel and make a mockery of my prayers.'

I was silent. I watched a fly swoop down on to my mother's hand. My throat muscles tightened. The fly took off again and I sat facing my mother without speaking, watching it hover over her dry white skin.

'Tamr, Tamr. Don't let me regret the past. Four years . . .'

I didn't want her to finish and I got to my feet irritably. 'I'm not listening. I'm not listening,' I shouted, and went into the kitchen. I put the kettle on the stove and waited for the water to boil. I felt as if I had something sweet like Turkish Delight in my mouth and it passed down over my throat muscles, making them relax. If I'd stayed in the other room I would have seen my mother put a hand up to her face to adjust her veil; she would have disengaged a finger to touch her nose and the sweat under the eyes, before shaking it in my face. 'Four years,' she would have said, 'and not a day went by without me saying my prayers, not a year without me fasting; I missed my period and the doctors said, "There's a child in your stomach," and I swore to God that I wouldn't break a fast or miss a prayer. I know my Lord will take this into account on the Day of Reckoning, although while I was pregnant I could have been exempted from ninety days of fasting and about two hundred prayers.' As usual I would have corrected her: 'A hundred and twenty days of fasting,' and, trying to calculate the number of statutory prayers my mother would have prayed in the course of four years: 'It comes to much more than two hundred.' I used to enjoy my mother's stories about how I'd had needle marks on me and been completely bald when I was born, especially since now my hair hung down my back and my eyebrows and eyelashes were thick, and there was no trace of the needle on my hands and thighs as far as I could make out from my mother's constant intimations; she was for ever grabbing my hand and peering at it, bringing it closer until her face touched my skin, when she would mutter 'Ha!' and let it go. But I no longer liked this story of her four-year pregnancy, nor the one of my aunt's about her daughter Awatef being born with her insides hanging out – imagine her swimming around in the womb with her guts trailing – and the doctors cutting her open and restoring every organ to its proper place. There was another one they told about two cats, sisters, who'd lived in their grandfather's house, which I didn't much like either: when the older cat was pregnant the other was jealous and after a while became pregnant too even though she never came out of her place in the box. The two went into labour together, cut each other's umbilical cords and couldn't tell their off-spring apart.

I used to look at my aunt and my mother as they finished off the tale and mumbled, 'God preserve us from the Devil.' They sat together morning and afternoon whenever my aunt visited the place, which she used to do a lot after she became half-paralysed. Their conversations wouldn't develop and take off in different directions until after lunch between cups of tea and coffee and fruit juice and biscuits. Each of them wanted to tell her own stories and my mother didn't listen to what my aunt said, nor my aunt to my mother. This was obvious from the way they behaved; my mother was absorbed in her fingers, my aunt poking about in her ear, then counting the beads on her necklace; or else my mother would get up for no reason and go off into the bedroom or the kitchen while my aunt continued her tales.

My aunt Nasab captured my attention more than my mother; her powerful voice, which had a huskiness about it, her gold teeth, her deep colouring, her gold heavy-looking neck chain, the henna reddening and blackening her hands and feet, everything about her was exaggerated; she put kohl on her eyes and the line along her lower lid was as broad as a finger; under her head cover she wore her hair in two black plaits which she sometimes untied; then she combed her hair with her fingers and replaited it, and I never once saw a single white hair among the black. She would sigh and say, 'Tamr, God is above and understands everything. Praise be, He is all-knowing. That Awatef's innards were tangled, and why, He knew. But He tries human beings and examines their faith. By God and the Kaaba, when I saw her come out as beautiful as the full moon, with huge eyes, looking at each of us in turn, and her guts hanging out on to her skin, I said, "O Lord, I'm not going to complain or abandon my faith. I want to love and cherish her as long as there's life in her." Darling Awatef. She was all eyes, eyes that took in everything. Sita said to me, "You moved when God was breathing life into Awatef." I realized that this was true: while I was asleep my feet would change places with my head.'

I noticed that the water had almost boiled dry and I was still standing right next to the whistling kettle. I poured what was left of the water over the tea bags and sugar, put the pot on a tray with glasses and took it into the sitting-room. My mother was watching television, although the picture was unsteady. I couldn't imagine that I'd be able to sit there as I had done before, content to drink tea and talk to the visitors who would surely come. The sunset call to prayer was stamped on my memory among the glasses of tea and the conversations, the noise of the television and the children playing, and the women praying wherever they happened to be.

Now I sat down at a distance from my mother and aunt, pretending to read, then pretending to write figures on a piece of paper, deliberately making a noise as I did it: the rent, the running costs of the workshop, the licence, the cost of bringing seamstresses from the Philippines.

My mother addressed my aunt: 'Nasab. When Tamr was in London someone must have put something in her food or drink; or perhaps the Devil appeared in the shape of a nurse or a doctor and whispered evil thoughts to her. They're idolators and evildoers over there, and they want to make the believers turn away from their faith so that they can increase their own numbers. And that foreign girl next door – the Virgin Mary or whatever her name is . . . '

I didn't laugh, because she never remembered the name of our neighbour Mary, and I didn't raise my eyes from the piece of paper.

My aunt replied, defending her, 'I understood that her name was Maryam. And I swear by God and the Qur'an that she came to see me in hospital one day.' She stretched her hand down to her healthy leg and went on. 'May this leg of mine become like the bad one if I'm not speaking the truth. I swear to you, Taj, she talked to me for ages, and she spoke in Arabic. "Sitt Nasab," she said, "My husband's not here. He's in a country a long way off, and I just have my children with me. I'll take Tamr on the bus to see the Queen's palace, Oxford Street, Big Ben, the Zoo." And I was nodding my head, making out that I was sometimes unconscious, not always listening, not talking much.

'Tamr had melted the foreigner's heart, but as my own heart softened towards Tamr, because I saw her crying, I muttered to myself, "Lord deliver me from the devils of the cold and the rain; if anyone sees Tamr or she gets into trouble, Ibrahim's family and the sheikh's family will come buzzing around like bees," so I said aloud, "No. No." '

My mother beat her chest and said in a quarrelsome voice, 'Let me understand this. Let me understand it. What turned her mind upside down, and who put two bagsful of tears in her eyes? When they kidnapped her son, she didn't let out a whimper.' My aunt interrupted: 'Didn't you see her? When they stole Muhammad she was as white as a ghost.' She sighed and drummed on her chest with her hand. 'I'm telling you the truth. For twenty days and twenty nights when I was in hospital Tamr didn't leave me. She was always on the sofa or at the window. When Awatef came they went to Oxford

Street and bought perfumes and material, and I said to her, to Awatef, "You and your husband are free to do as you please but Tamr has to stay with me. I want to see her on that sofa." '

I found myself listening intently but I didn't comment on their conversation as I normally did, or shout when my mother said, 'Rashid was right all along. The Institute has turned her head, and the Lebanese teacher, and the cars. She needs a home of her own and children.' Then she looked in the direction of the door, afraid that Batul, who was in the kitchen, would hear her, and whispered, 'I'd like to live with her and relieve Rashid of the responsibility. It's true that Rashid – God grant him a long life – doesn't ask for a thing from us. He has a sense of duty towards the family, but what concerns him is his sister's future. Nobody believes that Rashid's only my stepson, and in the past I've bitten his mother and she's spat in my face. He acts as if I were his own flesh and blood.'

My aunt listened thoughtfully, then remarked, 'God bless Rashid, and God bless us. English people are born and die strangers to their families. When the English doctor found out how we live, how we don't abandon members of our families, he said to me, "You're more civilized than we are." I asked the English girl Maryam who was there with Tamr – my dear Tamr who stayed by my side and never ever left me – what the doctor meant and she explained the word "civilization" to me in Arabic: it means progress and modern life, aeroplanes and machinery. I said to her, "Tell the doctor I've got faith in aeroplanes because I've travelled in them, and in steamships and cars for the same reason. But I don't believe that a person's landed on the moon and I wouldn't even if I saw a million pictures of it. How could a man stand on it when it's the size of a loaf of bread or a water melon, without it falling down? And tell the doctor that I don't believe the earth rotates and is like an apple. If the earth went round, this bed of mine and that table over there would change places.

Tell him these are fantasies. Or perhaps it's better not to make him angry so tell him my aunt believes in the radio and the television; they're excellent and they help to pass the time – even though when we listened to the radio for the first time we said it was the Devil, and when we watched television we said it was the Devil's grandfather." '

I put up my hand to touch my hair, all that was left to me of London. A stylist there had cut my long straight hair and given me a light perm. London, with its shops, the white bathroom, the clean hospital corridors; the green expanses there reminded me of the gardens they tell us are in Paradise with rivers flowing underground. I loved the rain, the red buses, tea and biscuits in the cafés, and the respect shown me by every man I met: the air steward, the nightporter at the hotel, the doctors at the hospital, the taxi drivers.

In London I decided that when I went back to the desert I'd enrol at the Institute and study. Learning to recite the Qur'an with the teacher of religion wasn't everything. I would take English lessons too so that I could reply when someone spoke to me. I couldn't say a single word as it was, and I couldn't fill up the forms at the customs even in Arabic. I pictured myself sitting in front of the television explaining to Batul and my aunt and my mother what was really going on in the foreign films: the woman whom Mr Rochester kept shut away in *Jane Eyre* was his mad wife, not his mother.

3

The following day I collected the divorce certificate from the sheikh. It was as if a chicken had taken a pen and scratched its name. When I reached the government building I said to Said, 'Ask the official to come to me here. I'll wait in the car.' Said didn't show any surprise. 'One moment, Aunt Tamr,' he said, getting out of the car.

Although I stayed in the car my heart was knocking against my chest just as it had done a few days before when I went into the bank. On that occasion I'd known that what I was doing was wrong; I was probably the first woman to cross its threshold, but women went into shops and stores and bought things. Who was going to stop me? The thick black cover was over my face. Through it I could see all the eyes, all the bodies. Nobody said to me, 'You're not allowed to come in,' and I went forward confidently and handed the man a paper. He went away for a little while, then came back and asked me if I had my identity card with me. I said yes, thinking a few seconds and this tension will be over, but then he told me that my money was in Muhammad's name. I gasped. 'He's my son,' I cried. 'He'll have to come and see us himself,' said the official. I went out of the bank, wondering why Rashid had entered my money in the name of my son who'd been five years old when my father had died and left it to me.

The next day when my son came, I made sure that he had his identity card. Without delay I wrapped my abaya around me and went towards the car. His astonished voice made me halt. 'What are you doing, mother?' Embarrassed, I answered, 'I'll come with you and wait for you in the car.' In even greater surprise, he replied, 'You're coming with me to the bank? And waiting in the car? Have you gone mad?'

I didn't argue with him and went back into the house with my hand on my heart. Twenty-five thousand, to be handed over to my son who wasn't even sixteen years old. I didn't take my hand off my heart until he came back with the money in a paper bag.

The same sensations had returned the first time I came to this building to apply for a permit for a workshop and hairdresser's. Silence hung over the place, and when I approached an official sitting at a table he appeared tongue-tied and waved me over to another table. From there I was passed from one person to another, and I realized that by coming into a government building I had made another big mistake. But it wasn't forbidden, and why should it be? The black cover was on my face, the black wrap around me decorously hiding my charms, and the hem of the dress I wore underneath it trailed behind me on the floor. I knew that Rashid would be furious. He'd kill me. Too bad. I returned to the first table. The dejection which had taken hold of me was transformed into a kind of daredevil courage. 'My name is Tamr daughter of al-Tawi,' I declared, not caring if anyone heard me or not. 'I want to open a dressmaking business and a ladies' hairdresser's.' The man answered in spite of himself, as if he had come under my sway: 'The dressmaking business is possible. Not the hairdresser's. Are you married?' 'Divorced.' 'Get a certificate of your divorce, then let your guardian bring us the lease and we'll examine the premises, and afterwards if everything's all right we'll give you a permit.' Looking down at the ground, he went on, 'But next time, stay in the car and send your driver, and someone will come out to the car with the papers for you to sign.' I thanked him and left. A certificate of my divorce? I hadn't seen such a thing when I divorced my first husband or my second and I didn't remember signing my name on a single official document in my life.

I ran away from my first husband Ibrahim one hot noon-day, with my son Muhammad in my arms. My husband's family were asleep because their stomachs were heavy with food. I was divorced by my second husband early one morning. I woke up at the sound of knocking on my bedroom door which was locked from the inside. As I hurried to open it I remembered the sheikh, my husband, saying to me the day before, 'Lock your door. My friends are sure to get drunk and one of them wants to see if it's true that you look like Nabila Ubaid. You know the wicked notions they get.'

I looked like a film star? I'd examined myself that night. Brown skin, large eyes, small nose, even white teeth, average height; my body wasn't bad except that my bottom was too fat.

I opened the door hastily and found the maid outside, holding Muhammad's hand. I smiled at him and held him. 'Good morning. Good morning, Hammouda.' The maid said shortly, 'Your brother Rashid's downstairs.' This astonished me, and I wondered what could have happened. Batul wasn't due to have her baby for another month. Ibrahim's family must want my son. I flung my dress over my silk nightdress and rushed downstairs.

Rashid greeted me angrily, but with some malicious satisfaction in his voice: 'Congratuations. The sheikh's divorced you.'

I didn't believe what I was hearing. The previous day the sheikh had calmed me down when he saw me crying, terrified by Ibrahim threatening to take Muhammad away from me. He'd said, 'Nobody's going to harm a fingernail of yours while you're my wife.'

Confronted by the news that he was divorcing me, I felt surprise and curiosity, and didn't know whether I was glad or sorry. I learnt from the maid as she helped me to pack that she'd been woken up by the sheikh shouting. He was very drunk but she'd seen him hammering at my bedroom door. When the door remained closed, he'd fetched a revolver and started trying to break in. He'd had to be restrained by the driver and the servants, and even then he wouldn't give in until he'd sworn to divorce me, asked for two witnesses and done it. No one believed me when I swore by God and his prophets that I'd heard nothing but the roaring of the air-conditioner, although it was rare for me to sleep so deeply.

After a few days in Rashid's house I realized that I was pleased to be divorced. The sheikh was a drunkard, with a bottle to hand twenty-four hours a day. He would sit all day long, never rising except to shake hands with a visitor, drinking glass after glass until his head slumped forward and he slept. He would wake up in the afternoon sometime and call until I came to him. He smelt strongly of drink and I would remind myself that I just had to bear it for a little while; soon he would leave me. Sometimes he would fall soundly asleep when he'd barely climbed on top of me. This delighted me and I longed for it to happen every time, for I found the smell of drink hard to take. I knew that my aunt and my brother and all of them were happy that I'd married into a big house that was like a palace and had servants and cars and drivers. The sheikh was an important person, and he was affectionate and generous; presents and money, like drink, were always available and he distributed them lavishly. He treated me like a daughter although he was no more than fifteen years older than me. Every day he asked me, 'Have you had something to eat or drink? Thanks be to God. Has Muhammad eaten? Thanks be to God. Has he had plenty? Thanks be to God.' Muhammad was my son and thanks be to God the sheikh rarely saw him, and even when he did see him he didn't play with him.

When I told Rashid all of this he said, 'What business is it of yours? It's not you doing the drinking, is it?' But coming back to my brother's house, living among them all, me being unmarried, was hard on Muhammad. I began to sell my jewellery and clothes to the neighbours at low prices so that I could buy Muhammad what he wanted. He was always telling me that his cousins were much better off than he was and instead of studying and doing his homework he would deliberately set out to annoy me. I knew that my separation from Ibrahim had changed him into a nervous, unpredictable boy, uncertain which of us to go to. When he was staying with me he rejected me and the life he lived with me, and asked to go back to his father; two days after he'd gone, Ibrahim would contact Rashid and say that Muhammad wanted me. On one such occasion Rashid came with me to fetch Muhammad. The boy looked happily out of the car window until we'd been travelling for a few minutes, then a scowl decended upon his face and he didn't say another word until he asked his uncle to stop the car because he felt sick. He got out and ran off and up on to the dunes where he sat crying forlornly. He refused to come down and began to throw sand at me and Rashid, but he wouldn't go back to his father's house.

4

Rashid agreed with my plan for a workshop once he'd read the permit and saw that it was registered in my name. He agreed to bring in the Filipino seamstresses on condition that Batul came in as a partner but didn't visit the place, and the Filipinos slept in the workshop and didn't cross the threshold except in my company. My aunt trilled, I jumped for joy, Batul cheered, and my mother wept.

I didn't pay any attention to the fact that my mother went on crying and her tears turned into a convulsive fit of sobbing. My thoughts revolved happily, busy with images of the workshop: the reception, the sewing room, mirrors, cupboards, the fashion photographs in Suha's magazines, the Filipino seamstresses – one of whom would have to be a hair stylist. I had an exact idea of the table and chair I would have to work from, just like I'd seen in the shops. And all the big families and the sheikhs' wives would be my customers.

Between her sobs my mother said, 'I swear, I carried you in my womb and gave birth to you but you cling to Nasab. It's as if she's a hyena who's pissed on you and got power over you. Four years I was pregnant with you . . . '

She cradled her head in her arms and I didn't know how to answer her. I knew she wouldn't stop crying for days and nights as usual, and I was scared that she'd revert to her raving and chattering, losing her mind as she always did when she became very angry. I approached her and spoke soothingly as I would have done to a child. 'No, mother. I swear by my son, you're wrong. I listen to you and I do what you want. You know Rashid and his stubbornness, but my aunt has an influence over him and she makes him embarrassed. You know he owes her a lot. She's like his mother.' Tentatively I touched her red plait. I saw the little white hairs at the roots. Her head appeared small. Even the henna didn't colour the original red of her hair or the striking whiteness of the palms of her hands. I stared at the fine blue veins in her neck and caught sight of one of her bare feet, small and slender, looking as if it were made of glass.

I pulled her hand away from her red face. When she lifted her green eyes to me they were swollen. As usual when I noticed her colouring, I thought that she couldn't possibly be my mother. 'God forbid,' I uttered involuntarily, warding off this notion of mine, and my mother cried out, 'Even you, Tamr, say "God forbid". By God, I'm not mad!'

I kissed her on both cheeks, tasting the salty tears, then kissed her hands and embraced her, saying 'You're Taj, Crown of the Bride and Crown of Kings.* You're no more mad than I am!' This last sentence made my mother's weeping rise almost to a lament, and she made a noise like a cat in distress.

*Taj means 'crown' in Arabic, and Taj al-Arus 'the bride's crown'.

She rocked her whole body and covered her face with her hands again.

Gradually her sobs abated and she indicated in the direction of her nose, then reached out a hand to me. I gave her a handkerchief from my pocket, and when she'd cleaned her nose and wiped her eyes she tried to speak without crying. Out came one sentence that I knew by heart: 'I felt you between my shoulders.' I wanted to say to her, 'I know, I know,' but I was afraid of annoying her and I let her go on. 'I felt you between my shoulders, and I never once slept on my back, always on my stomach or my side. Every day I drank camels' milk and sheeps' milk and ate three dates, and the doctors injected me with a needle a span long. When you were born I saw the needle marks in your hands and thighs. God is great! You had no hair, no eyebrows or eyelashes, not even any hair in your nostrils. I began to put henna on you every Friday night. The other wives and their children laughed at me and said, "You're wasting your time putting henna on the Safwan stone." And I made myself deaf and dumb and blind. I hennaed your scalp and bought you combs and hairbands and even medicine for headlice. In the woman's market they all made signs behind my back when they saw that damned Mawda trying to sell me a big bottle and saying to me, giggling and winking, "Perhaps Tamr needs this medicine from India. Everybody swears it's like Solomon's devils. One drop applied to the head does away with lice as if they'd never existed." Just to show them all I said, "It can't do any harm to have some," put my hand in my bosom and paid for it.'

I looked at my mother's breast, which was scarcely visible in the folds of her voluminous dress and answered, bored but sad at the same time, 'I know, Mother. I've caused you anguish in the past and I'm still doing it. I know. I mustn't talk to Aunt Nasab so much. In any case she's just a guest, and in a couple of days she'll be going back home.' Then I added hypocritically, 'From the way she was so hard on me and spoiled Awatef when we were in London, I know where I really stand with her.'

My mother gulped in agreement. 'You don't have to tell me about Nasab and Awatef. When the sheikh divorced you your aunt didn't tear her hair or claw her chest in sorrow. Maybe she was glad. How could Tamr be married to a sheikh and not Awatef?'

'God forgive her,' I replied appeasingly.

Then I took my mother by the hand and pulled her up off the bed. 'Come on, Crown of the Bride and Crown of Kings. Wash your face, put on your dress and do your hair. We've got lots of work to do.'

As I picked over the rice, minced the meat and chopped up the vegetables with enthusiasm, Rashid came in with the permit in his hand, still not able to believe that the ministry had given it to me. I smiled triumphantly and said nothing. I had to cook quickly. Batul had offered to help me with the cooking that day but I'd refused to let her. I wanted to prove that my opening the workshop wouldn't mean I did any less housework.

I had many things to occupy my thoughts – such as pur-chasing machines, curtains, pins, scissors, a small fridge and two beds for the Filipinos – but still I was concerned about my mother. I thanked the Lord she was continuing to recover. Her anger and her sadness were normal this time and she didn't refuse to leave her bed.

When I was little I lived with my mother in one room of a three-storey house. I used to wait for her to come to bed, watching her as she plaited her red hair and dipped her fingertips in warm oil. She would say to me with a smile, 'You must be sleepy, Tamr. Don't you want to hear about the Little Fish?' I would be smiling too, knowing that she was teasing me. She never changed her way of speaking even when she was ill. She adjusted her veil as she said the story's name, and always began by biting her lips. 'Tamr, O Tamr, the Story of the Little Fish is the story of a poor girl whose mother had died, and whose stepmother was harsh and wicked. She made her stay in the kitchen, polishing the brass, fetching water, sweeping, dusting, stoking the fires and cooking, doing the washing, preparing the incense burner and putting henna on her stepmother's hair.

'O Tamr, O Tamr, one day her father caught one hundred fish, and the poor girl had to stay up all night gutting them. Her stepmother said to her, "You must clean all the fish tonight. If they weren't full of evil, they wouldn't make such a horrible smell." When the girl took hold of the last fish it slipped from her grasp. She thought to herself that her swollen red hands must have grown tired, but the Little Fish cried and said in a loud voice to the girl, "Spare me and I'll make you rich." The girl was astonished that the fish had spoken, and she took fright. "God preserve me from the Devil's curse," she said. She looked hard at the Little Fish and saw that it was beautiful: its eyes were black, its nose small as far as she could see, its mouth a tiny opening; it had little even teeth and a shining silver skin. The Little Fish cried louder and begged the girl again, "Spare me, and I'll make you rich." The poor girl took pity on the fish. She put it under her arm and slowly opened the door. The snores of her stepmother and her father rose to the sky. She ran until she reached the sea. There she took the fish in her hands and said to it, "Little Fish, Little Fish, don't cry and don't wail. Go back to your mother and father and sister and brother, and to your neighbours and your Qur'an teacher. Goodbye." The girl went back to the house, and when she heard the snores of her stepmother and her father still rising to the sky, she heaved a sigh of relief. The next day the Sultan's son was giving a party to end all parties, with meat and rice and sweets in abundance. And every boy and girl and every man and his wife went to the party, all except this poor little girl. Her stepmother left her in the kitchen with a big bag of rice and ordered her to pick the weevils out of it grain by grain. Then she sprinkled salt on the floor and ordered her to gather it up grain by grain, and scared her with stories about the Judgement Day and how God would make her spend eternity sweeping salt off the floor with her eyelashes if she didn't do as she was told now. The poor girl sat on the floor crying, and began trying to pick the weevils out of the rice, but the creatures slipped through her fingers. Suddenly she heard a sweet voice saying, "This is the Little Fish. I've made you a dress of coral from the sea, and jewellery of shells and pearls so that you can go to the Sultan's palace." The poor girl turned in surprise and called out, "Where are you?" Then she looked back at the floor and said, "What about the weevils and the rice and the salt?" The Little Fish replied, "Don't bother about them. I'll make the rice clean and white for you and drown the weevils and put the salt in a jar. Off you go. Goodbye!"

'The girl looked down at herself and found she was wearing a lovely dress, and from the window she saw a coach with a huge shell for a seat, driven by a young giant. So off she went to the palace and the Sultan's son fell in love with her beauty and her sweet disposition, and she married him, Tamr, and lived till the Judgement Day and had both sons and daughters.'

Only when I was stretched out in bed listening to the tale of the Little Fish did I feel happy, for my mother looked peaceful and beautiful, and the smell of food and coffee and laundry soap had faded from the room which was our home.

My mother cooked our food and washed our clothes in this room, and we didn't leave it except to rush down the long staircase and back again, my mother clutching meat and vegetables in her arms as if she were a thief. I grew used to hearing her voice cursing and threatening up the stairs from the first floor. Sometimes the sound of another voice mingled with hers. I was glad whenever I saw that she had the bucket, because then I would run out of the room and lean over to watch her hauling up the rope with a frown on her face.

Because she was in such a hurry, most of the water in the

bucket slopped out on its way between the two floors, and sometimes one of the boys, in spite of the speed at which it was moving, dropped a pebble or a date stone or a bit of paper into it, to see my mother Taj go crazy with anger and curse Jauhar and Najeeya at the top of her voice. I rarely left the room day or night except to go to the lavatory, and then I went with my mother. As we descended the two flights I would try to loiter and she would scold me in annoyance: 'No time ago you were clutching yourself, and now you're prancing about as if you've got all the time in the world.' I wanted to see the other children, and Jauhar and Najeeya, and stare into their faces, for I could see more likeness between me and them than between me and my mother. But without realizing it I lowered my gaze each time I met one of them in the hallway of the house or at the bathroom door.

I felt as if I lived with them because I could hear the sounds of their voices and the noise they made as well as if they were in the room, and when I couldn't hear them I waited expectantly until I could. My mother told me their life histories from the moment she opened her eyes in the morning until she went to bed at night; she recited stories that I didn't understand, but I recognized that at the core of them lay a deep hatred. All the same I was curious about them, and longed to go down to the rooms where they lived and talk to them and play with their children. More than once I'd seen Jauhar and Najeeya pulling my mother's hair and jumping on top of her and hitting her; they would shriek when my mother bit their hands and their thighs, while the children cheered them on delightedly, chanting, 'The Turkish woman's mad! The Turkish woman's mad!'

I even began to long for us just to open our door because they used to leave their rubbish beside it, a dead rat, potato peelings, a gold paper crown, all of which, as far as I was concerned, formed part of a dialogue between me and them.

How I wished I could explain to them how much I longed to know them – even though our mothers fought and I'd once seen goat dung thrown outside our door – and how much I'd loved the gold paper crown which they'd discarded there; I'd tried it on and I wanted to keep it, but my mother pulled it off and tore it with her teeth.

It was when my mother lost my gold bangles, a pendant formed of the words, 'What God has willed', and a Qur'an studded with diamonds and sapphires which had been a present from the Sultan, that my aunt came to take us to live with her, for my mother was frantic. When she discovered the things were missing she'd rushed down the stairs to Jauhar's like a tornado, as if she were certain that Jauhar was the culprit, and overturned the furniture and even ripped the bedding and began feeling around in it. Jauhar and her children couldn't do anything to stop her, and my mother turned her fury on Najeeya and twisted her arm and spat in her children's faces. When she found the door locked in her face, she began to retreat, then returned to the fray, charging the door like a bull. It withstood her assault and she raised her eyes to heaven, beseeching God to destroy them one by one. Nejeeya and Jauhar were afraid of her coloured eyes and the red freckles on her face and her red hair, the like of which they'd never seen before. Each of them hurried to protect her own children, covering their little faces with the hems of their dresses.

Life was different in my aunt's home, and I couldn't help wondering why we hadn't moved there before instead of staying in that room, why indeed we'd never visited her, nor she us. For my aunt had an abundance of love, a broad smile, and a laugh which everyone in the house could hear.

Even my mother sat calm and beautiful at my aunt's side, except sometimes when she remembered episodes with Najeeya and Jauhar. She was the focal point of any gathering. Her appearance was so different from all of theirs that she dazzled and shocked them, but what she said must have fascinated them, for all the women, even my aunt, listened as if they were bewitched. I began to enjoy playing with my cousins, especially Awatef who was the same age as me. The boys went to school and came back with books full of pictures, which opened my mind to things I hadn't known existed: once I asked about the pictures of fishes that caught my eye, and one of my cousins told me all about them. I waited for him at the door in the heat of the sun and afterwards I shook my head sorrowfully and said, 'If only the woman who teaches us about religion gave us books like the ones you're allowed to read.' I took the books in my hands, staring at the pictures. Once I read the word 'God' and was amazed to find that I could read and understand a book that wasn't the Qur'an. When I began to be able to read what he read, and study what he studied and write what he wrote, the tears that I had shed regularly every morning when it was time to go to the Qur'an teacher were replaced by a sense of gratitude. I no longer minded her hard eyes, and I gave up counting the buttons on her veil and lavished all my attention on her mouth, deciphering the symbols for the words and then asking her if I was writing my name correctly.

With my aunt I visited the market, rode in the car, went into the desert and slept in a tent, and with my aunt looking on, I stood while our Indian neighbour fitted material on me for a dress. Running my hands over the gold and silver threads, I asked my mother curiously if a feast day was approaching. It was my aunt who answered: 'No, Tamr, this is for the daughter of one of my relations in Iran.' I didn't ask which one as she had many relatives over there. Not a month went by without her inviting a family from Iran or Bahrain to stay; I used to think that every woman wearing an abaya and a veil was a relation, and I would stop in the street and refuse to go on until my mother had said hallo to the moving abayas.

But the nice clothes were for me: they hennaed my hands and feet one morning and dressed me in one of the dresses that same afternoon. They took me to my father's house where Jauhar and Najeeya and my father's fourth wife were waiting, and for a moment I thought of the bucket and the rope and the servant. My mother and my aunt were there to accompany me, and I suddenly wondered if this could be my own wedding. The neighbour's daughter once told me that she'd known about her father's second marriage because there had been so many baskets and metal containers around, full of cooked rice and meat, and here I was confronted with bags and boxes of provisions, and my mother tasting a bit of rice and saying, 'They're obviously mean. God help us! You can count the cardamon pods and cumin seeds with the naked eye. God help my precious Tamr!' Then I heard drumming and women trilling. 'Mother, mother!' I cried. 'Are you marrying me off? I'm not even a woman yet!' I knew about puberty from the Qur'an, although it was the teacher who had described monthly periods as 'dirty'. 'Are you marrying me off when you know it's wrong?' I asked again. 'It doesn't make any difference whether it's to a boy or a grown man.' 'Hush, Tamr,' replied my aunt. 'Don't be ungrateful. A man is an adornment, a crown for your head, a staff to strengthen your heart.' I wept, without knowing why. 'Mother, mother, will you be staying with me?' I asked her, and when she nodded I felt reassured.

The women beat the drums and trilled and sang. Women I didn't know entered the gathering. The chanting and songs rose higher, and I saw the professional entertainer whom I'd seen singing at other weddings. I'd always wondered why money was showered upon her and watched her hiding it in her breast, as she was doing now. When I saw the neighbours and their daughters kissing my mother and looking at me, I thought, 'Perhaps I'm already married,' but I pushed the thought away. I'd heard that the bride was wrapped up in a carpet or rug. Before my father came in my aunt shouted, 'Anyone who's unveiled should cover herself!' The women gasped and if they saw my father picking me up it was only by sneaking a glance, but when I screamed 'Mother! Mother!' they couldn't resist throwing back the covers from their faces.

He carried me to his room at the centre of the house and I saw a young man sitting on a mountain of mattresses with a white cover draped over them. I screamed. When my father had gone, the young man stood up. I screamed again and took a few steps backwards. He didn't move or speak, and I retreated to the door. I stood there for about an hour and whatever he did, whether he took a step in my direction, climbed up on the bed, or said something, I screamed. I wanted to open the door but I could hear the tambourines and drums and the women's trilling. I kept my face to the door and when the noise died down and the drums fell silent, I opened it and closed it again. I stood for perhaps another hour before I opened it and this time went out and ran from room to room searching for my mother. I found her in her bed and squeezed up next to her, and put my arms around her, sobbing. She put out an arm to hold me and I wished she'd recite the story of the Little Fish to me until I was calmer. I couldn't sleep because of the long gold ear-rings and chain and belt that I was wearing. I took them off and put them down on the floor. When I heard the dawn call to prayer, I started up in fright and found that my mother was no longer beside me in bed. She was doing her ritual ablutions. Kissing me, she said, 'Good morning on this blessed morning, Tamr.' I didn't answer: I wanted to cry, but I didn't.

My father's fourth wife made the breakfast, and my mother arranged the dishes on the mat. I sat by my aunt who hugged me and quoted some expression about the musk from deer. I didn't know what she meant but the phrase stayed with me until I was grown up, and one day I asked her what it meant. She didn't remember saying anything about musk on my wedding morning but told me that it was the most precious of all scents, and they gathered it from sacs under the bellies of certain male deer. She had some which she'd acquired from a woman whom she met on the pilgrimage, in exchange for a sheep. Then I remembered that distinctive smell which had dominated every detail of the wedding and stayed in my sensory memory, so that whenever I smelt it the wedding came back to me.

That morning they put me in another dress and replaced all my gold jewellery and sat me on mats piled high in the heart of the gathering. The tambourines began to play and the dancing and singing started up again and went on till nightfall. Everyone enjoyed themselves enormously. I saw the boys and girls I used to play with, and even the younger ones were peeping round the door, sticking out their tongues and rolling their eyes, making me laugh. Amidst all this excitement I forgot the coming night, although I hadn't thought about what was going to happen and why I was afraid. This time my mother took me to the room, and before my eyes had adjusted she left abruptly, and the confused young man took her place. I screamed and shrank against the wall. He took no notice and said nothing. Now it was his turn to stand for ages with his face to the wall. When I stopped shouting, I stood where I was and only moved my eyes when a sound came from the bed and I looked to see him stretched out there facing the wall.

I undid the bolt and pushed the door but it didn't open, so I lay down on the floor far from the bed with my face touching the wood of the door and my arms hugging my chest. I don't know whether I slept at all: I remember staring into the darkness in the direction of the bed and feeling reassured. The gold chain and belt were in my way but I didn't want to take them off; they were protecting me. When I heard the dawn call to prayer I pushed the door with all my might and found out that I was also pushing a table wedged against the other side of it. Once I was through, I ran off to my mother's room.

After that, a pattern of events developed which repeated itself every night: when the door wouldn't open, I screamed and screamed and bit his hand and my hand and any flesh I could reach with my teeth. At this the youth lost patience and opened the door and let me escape.

When I'd escaped, I ran straight into another trap: all the doors were locked from the inside, including the kitchen and the bathroom, and the only one that opened was the outside door. I opened it and stepped out into the street, then went back in again, closing it behind me.

It was my aunt who made me change my mind; she sprinkled cold water on my face, heated up some milk for me and fed me with sweets and chewing gum while she sat with me in the kitchen. She asked me if I remembered the girl who'd been tied up to the palm tree. I remembered her without hesitation, as I remembered in detail anything which happened to interrupt the daily routine: weddings, funerals, births, swarms of locusts, riding in a car, riding a camel, my gold dress, my mother's quarrel with Najeeya and Jauhar, and the story of the Little Fish. I remembered the girl tied to the palm tree; she was there till she and the tree looked like Siamese twins. My aunt and my mother had taken me and Awatef in the car to visit one of my aunt's relations. There were women and children standing between the houses and on one side of a big open piece of ground, and there were men on the other side of it. My mother didn't like the idea of stopping to watch with the women, in spite of my aunt's entreaties, and she forced the relation to come into her house with us. Inside the house, the women began to take turns at the window, while Awatef and I tried to squeeze our heads between the grown-ups' bodies. My aunt's relation said, 'The girl's been without food and drink for three days.' Then she pointed out the girl's mother; she was with the other women, circling around the girl, shouting and singing, weeping and laughing. The women were touching her and striking her, wiping the sand off her forehead then throwing it at her. Her mother replaited her hair and struck her face with her plait again, held her dress together where it had been torn and then started to tear it again. The women swarmed around the girl like hungry locusts.

'What's the girl done?' I asked excitedly.

'She hasn't bled this month,' replied my aunt, 'and her stomach's grown. Listen to me, Tamr and Awatef. When you become women, you have to bleed every month; if you don't, dig yourself into the sand like cats do. Lie down and stay quiet and never get up again. That girl didn't find any blood and yet she didn't dig herself into the sand and lie low.'

Awatef, who had sometimes seen spots of blood on her mother's dress, said, 'Why didn't the girl bleed?' The women laughed loudly and my aunt answered, 'Someone who was playing with her must have left his stick behind in her.' Before Awatef could ask her what she meant, the relation addressed my aunt and my mother: 'The slut. She swore on the Qur'an that she and another girl were playing around and what had happened was a miracle. Her mother and all the rest of the women told her not to tell lies.' But an old woman called Watfa couldn't stand it and shouted, 'A girl with another girl is like two hands.' And she pressed her palms together with all the fingers touching, and the thumbs, so that the two hands became one, and gasped, 'Is that possible?'

We all moved away from the window to eat. In the morning of the next day when we left the place we saw the girl still tied tightly to the tree. She was dozing with her eyes closed and her black hair was touching the ground. Two days later her cries rent the air. The knife had descended on her lower abdomen. There was a woman called Aleeya Tattoo, because she'd punctured the hands and faces of so many young girls with her needles to draw black tattoos on their flesh. When they screamed she swore that she would stick needles in them and leave them there if she heard another sound. She was the first to meet newborn children, the first to see the dead and bury them or help bury them. This woman was muttering there, almost raving to herself, the knife in her hand along with a small piece of the flesh which had been in direct contact with the other forbidden flesh. She screamed as she tried to force open the mouth of the girl tied to the palm tree: 'Open your mouth and eat this. Chew it up.' She brought the knife down again rapidly as she did when she was slaughtering a young lamb on a feast night. She shouted as she tried to feed the girl with the piece of flesh; and the girl, as if finding relief from her pain, bit Aleeya Tattoo's fingers, which were as dry as a billy goat's horns. Perhaps sinking her teeth into something helped her bear the wound which must have been oozing blood by then. It extended up to her stomach and the pain around there grew, and the girl screamed and screamed. The sand seemed to be joined up to the sky, and it was as if little grains of salt were covering her wound. 'Eat this. Open your mouth. Chew it up.' This time it came forcefully, for Aleeya Tattoo felt the teeth digging into her fingers. The girl moved her head away, to the left, to the right; the palm tree hurt her face. When she tasted the blood and the flesh she closed her eyes and vomited, and was no longer aware of anything.

I was twelve years old and I was jumping around on the roof of my husband's family house with the neighbours' daughters. I rushed down into the house to see the white dust come rumbling from the ceiling, then went back up to the roof. This was the only time when I forgot that I was married and playing in a strange house. I played only for two days, in the time after lunch when my husband's family were sound asleep. The noise I made woke them up and they found out what I was doing. My husband's mother, Reehan, disapproved of my game and frowned into the faces of the little neighbours who had been delighted with the young bride. They no longer came to amuse her because of that, and because their mothers told them the bride had begun to know about other things and might unsettle their minds. The days began to grow interminably long in the new house. The burning heat of the sun made its way inside in spite of the fans constantly revolving. The only things I liked about it were the designs carved on the ceiling and the wooden doors, because they were more beautiful than the carvings in my aunt's house, and their colours were not the same, but after a few days they no longer interested me. Silence hung over this house. There was no laughter and noise in it as there had been in my aunt's house. Reehan and her daughter wore stiff expressions and I didn't once see them laughing. Even seeds and chewing gum were in short supply, and when I asked about this one day, Reehan replied, 'We don't have small children in the house.' I wanted to tell her that even my aunt and my mother like seeds and gum, and I used to stock up with them whenever I visited my family or my mother and my aunt came to see me. I hid them in the bottom of the chest in my jewel box between the nose ring and the other rings, just as I had earlier hidden two photographs, one of me dressed up for a feast day, and the other of me and my mother holding palm leaves. As the days went by I became certain that Reehan didn't like me or my mother or my aunt. She shouted at me when I fidgeted as the dressmaker fitted me for a dress: 'Stand absolutely still or you won't have any dresses to wear.' Stubbornly I replied, 'I've got some other dresses. My mother and my aunt'll bring them for me.' 'Do you mean those rags?' she asked sarcastically.

I started to cry, defending my aunt and my mother. I decided that I would tell them as soon as I saw them. I realized too that I didn't like Reehan and that I was bored: I wanted to play and run and learn about the fish and the animals which I'd seen in my cousins' books, and I longed to be with my mother and my aunt all the time, not just for the one day in the week when I regularly visited them to share in the hustle and bustle of the house and listen to songs all day long. Going back to Reehan's house was always hard. Just before it was time for the servant Khaizuran to collect me I used to pray 'O God, please don't let me see Khaizuran,' but her tall thin shape would always loom into view. I would fly to her inviting her to have a cup of tea, some sweets, to delay her for as long as possible, but Khaizuran would remain –

like her name which means bamboo – as dry and unyielding as a bamboo cane.

I thought of running away from the new house whose floor was unwelcoming to my jumping step, and whose walls rebuffed my laughter. Then one morning I felt blood on the inside of my thighs and knew that I'd grown up. I remembered what I'd said when I wanted them all to have pity on me and change their minds about making me get married: 'Are you going to marry me off when I'm not even a woman yet?' My aunt had answered, 'God willing you won't become a woman before he's been in you! As well as marrying Tawi's daughter, he's getting you when you're still a little girl so you can grow up at his house and he can raise you.' I asked Khaizuran for a piece of cloth, refusing to tell her what it was for. Then I began to cry. I wanted to go home for an hour, but Reehan refused to let me, insisting that there were three days to go before I was due to visit my family.

Khaizuran discovered that Ibrahim had fewer and fewer headcloths with every day that passed, and that some of the family's sheets had had strips torn off them. Then Reehan found bits of sheet, headcloths and even underclothes with bloodstains on them, tied up in a dress and hanging in a bundle on the back of the bathroom door.

Every time I woke to the sound of the dawn call to prayer, I thought of my mother and my aunt listening to the same call without me there; all that separated me from them was two streets and a few houses, and I sat sadly, unable to understand why they didn't love me, and why they'd sent me away, since I hadn't been greedy or made my clothes dirty. And why did I have to take Reehan as my new mother and aunt combined, and listen to her and sit with her relations and her neighbours instead of with my family?

I cried every time I visited them, refusing to go back to Reehan's house with Khaizuran, and when my mother and my aunt visited me and brought Awatef with them I was overjoyed and my courage came back to me. I walked about the house with firmer footsteps; even my voice changed: there was a ring to it; and I felt secure and happy as if I knew that Reehan couldn't criticize me or tell me off in front of my own people. I took Awatef into my room. She tried on my eight gold rings and the silver one off my thumb, then my gold dress, and said enviously, 'You are lucky!' She asked about Ibrahim and what we did when we were in bed. I pushed my hair back off my forehead and didn't answer.

When my mother heard that I was pregnant she trilled for joy, kissed me on the cheek and put out a hand to feel my stomach. She closed her eyes and even though Reehan had come in and was standing waiting for my mother, Taj al-Arus, to open her eyes, she said, 'God willing, your child will be in your womb for nine months and not a day longer; God willing your child will come out with thick eyebrows and curtains of hair in his eyes, and with hair on his head and on his stomach and between his legs.' I wished my mother would be quiet: I didn't want Reehan and her daughter, or even Khaizuran, to hear this talk. I didn't know that the details of my birth and the story of my mother's four-year pregnancy were known near and far. To my surprise Reehan adjusted her veil and remarked 'That's just talk, Taj. Fairy tales. The Almighty doesn't make mistakes, and He has power over all things.'

My mother was nonplussed for a moment, not knowing how to answer Reehan who'd just accused her of lying. She was visiting us alone; for the first time she'd come without my aunt, who was unwell. She wanted to speak up for herself but she was afraid that Reehan would be angry and take it out on me. She changed the subject: 'O Tamr, my precious, O Tamr, my love. Perhaps you're tired and you ought to lie down?' 'No, mother,' I replied eagerly, then after a pause I added boldly, 'But I want to go with you and visit my aunt.'

There was a general silence broken by my mother who said, 'And leave your husband Ibrahim at night? You shouldn't do that, my daughter. The day after tomorrow you can visit us and your aunt will be better.'

I began to cry and found that I was shaking. I would have liked to throw myself into my mother's arms and hold on to her and ask her to tell me the story of the Little Fish. I didn't feel married or pregnant, even if Ibrahim had lain on top of me and jiggled up and down and made a sticky liquid come out, and now my stomach had swollen out. I cried louder, picturing myself left alone with Reehan, and my mother Taj al-Arus rebuked me: 'No, Tamr. I don't like the way you're behaving. How can you cry when you're at home with your family?' Later on she told me that she'd been thinking something quite different: 'Their coffee's like hot water and so's their tea; there's no taste to them. And the dates aren't easy on the teeth or sweet to the tongue.' She said that she'd been wishing she could have seen me living like a sheikh's wife, with dresses which shone as bright as stars and my hair smelling of jasmine, henna patterns on my hands and dozens of maids in attendance bearing trays of tea and coffee and dates. Then she'd heard me shouting, 'I want to go home. I don't like this house.'

I didn't come back to life properly until the next time I visited my family. My aunt was bent on taking me and all the women of the house on a trip, once she'd persuaded Rashid. We climbed merrily into the car, which was to take us wherever we wished: into the desert, to the streets where the only shops were, to the hill always known as the mountain, and to the seaside. She made the car stop so that we could look out of the window. We pointed to some beautiful birds and cried out in wonder, 'Glory be to God.' My mother put out a hand to cover my eyes. 'Don't look,' she ordered. 'Don't admire them. If you gasp in wonder and say that those birds are beautiful, the child in your womb might grow feathers.' The return trip to my aunt's house was another excursion in itself, and when we arrived there was drumming and singing and dancing all the afternoon and into the night. 'You're pregnant. Don't dance,' they told me, proud of me.

They swung their long hair about; my mother danced, and Batul danced a dance which was different from the others except for the swinging hair. They all sang to me and smiled at me. I sat with my hands resting on my stomach and counted the days to my next visit.

When my mother left Reehan's house, Reehan ignored my bad mood, perhaps because my mother had entreated her to remember that I was still young and ignorant. But she did remark, 'I've never known your poor mother Taj to hold a conversation before. She's quite normal.' I didn't make any comment, but I felt angry. I couldn't defend my mother; everybody knew the story of Taj al-Arus, and nobody – child, girl or woman – left my mother without having heard her life history.

When I felt the labour pains starting I fled to my aunt's house. I didn't want to be in pain and to push and strain in front of Reehan. To my mind she didn't deserve to be there even at this special event.

They fetched Aleeya Tattoo to me; she forbade me to make a noise then she shouted herself as she pulled and pushed, as if she were the one giving birth. 'It's a boy! It's a boy! ' she cried as she pulled him out. 'Glory be to the Creator! His eyes are dark, he's as beautiful as the moon, and he's got a big prick: he'll only have male children. His chest's powerful. You can see the breeding in him. Naturally, since his mother's descended from sheikhs and his father from merchants.' She was lying: we weren't descended from sheikhs! Then she turned to Nasab and Taj al-Arus, screaming, 'Cover her eyes! She mustn't see the afterbirth. Go and dig deep, deep and bury the afterbirth deep, deep, because the dogs are always hungry.'

Once again I fled from Reehan's house and my son Muhammad was in my arms. It was an ordinary afternoon, the same as all the rest, and as usual Awatef had slipped in to see me when everyone in the house was asleep and the fans and air-conditioners were going full blast. We laughed a lot and chewed gum and cracked seeds between our teeth, tried on rings and imitated Reehan's glowering expressions and Khaizuran's walk, and Awatef snored, imitating the sounds rising up from Reehan's bedroom and the sitting-room where Ibrahim and his father had stretched out directly after the meal. Awatef wanted to scribble in Ibrahim's school books but I stopped her.

We padded cat-like to the kitchen. The smell of onions and garlic and the recent meal pervaded it. We began opening the cupboards, poking around for nothing in particular. Awatef took two sticks of incense and hid them in her pocket and I took a packet of sugar candy. We went on opening more cupboards until we heard someone clearing his or her throat.

Muhammad was still in his bed. I picked him up and he went on sleeping. I said to Awatef, 'He's my child and they don't even let me hold him. I want to take him and leave. Yesterday Reehan boiled a piece of lead to protect him from the evil eye and it shot out of the pot and grazed his forehead.'

Awatef winked at me and said, 'Come on, let's run away.'

I wanted to put the idea out of my head because I knew that this time I wouldn't come back. Ibrahim's family wouldn't even try and fetch me back. The scandal of my running away to have the baby in my aunt's house still occasionally cropped up in conversations and caused a stir. But all the same I took down a small suitcase from on top of the chest and put Muhammad's clean nappies and a packet of dried milk in it. I whispered to Awatef, 'You take this and I'll carry Muhammad.'

Without hesitation Awatef nodded her head, stifling her laughter. We held our breaths and went along on tiptoe. We didn't talk until we were just a few metres away from our house. The first words my aunt spoke when she saw us were, 'O Tamr, O Awatef, you're the colour of turmeric.'

5

Women normally flocked to my place in the afternoon and at
sunset with their children and their relatives, bringing lengths
of material and cuttings from fashion and hairdressing magazines. But during this month of Ramadan, I opened from nine
in the evening and was closed all the afternoon just like the
other businesses. I stayed in the shop from the morning
onwards, the hair dryers idle around me, the clean towels
folded one on top of the other: around the walls were photographs of hairstyles, a nature scene, and in the middle of one
wall there was a clock which wasn't working; Filipino music
played and a smell of food made its way down into my lungs.
I felt hungry; the seamstress and the stylist were in the
kitchen cooking, singing along with the cassette tape and
writing letters. I wondered anxiously how I was going to get
back to my brother's house in the early morning; the place
wouldn't close before five and sometime tonight Jameela and
her six daughters were coming to have their hair done before
they went away the following day. I couldn't sleep in the
shop: my brother's orders. 'Sleep by yourself in the same
place as the Filipino women?' Perhaps I would ask Jameela to
accompany me to the house to keep Rashid quiet.

I forgot what was troubling me as the women came cheer-
fully pressing on the doorbell, knocking at the door, and sat
down, chose fashions, posed in front of the mirror, went into
the other room to have their dresses fitted or stuck their
heads under the sprays in the basins to have their hair
washed. They left their abayas flung down on the chairs, all
except the client waiting her turn, who kept hers around her
shoulders. I sat at my table content at the throngs of women
around me, the heads under the dryers and the money in the
till, already more than I'd expected to take that night.

I got up from the table and walked proudly around, at ease

with every step I took now among the women who sat waiting to be called, as if they were in a government clinic. I'd felt that I had to open up a place like this to establish my independence, and I'd become well-known among families here and in other areas. The old women who accompanied their daughters, just to watch, made me pleased because the fact that they came and sat there in my shop meant that they trusted me and gave my venture their blessing.

Gradually I became unafraid of the morning and of Rashid. The door bell rang insistently. Before I opened the door I asked as usual, 'Who is it?' and heard my mother's voice reply. I turned in delight to the women sitting behind me and said excitedly, 'It's my mother and my aunt.' To myself I added, 'My aunt must have convinced Rashid.'

I turned the key in the door and before I opened it, I said to the women, 'Veil yourselves. My cousin will carry his mother in.'

They rushed into the inner room while the women under the dryers threw their abayas over the hairdryers so that their heads and the dryers were hidden from view. When I saw that my son Muhammad had come to help his cousin I was overjoyed: I cried, 'God protect you from the evil eye; stay alive for me, Muhammad,' then I laughed at myself for what I'd said. My aunt didn't want her son and Muhammad to lift her out of the wheelchair on to the ground where I'd spread out a mat in the twinkling of an eye: 'I want to see Tamr's place,' she said to the men, 'So goodbye to you.'

I locked the door behind the two of them and bent eagerly to kiss my aunt who took my face in her hands, saying, 'I said to Rashid, let's go and give our blessing to our darling Tamr's new place.' I wriggled free from my aunt's hands and went up to my mother to kiss her, and joked, 'Crown of the Bride and Crown for my Head, welcome. What do you say? Shall we take my aunt around and you can both give me your blessing for opening this place?'

I didn't let go of my mother's arm until she had wheeled

my aunt's chair into the sewing room. They touched all the
dresses hanging up there, the sewing machines, the scissors
and the clippings of material. My mother shouted, 'God is
great! A headless jinnee!' and pointed to the mannequin
which the seamstress had made out of cloth stuffed with
paper and rags because she hadn't been allowed to buy a
wooden dressmaker's dummy. She began striking it with the
flat of her hand until it toppled over. I introduced them to the
two Filipinos. My mother smiled at them and said, 'I
wouldn't like to see them in my dreams.' Then she added,
'Poor things. They haven't much money and they're far away
from home.' We proceeded to the next room where the
Filipinos slept. The two women examined everything, even
the calendar on the wall; they fingered the two girls' letters
and their numerous lipsticks, the little magnifying mirror, the
rush fan, and their clothes which were folded on their beds. If
the stylist hadn't come into the room pretending to look for
something, Taj al-Arus and Nasab wouldn't have agreed to
leave the room unti they'd discovered the secret of the large
orange candle burning in the centre of the table. Meanwhile I
was keen to know the details of Rashid's allowing them to
visit the shop; I asked them, 'Where's Batul?' 'She's coming,'
replied my mother. 'She's waiting while Rashid takes Ahlam
to her friend's house.' Rashid hadn't commented when Batul
had said to him, 'I was going to take Ahlam with me to the
salon, but she's scared that one of the women'll see her and
like the look of her and tell her son or some other male
relative about her. I know these young girls go around in
wraps as thick as camel hide, and it's certainly not because
they're thinking about what's forbidden and what's allowed
in religion – they just don't want to get married yet.'

The telephone rang. I hurried to lift the receiver and replied
with a smile, 'Yes, we do henna patterns. No massage. We
can do it. Of course, I've a Filipino who knows how to do it
but it's prohibited. We've got facial masques. Egg and milk,
yes. The Filipino girl knows how to do it all. She's specially

trained.' I replaced the receiver and announced proudly, 'That was the daughter of the Shufan family. Her mother want a massage.'

When one of the Filipino girls brought two cups of coffee, Nasab refused hers. 'I don't want it,' she said. 'I'm hot.' In English I asked the girl to fetch her a carton of juice and my mother exclaimed delightedly, 'You've got a place of your own *and* you speak English? God is great, Tamr of Tamrs.' But my aunt refused to let the Filipino pour out juice for her, and she wouldn't have any tea. She drew me close to her and whispered something to me which made me laugh. 'O Aunt!' I chided her playfully. The Filipino girl went off into the sewing room and so my aunt spoke out: 'Tamr, listen,' she said. 'There's nothing unclean about her sewing. When the other one washes hair, the women should say, "In the Name of God, the Compassionate, the Merciful". That doesn't matter too much, it's a minor uncleanness. But to take food and drink from an infidel like her is a huge uncleanness. It's forbidden. We're in Ramadan.' 'Never mind, Aunt,' I replied, irritated.

She interrupted me: 'I know. Ask any man of religion and he'll confirm what I've said, word for word. When I came into the town from the desert I wouldn't drink coffee or tea, or eat town bread or meat. My husband and his family didn't understand why. They felt sorry for me and thought I was shy. His sister Zaynab said, "Your wife's growing weak. She won't eat." My husband replied, "She's weak, is she? Every time I get into bed with her she throws me out. And when I pick myself up and try and huddle up in the bed with her, I find myself back on the floor." '

The women laughed loudly, while my aunt arranged her plait of hair. She sighed and put a hand down to her leg. 'Where's that strength gone now?' My mother reminded her of another story: 'And when they brought you a nightdress . . . ' She seemed to be encouraging my aunt, so as to make it an entertaining evening. Nasab laughed and picked up the story: 'And when they brought me a nightdress I left it where it was. Zaynab said to me, "Put that on." "Why?" I asked. "Put it on and you'll see," she said. So I put it on, and before we went to bed she asked me what had happened to it and I said, "I've got it on." She didn't believe me and began to look for it under the bed. I lifted up my dress and said, "See. I told you I was wearing it." She started to laugh. "Take your dress off," she said, "and just wear the nightdress." When I asked why that time, she just said, "You win," in a weary voice.'

'What did you eat and drink in the end?' asked one of the young girls. My aunt drew herself up haughtily, seeing that she'd become the centre of attention. She struck her thigh with the flat of her hand for emphasis and replied, 'I saw Indians and Ethiopians and I was afraid that the animals hadn't been slaughtered according to religious law and that the bread had been baked by an unbeliever. I got hold of more flour and made dough, and cooked the bread in the frying pan myself, and I didn't trust the coffee unless I'd ground the beans. I knew that they were lying to me when they said that my brother-in-law had slaughtered the sheep. I ate it the first day, but not the second, and I told them that meat wouldn't pass my lips again unless I saw the animal being slaughtered with my own eyes.' An old woman who'd accompanied her daughter and granddaughter was listening to the conversation. She took out her dentures and polished them on her dress and remarked, 'I said to my son to get me a human cat like that one there,' and she waved in the direction of the Filipino girl who was bending to pick up the tray in front of them. 'He said to me, "What use would she be to you when you won't even take a drink from her?" "Turn her loose in the valley," I said, "and she can work the land, use the scythe, and harvest the crops."' 'What did he say?' asked my aunt, annoyed at being interrupted.

The old woman didn't understand; she didn't even hear the question and went back to shifting her gaze around, intently studying everything that was going on in the shop.

My aunt was playing with the coral in her necklace; between every coral bead silver coins were threaded. She continued, 'We came from the desert, your father and I,' and she turned to me. I was busy trying to add and subtract on my fingers. 'We didn't know any sweet things except dates. When we saw grapes and oranges we burst out laughing.' Then she began to laugh and slap one palm against the other. Every time she tried to stop herself she only laughed more and curiosity spread and mounted among the women around her and they begged her to tell them what she was laughing at. 'Next I found out that the drainage holes in kitchens and bathrooms weren't for squatting over and doing your business. I was visiting the sheikh's wife and they showed me the bathroom. There was a white seat in it. I lifted its lid and saw water in the bottom of it. I said to myself, "That's to protect it from flies," and washed my face. Thank God I didn't drink from it. Then I looked around for the lavatory. I got out of the place and went to ask again. They took me back to the bathroom, but this time the Ethiopian maid came in with me and opened the lid of the seat and pointed.'

The women laughed briefly, then were distracted by the hairstyle on Jameela's daughter. But my aunt didn't want to be quiet, so she found herself having to direct her conversation to me. 'Your grandmother wouldn't leave the desert except on my wedding day, and when your father married Najeeya, poor mother, the heat was enough to dry a gazelle's tears and she wouldn't leave the desert. Your father and I looked for her and when we saw that the water had dried up we went from oasis to oasis. She didn't realize this. She sent us messages – desert lavender and camels' milk. She didn't like townspeople; when we were having an argument she would scoff at me for sleeping in a bed, using electricity, letting my voice be carried in and out on a telephone, not knowing the difference between a lizard and a gazelle, nor how to stop a locust sliding around in the cooking fat. "O mother," I would ask her, "who married me to someone from the town? Who said that she wanted Nasab to live in a house built of bricks, with a television, and to buy seeds and chewing gum from the shops?" ' Nasab took a deep breath and continued, 'Even when my father, your grandfather, came into the town complaining about his gut and your father took him to the Sultan's doctor – as he and the Sultan had become like brothers – your grandfather wouldn't leave his camel. Your father agreed to tie the camel up at the door of the house. Your grandfather fled from the house whenever Najeeya turned on the radio. He didn't like sitting at the table to eat: he would put some food on his plate and go and keep the camel company.

'Poor thing. He didn't like Najeeya going into the room where he slept; your father had to give him a clean towel and sheet and do his washing for him and bring him his food. Whenever Najeeya wanted to go and visit relations your father lied to him and told him that Najeeya was ill and was going to the doctor, because as far as your grandfather was concerned women were forbidden to leave the house.'

One of the women opened a bag of ear-rings and bracelets and combs which she'd brought from Beirut. I was glad for her to display them in my place. The women and children fell on them and they were scattered, some on the floor, some picked up by the children, some stuck in hair, or hung on ears. In the twinkling of an eye the women had bought everything in the bag. My aunt was plainly irritated: she wanted to say a lot and found herself with no one to listen to her. So I said to her, 'And what next, Auntie . . . ? ' and she took a deep breath and laughed loudly to attract attention to herself again, then continued: 'We missed the desert, the smell of sand and goats and coffee and roasting meat and fires being kindled. But I liked the easy life in the town and quickly picked up the ways of the people, and my mother-in-law was happy with me because I had an enormous capacity for hard work. Although I must say, at the beginning I thought the people odd: they liked useless things and put them in their houses. It was hard for me to eat three times a day, and as for the amount of meat they ate . . . I refused to take hold of fish without covering their eyes with the edge of my handkerchief. I used to say, "There is no strength and no power save in God," to allay my scruples whenever my mother-in-law took a needle and thread and sewed up the chicken's backside after she'd stuffed it with breadcrumbs and rice; it surprised me to see them cooking tomatoes when they were so precious. I'd never imagined that one day I'd move freely in town dwellers' houses even when my father married me to one; I thought that he'd live in tents with us. But I went back with him, and I could have gone back with one of his friends instead, except that when my father told the two of them that he had a girl of marriageable age it happened to be him who shouted first, "I'll marry her." '

The women were bubbling like a hive of bees. My mother and my aunt laughed secretly at the hairstyles, comparing them to goats' horns, bananas, roosters' crests, especially when the woman covered her head and the cover was raised up high. They signalled comments about the Filipinos to one another, wiggling their eyebrows about every time one of the girls passed in front of them. 'That one's lust incarnate,' remarked my aunt, 'because she hasn't had a taste of her husband for three months; she's got children of her own. Every day she has a fight about something. She wants to go out to the shops and Tamr knows that it's to chat with men of her own type and religion. Tamr said to her, "You're not going out except with me." Anyway the neighbours and the shop owners round about are just waiting for a sign: they don't want a woman to start up in business and they're watching for evidence in any shape or form to use against her. The Filipino girl knows that.'

I shut the ledger and locked it away in the drawer, then moved my chair round until I was facing my mother and aunt. 'Guess who came this morning!' 'The men who close down shops owned by women,' surmised my customers.

Laughing, I replied, 'No. Not this time. They came the day before yesterday and asked if we had any men in here. I said to them, "Can't you read what's written on the door?" but they asked me again if I was quite sure. So I said to them, "If you like I'll open the door for you. Wait a minute while we get veiled." But they didn't come in.' My mother and aunt couldn't guess who'd come to see me and they began to look impatient, so I said enthusiastically, 'Reehan, Ibrahim's mother, with her granddaughters. They were going to a wedding. If you'd seen her clothes: they were all silk and her jewellery was Italian and her handbag was real leather. But she was still mean: she asked the price of henna and when I told her she said, "Hell!", and wanted us to use some that she'd brought with her, but I refused. The Filipino gave her granddaughter a facial – what's the girl's name? I remember, Khulood – and for a whole hour Reehan didn't stop cursing and complaining that the prices were too high while the girl tried to make her be quiet. Anyhow, those are days I'd rather forget.'

It was all quiet in the room except for the sound of my mother's voice as she spoke to the old woman: 'And Mauza said, "You can have contact with this other man, Antan, as long as there's a door between you and he doesn't see you and you don't see him. Nobody'll know and you'll become a Sultana and your son will be a Sultan . . . " '

I rose and went over to my mother, annoyance showing on my face. But the old woman looked confused and I felt reassured; it appeared that she hadn't understood a single word of what my mother was saying. 'Would you like to have a dress made, Taj? ' I asked her, relenting.

6

I became irritated every time I was with my mother in a gathering of women, and could no longer bear sitting like a shepherd, frightened to close his eyes even for a second in case his flock should stray. Taj al-Arus could never resist telling the story of her life, and I'd threatened more than once not to accompany her over the threshold of a house.

While she sat waiting for my aunt and me to come home, she would think in anguish how I was no longer a sheikh's wife, remembering how my aunt Nasab had brought embroidered cloth back from Iran to make a nightdress for my wedding night, and how she herself had insisted that the cloth be cut in the shape of a big heart at the navel and a little heart at each breast, and then that there should be henna patterns in each of these openings.

Taj al-Arus had been certain that this wedding nightdress would ensnare the sheikh's heart for ever, for the Sudanese girl whom the Sultan had taken for his wife and kept as his wife for a long time, asking for her and no other every night, had once told them her secret. In front of them she put on her white wedding nightdress and showed them the hearts on it, some embroidered and some open to show off henna patterns on her skin. She told them that night that the Sultan used to open a jewel box and play with her for hours, trying to fit pieces of jewellery into each heart-shaped hole and, where he succeeded, giving the ring or trinket to her for her own.

Taj al-Arus had heaved a sigh as she listened to this story, and thought that perhaps the man who'd been waiting in the room when Mauza pushed her through the door, and who'd lain on top of her and hurt her while she kept her eyes tightly shut, wasn't the Sultan: he hadn't played with her like that even though his room had been large, his bed gold, the carpet soft, and an air-conditioner had been humming in the room.

She wanted to hear more and she felt envious of the Sudanese girl, although the others talked about what she'd said and called her a liar.

Whenever she was in a gathering of women it always struck Taj that she might have been Sultana over them, and she found herself interrupting them and telling them her story however much she'd promised not to anger me in future, and not to open her mouth except to eat.

She used to sing traditional Turkish songs in a gentle voice, and the kohl round her green eyes was washed away by her tears; these eyes were sometimes cloudy, sometimes clear, and her cheeks turned the colour of roses. Her long neck grew longer as she looked constantly at the ceiling or out to the horizon, never meeting the eyes fixed upon her. It was as if she were pursuing her memories, or as if they had been there with her constantly since the day she went bewildered to the train, and saw her father bending to kiss the Sultan's hand and heard him saying in Turkish, 'Taj al-Arus is your lawful right, as she is your wife, and your sister should you divorce her. She's my youngest daughter and the apple of my eye.' The Sultan pressed his hand, and he walked away gathering in the skirts of his abaya which were flying up in the wind. Her curiosity was directed at the prospect of travelling in a train, and she felt a simple pleasure at the thought of seeing another country, mixed with fear because she couldn't understand the language which these men were speaking. 'You're a Sultana,' her mother had said to her, as she searched her long red hair for lice, massaged it with black mud and poured rosewater over it. Then she rubbed her body all over with a loofah and olive oil soap, poured water over it and dried it, saying, 'The Crown of the Bride has become a Crown of Kings.'

Their house was the largest in the village, and her father was the village mayor. The Sultan had come from the desert with his retinue to take a water cure, and had been her father's guest. In the time it takes to blink, Taj al-Arus, her seven brothers and sisters and their mother had been moved to her uncle's house, the whole of which was transformed into a giant kitchen. The women and girls stuffed ducks, rolled up vine leaves, plucked and roasted sparrows, and impaled meat on skewers for kebabs. Her father, her brothers, her uncle and her cousins carried the trays of food. On the last night her father bowed so low that his head touched the ground, and the Sultan presented him with a gold watch with his picture on it, and a gold ring set with a diamond; her father found himself telling the Sultan that he was ready to give him his soul, and the most precious thing in the world to him was Taj al-Arus.

One of them translated her name for the Sultan – 'Crown of the Bride' – and it pleased him and he said, 'I accept her.'

Before Taj boarded the train she turned to look behind her and saw all the people of her village waving brightly-coloured handkerchiefs; the women were trilling and the children running along beside them. As the train moved away and Taj's heart sank, she stretched her long neck out of the window and saw all the village dogs chasing the train, barking wildly, and she felt a surge of affection for them and laughed out loud. As the train drew away the dogs were still running.

When the train halted after many hours, Taj stuck her head out of the window again, and all she could see was sand. Then the men got down and she was left by herself. She wondered if they'd forgotten her but they came back for her and sat her in the back seat of a car, and the party set off again. After some time they stopped and got out and again she stayed where she was, wondering if they'd forgotten about her, until in the end one of them came back and pushed a black wrap at her, and an abaya, and indicated that she should put them round her: she was wearing a dress with trousers under it, and her head was covered by an embroidered scarf with little silver beads hanging from it.

All she could see was sand and a few houses, and tents;

they went into a courtyard without a single plant growing in it; there was sand here too and small stones and beyond it a large colourless building. She could hear noises of children and women's voices, but saw no one. She didn't move until the driver opened the door and signalled to her to follow him into the big building. When they were inside he shouted 'Mauza!' three times and disappeared. A woman emerged. Only her face was uncovered but Taj could see that she was tall and broad. She kissed Taj on both cheeks and took her by the hand. They passed through a large room with huge brightly-coloured sofas ranged around the walls, and into a corridor with numerous other rooms opening off it. Taj found it extremely hot. The woman opened a door at the end of a passage. The room turned out to be taken up almost entirely by a brass bed. Taj stood with her eyes downcast until the woman vanished, closing the door behind her. Taj had scarcely poised herself on the edge of the bed when the woman came back, handed her a towel and soap, and led her along the corridor to a bathroom; here she pointed to some water in a barrel and to the soap and then reached out a hand to Taj's chest. Taj understood and began to wash, her eyes on the closed door, thinking uneasily that she would lose her way as soon as she went out of the room. But the woman was waiting for her; she took her back to her room and signed to her to undo her bundle of clothes.

When Taj had done this, the woman looked through them and threw them aside. She went out of the room, and Taj al-Arus fingered her clothes and the things which her mother had collected for her from the neighbours and her female relatives, and thought about what the woman was doing. The woman returned with a long dress which she gave to Taj to put on. It was tight across the chest; Taj al-Arus held her breath and climbed into it, then sat back down on the bed. The door opened and the same woman entered with a tray with a glass of very sweet tea on it. Before she'd drunk it the woman handed her some dates, then poured a green fluid

from a copper jug into a little cup. Taj ate the dates vora-
ciously, but when she tasted what was in the little cup she
moved it abruptly away from her lips.

'That's our coffee,' said the woman. 'You'll have to get to
like it. It's nice.' Taj al-Arus smiled at her, not understanding.
The woman turned to leave and gestured to Taj to follow her.
They passed through silent rooms, then through rooms noisy
with shouting and boisterous laughter. Through the black
cover which the woman had thrown around her face Taj saw
a man's face, and then another.

It was difficult to walk with the black abaya wrapped
around her. All of a sudden she was met by a stinging heat
like the heat she'd felt when she put her hand on the coals and
glowing ashes in the copper stove at home. It didn't leave her
until she went inside again, this time into another building in
the yard itself, and found out where the noise of children and
the women's cries were coming from. The woman took her
into a long chamber where there was a table with chairs all
round it, laid with a plastic cloth and trays of rice and meat.
She thought it must be in her honour, but soon changed her
mind, and turned away from the eyes which bored into her
with scorn and hostility as their owners talked to the woman
who'd brought her; then she heard laughter interspersed with
words. When she reached out a hand to eat she found her
plate heaped up with rice and pieces of meat. She sat for some
time until the woman got to her feet, wiping her mouth on
her sleeve, and signalled to Taj to get up and go with her.
Again the heat struck her and seared into her until she
reached the other building. Taj realized that it was the first
building when the woman opened a door and she saw her
bundle. The woman went away for a few moments and came
back with a bottle of perfume in her hand. She sprinkled it
over Taj and asked her, 'Is that nice?'

She went away again briefly and this time she came back
with an incense burner which she placed near Taj, gesturing
to her to fan the smoke about. When Taj clearly couldn't

understand what she had to do, then woman held the incense burner close to Taj's chest, then she bent down to lift up Taj's skirt and Taj felt warm smoke on her thighs. The woman raised her own dress and wafted the burner around her thighs, then set off in front of Taj still carrying the burner. She went up a short flight of stairs and knocked on the door at the top. When she heard the sound of a voice, or a throat being cleared, she pushed Taj al-Arus gently forward.

The following day, the same woman came to her and gave her a Qur'an inlaid with diamonds and sapphires, gold bangles, and a pendant with 'What God has willed' inscribed on it. 'From the Sultan,' she told her. Taj was delighted with the jewellery which shone like nothing she'd ever seen in her life before.

She found herself thinking of her family and her neighbours and friends for the first time since she'd arrived, and she pictured their eyes and their fingers pursuing the sparkling treasures, not believing that it all belonged to her. The woman took Taj down to the ground floor, across the yard, and into the other building which resembled a Turkish army barracks. The woman no longer summoned her to eat with her. Taj felt as if she was in the middle of a market: movement and noise; women, girls, and boys of every race, age and colour. She began imitating the others, sitting down to eat when they did, going out into the yard if they did, then attaching herself to groups of them, sitting as they sat, even beginning to drink the thread of green liquid when it was poured out into the tiny cups.

The day after that Taj al-Arus began to learn how she should behave in the yard, in the gatherings of women and in the bedrooms. The noise no longer bothered her; she grew accustomed to the presence of large numbers of black and white children and their loud voices and their talk and laughter. She was no longer shy at table and she picked up the rice just like all the rest of them, gathering it together in her fingers and throwing it into her mouth. She tore the meat apart, remembering her sisters and brothers and how at home everybody had shared out the food together; now she was on her own.

In the yard a fire was burning with a giant spoon resting on the coals containing green beans – coffee beans; she saw a woman roasting them for several minutes then pounding them until they looked like cracked wheat; then she stood close to the fire and watched the coffee powder and sugar and fat simmering together. She wished that she could take the old woman's place at the fire; she wanted to know how she was going to live, what she was going to do: in Turkey she had been used to starting work at daybreak.

Had she done something wrong when she'd gone into the vast room and the Sultan had approached her and lain on top of her? Even when it hurt her she hadn't started to cry. At the sound of the muezzin she'd thought of her mother and father and brothers and sisters, and of the walnut tree, and how she used to pick a nut and rub its shell on her lips until they were stained red, turning to a deep dark brownish crimson after a few moments.

She forgot about her family when she heard a loud voice echoing all round the building: 'Prayers! Time for prayers!' She had to hurry like the rest of them to do her ritual ablutions and pray with the other women in the large chamber, while the men had their own mosque. She copied the others and prayed humbly to God.

That evening when she met the first woman's eyes and she didn't call her over, Taj wondered if she was expected to sleep in the Sultan's room like the night before. Then she remembered her bundle of clothes and went off to try and find the way to the outside door. It was locked. She tried to ask a woman but she couldn't understand a word she said and didn't know how to get rid of her. She made her way back to where the other women were and smiled at them and searched for Mauza, the one who had looked after her on her arrival, afraid that there was nowhere for her to sleep. Taj slept in her clothes in an empty bed surrounded by four other empty beds, her hand on her brassière where she'd hidden the Sultan's presents.

In the morning she woke early and lay there taking in the room, which was bare except for big ceiling fans: the centralized air-conditioning wasn't enough for all the rooms. She thought of the mirror at home which had pictures pinned all round its wooden frame. The bedrooms here were more or less empty except for beds, chests and cushions propped against the walls. When she bent down to get her shoes she noticed dust under the beds and all over the floor; in some places it had accumulated in little fluffy balls which looked to her like grey mice. How she wished she could swill water over everything and give it a thorough cleaning from top to bottom, but she remembered that she was a Sultana.

She knew for sure that the Sultanas in this place were different from the Queens she'd heard about. Here a Sultana ate, drank, prayed, slept, danced, sang, and didn't work, unlike a Queen in a story who sat on a throne with a crown on her head and a whip in her hand, ordering the sun to set and the moon to shine. And the Sultan didn't sit counting his jewels: indeed, a lot of his time was spent travelling. When she came to think about the small children, of whom there were perhaps more than a hundred, her mind became confused.

The place had a smell, incense and food; even the clamour, the running and movement from room to room, the lying on beds and on the floor had a smell. It was the women's perfume floating out into the air. Strange perfumes; Taj didn't know that they were Indian and desert perfumes, and that only the Sultan's paramour wore European perfume. They rose up from the tinkling of the gold bangles and the belts and jewelled Qur'ans, smells of henna and oil and jasmine.

She grew used to the comfortable noisy life, the mixture of sleeping and staying up late, sometimes till dawn. All the same she didn't open her heart to a single one of them; the only points of similarity between them and the women from her village were their plump bodies and the gold in their teeth.

She no longer thought of the language as the obstacle, as she had done previously. The reason she felt distant from them lay in what she saw at nights, the rustling and whispering which she heard; Fatima's sighs and the creaking of her bed; the uproar around the door as Belkis clung to it. These things kept Taj awake for hours. After some time she found out why Fatima was sighing; one night another of the women who slept in the room crept up and whipped back Fatima's covers while at the same time another switched on the light: her lower half was naked. The more she swore at them, the more they laughed and when she screamed at them they imitated her. Since she could do nothing against them she rolled herself up in a blanket and closed her eyes.

After this episode Taj refused to eat for two days and was moved into another room. It was Mauza who arranged for her to move and she also brought her the bundle of clothes she'd carried from Turkey. The new room only had a few beds in it; the girls were beautiful and they were Taj's age or slightly older, whereas Fatima and the others had been much older, and more than once one of them had tried to be affectionate to her by putting a hand on her chest: at first Taj had thought she was trying to steal her jewellery.

The first night in the new room didn't pass as peacefully as she had expected, and nor did the following nights. It agitated her the way Belkis stood waiting for so long, then leant against the locked door after Mauza had gone round locking all the rooms, turning out the lights and listening to the complaints.

Taj al-Arus didn't dare to ask Belkis what she was doing every night at the locked door, supporting herself against it with her hands held above her head, although she didn't think she was trying to open it for she emitted faint noises as

she stood there. By the time Taj al-Arus found out the reason
she knew, despite the fact that she was only fourteen years
old, a lot about men and women; she also knew the secret
shared by all the women there, the young and old, the black
and the light-skinned; she knew about the children, the
Sultan, the Sultana, and about herself: she knew that she was
waiting and they were all waiting with her, even the Sultan,
for the end of the month. If she didn't have a period, all the
rest of them would envy her, and the Sultan would be told
that he was expecting a son or a daughter from his red-haired
Turkish bride; she would still be his wife and the contract
which had been drawn up in the village between her father
and one of the Sultan's aides would remain valid. 'Shall I
become a Sultana?' Taj al-Arus asked Mauza, who clearly
knew all languages: Ethiopian, Somali, Syrian, Albanian,
even a bit of Turkish. Mauza nodded her head: 'A Sultana.
He'll give you an allowance, gold jewellery, dresses. You'll
have a room of your own, maybe even a palace. And the
Sultan will come and see you and his offspring. Everyone will
listen to what you say; in social gatherings they'll bring the
incense burner to you first and give you a leg of mutton and a
cup of coffee before the other guests, and you'll have two
personal attendants.' Because all the women wanted this for
themselves Taj al-Arus wanted it too. Her eyes were aglow
with the heat of her enthusiasm, and she looked upwards,
supplicating God. For the first time she understood the secret
of the eyes fixed on the ceiling: the young ones must have
been praying to be pregnant, the old ones devoutly hoping for
the opposite.

   Taj seized Mauza's hand beseechingly. 'What if I don't get
pregnant?' she asked, pointing to her stomach. Mauza
smiled. 'You'll get pregnant, God willing,' she said. 'You
follow my advice and your stomach will swell up under your
chin, and when the Sultan hears the cry of his newborn son
he'll give you his weight in gold, and if it's a girl half her
weight in gold. And you remember Mauza and give her

whatever you feel you should.' Quickly, Taj al-Arus asked again, 'What if I don't get pregnant?'

'You'll get pregnant if you trust Mauza,' she replied.

Taj al-Arus learnt that she would have to lean against the door after the rest were asleep, and when she heard a rattling, she should lift her nightdress and drop her pants down around her feet and press up against the door just where there was a big wide hole, and there would be a man outside ready.

Taj al-Arus hid her face in her hands, not wanting to hear more, while Mauza, seeing the girl's reaction, hurried to make light of it and said she'd been teasing her. Taj al-Arus discovered that even if she gave birth to a son or a daughter, the Sultan would eventually divorce her and she'd never become a Sultana; she'd been wrong to think that he had over a hundred wives; the fact was that he would even divorce her, his youngest wife, to give himself the chance to marry others.

Three of the women besides her were still the Sultan's wives and the rest were divorced from him but preferred to stay in the big house helping to bring up the little sultans; some of them married again to drivers and servants.

Taj al-Arus didn't get pregnant, but she didn't consider going back to her village because she was still enjoying the light blazing from the lamps, and admiring the water flowing from the tap.

Another month passed and Mauza came asking Taj to gather up her possessions and prepare to leave. She asked her for a keepsake. For the first time for ages Taj al-Arus thought about her family and her heartbeat quickened, but Mauza told her that the Sultan had divorced her and was going to marry her to a friend of his, and somewhere in the building the first chapter of the Qur'an had been recited and the agreement concluded in her absence. She left the big house wrapped in her abaya. She touched her jewellery; when she wore it she felt like a Sultana, because hers hadn't changed colour like the others'. She remembered how she'd heard some of them shriek when they saw their emeralds and sapphires changing colour as they washed their hands or rubbed their clothes in washing powder; after that they'd avoided washing powder like the plague. Through the black cover she saw the yard – sand and small stones without a single plant. She was told to sit in the back seat of the car. The roads were like the yard, only long, and the car didn't stop until nightfall. When the driver and the man who'd been sitting next to him got out of the car, she did the same.

When the Sultan's friend saw her he said, 'So you're Taj al-Arus? ' He took hold of her long red hair and pulled it, not believing that such hair could belong to a human woman and thinking she must be a jinnee. When she gave a cry of pain he was satisfied that she was human. He didn't leave her room for three nights. He'd put her in a high room the night they'd brought her to him. The two of them had climbed a long flight of stairs and he'd taken her into a room which smelt of dates. He told her not to leave this room except to go to the bathroom on the second floor, and not to talk to any woman she might see. She was brought food on a tray by a young girl, and on the third day the door was pushed open: two women stood there without speaking. They took her down the long staircase to the entrance.

One of them pointed to a bucket of water and indicated to Taj that she should pick it up and take it upstairs and empty it into a large barrel there. She followed her and directed her to go back downstairs again where she lifted up a plank of wood, hauled up another bucket on the end of a rope and poured water from it into the first bucket. She gestured to Taj to do as she'd done then looked up, pointing to the long flights of stairs. Taj al-Arus was frightened of the well and said nothing. When her husband came to her she cried. He asked her what was wrong and she told him, but he didn't understand. He left the high room and later when he tried talking to her again she didn't understand a word he said.

In time she found out that the two women were Jauhar and Najeeya, his wives, and that they had taken it upon themselves to order her about; they blamed her for everything that went wrong and even invented mistakes she was supposed to have made: burnt food, water spilt on the stairs; when the children screamed they accused her of hitting them. They even stole from her and her husband. Taj became pregnant twice, and gave birth to two stillborn children, a boy and then a girl. As soon as she'd learnt some Arabic she told Jauhar and Najeeya that she'd been a Sultan's wife, and that if she'd had his child she wouldn't have been there with them then. When she got pregnant again she stayed in bed in the high room and refused to get up because she'd realized that they'd made her carry the bucket as an act of hostility towards her: she'd seen the black servant letting the bucket down to his wife who was standing by the well, and then pulling it back up. She noticed that her husband had changed. He no longer called her 'Crown of Kings'; he shouted at her and inquired of her sarcastically why there had been all that trouble and waiting if she was going to give birth to two dead children. Sometimes he panted with excitement on top of her, but no sooner had his head touched the pillow than he fell asleep and started to snore. He no longer came to her each night. One morning she held the pillow in her arms wondering why her husband slept as soon as he rested his head on it. She felt it and her hand came up against something hard; she began pulling apart the fibres of the pillow and saw embedded in the cotton some charred pieces of paper with writing on them. That night she showed them to her husband. He seized them with eager rage and descended the stairs: she could hear him shouting and threatening as he went. Later on he came back into the room and shouted at her and beat her and told her that he'd found out about her being unfaithful to him with the servant. Then he pulled her by the hair down to the second floor and pointed to a rifle hanging on the wall. He screamed at her that he would wait for the black boy or the stillborn black girl before he fired it. She smiled and went back to bed and slept as she'd never slept before. She gave birth to me after she'd been pregnant for four years.

My father came back to the high room with silver and dates and a box containing English and Turkish gold sovereigns and necklaces of coral, sapphires, gold and emeralds and placed them all around me. I was beautiful and my skin was the same colour as his. From the terrace adjoining the room he made two big rooms, so that I could run about and go down without falling on the stairs. But Najeeya and Jauhar wouldn't keep their mouths shut. Misery and spite made them ever more inclined to accuse Taj al-Arus of everything that went wrong in the house, and she never knew why he came to her after a long trip to India and said he was divorcing her. She didn't leave the house, saying that she would wait until I was married, and she no longer saw him, although she heard him talking to me and playing with me, as he married a young girl he brought back from India with him. She didn't ask him why he divorced her and not Jauhar and Najeeya; she was told that they were related to him and what's more she wasn't from the desert. She asked, 'Why didn't he bring his wife to live in this house as he brought me?' Jauhar answered, 'The man's afraid of you. Glory be to Him who made you different. In the Name of God the Compassionate, the Merciful! Your head's like a piece of cloth unrolled and blown here and there by the wind. Your eyes dance and move around and never focus on a fixed point. And your voice – in the Name of God the compassionate, the Merciful! – one moment it's sensible, the next it's wild, and one moment you're a pious Muslim, the next you're the Devil's creature. Tell me, tell me, are you right in the head or crazy?'

7

The noise lessened with the departure of most of the women. When my cousin and my son Muhammad came I went down with my mother and we sat in the car and waited for my aunt. The two Filipino girls stood in the middle of the street, happiness written all over their faces; this was one of the few times they'd been able to go out into the street, see the night and breathe air which was hot and sticky but at least wasn't manufactured by the air-conditioner. They helped lift my aunt into the car and when they'd gone inside I got out of the car and locked the shop door behind them. I called out good night but didn't hear them reply.

I closed my eyes as the car sped along with us, wondering why they were so annoyed at not going out. How could I let them go out when the men here were like traps set ready for them? I felt happier as I began to think about renting a second flat now that there was no longer room for my clients, in spite of the objections raised daily by my son. My aunt remarked suddenly. 'Congratulations, Tamr, and God willing we'll be able to congratulate you on finding a new husband before long.'

Once in the past she'd given me the names of three highly eligible men and urged me to speak to all three of them on the telephone and choose one of them. I insisted that I should meet them: I would only marry a man whom I'd seen and talked to. The past was no longer clear, or painful. I felt tired and turned to my mother. Her eyes were closed and there was a half-smile on her face: she must have been dreaming of her homeland.

Later that same night everyone in the house was asleep except Taj al-Arus. She was afraid that if she closed her eyes an angel or a devil would whisk her away to Turkey, and the smell of the gaseous springs for which her village was famous would penetrate her mind, used by now to the smell of humidity and sand and the noise of air-conditioners, and make her lose it.

Taj al-Arus opened her eyes in terror and recited, 'In the Name of God the Compassionate, the Merciful.' She stared in front of her for a long time and could see nothing. The darkness had swallowed everything up. 'Tamr. Tamr. Rashid. Batul,' she screamed. She screamed until she saw the three of us bending over her; she didn't know why these faces looked scared and asked them what was wrong. Our hands shook her and our fingers brought water up to her lips and one face was crying: my face. When we were all gathered around her she could see everything she was used to seeing each day in the distorted mirror: heaps of bags and clothes in one corner, the cracks in the walls, a cord hanging from the ceiling with a bulb on the end of it; the room had no window.

'Rashid. Tamr. Batul.' She knew these names, but not the faces. She told us that she'd been with her mother and father and other relations and heard herself calling out to them and laughing with the village girls; she knew each one, remembered the dress each one wore, the colour of her kerchief. She remembered every house in the village, the colour of the earth and the mud, the distance between every corner, every street. She saw herself pushing her kerchief back off her forehead so that the pearls and gold rings didn't go in her eyes while she was plucking a duck and making kebabs, and she saw again the freckles on her firm white hands and on her face. She peered into the faces in front of her and muttered, 'God protect me from the accursed Devil,' and realized that she was dreaming, and that we were the faces that went with the names which she knew. Rashid and Batul went back to their room while I climbed into bed next to my mother; she closed her eyes and turned on her right side as usual. She didn't sleep, and she didn't cry out although her heart was pounding and there was a rattling in her throat which obstructed her breathing. 'What's wrong, mother?' I whispered. 'What's upsetting you?' And she was saying, 'Forgive me, Lord. Forgive me, mother, father.' She sat up in bed and told me that she'd remembered carrying her little brother and sister one on each hip, and running with them for fun, the chains around her neck chinking and rattling, and how they'd wailed and clung to her in fright. She could picture the dress her little sister had been wearing and her brother's bare feet knocking against her as she ran, and even the shape and size of the blisters on them.

Taj al-Arus felt a heat in her chest, and pushing the cover back she got up and paced about the room like a cat searching for her little ones, even though she's seen them all dangling from the mouth of a wild animal. The heat rose up into her head and she cried out to herself, 'Why so long? What's become of them?'

When the floor began to reverberate to the sound of her feet, even though they were so small and slender, I rose to take her back to bed. My aunt had heard her cry and called from her room, 'What's got into you, Taj? The Sultan's a heap of bones. Tamr isn't going to marry any sultans. For God's sake go to sleep.'

Nevertheless, Taj al-Arus sat describing the roads and pathways to me, telling me the names of the trees, recounting how the whole village thought that the hot springs were the Devil's bath. She described her mother, her father, her brothers and sisters, the earthenware jar of figs the size of stones, the snow, the ducks, the pomegranate juice; how they'd distilled rose water, fattened the sheep, made rag dolls, and cats of clay and water. When I showed interest and prompted her to tell me more, she settled into her stride and plunged ahead impetuously as if she were coming closer and closer to her village. All of a sudden she stopped and asked in Turkish, 'Do you think they remember me?'

In the morning I got up, my aunt grumbled restlessly, and it seemed as if the daily routine of the house had begun: Rashid's children made a noise; Batul shouted at them; the water boiled on the stove and the smell of coffee filled the place. Taj al-Arus gathered her nightdress around her as if she didn't want any person or thing to reach her or come near her feelings, in case they took away what she was bent on preserving. She withdrew, her rosary in her hands, telling its beads. She couldn't see any freckles on her hands and for a long time there hadn't been any on her face either. Jauhar or Najeeya had once said to her mockingly, 'God protect us. You've got eyes all over your face!' When my father stopped coming to see her, Taj never missed an opportunity to ask every woman she met, old or young, how to remove the freckles.

She got up from her corner and announced to us all that she was going to Turkey. My aunt laughed but I was afraid of the turn my mother's thoughts were taking, and replied quickly, 'They might have died a long time ago, then what would happen to you?' Taj al-Arus didn't make any comment but she was determined to go, and began bundling her clothes into my case, and preparing the reply she would give if anybody asked her whether she was really a Sultana. Her clothes were not the clothes of a Sultana, nor were the earrings and necklaces and bangles she wore now the jewellery of a Sultana. She deliberated and went off into corners by herself and wept constantly, until Rashid eventually decided to arrange the trip for her, although she swore that her village wasn't far from Bursa and that she had been to Bursa on foot. Rashid made enquiries about the area she came from, but unexpectedly no one could help him: the countless women who'd been brought to the Sultan were from every country under the sun. Rashid didn't feel at ease about her until he'd entrusted her to some Turkish pilgrims who were on their way home, and who assured him that they would bring her back to the desert whenever she wished to come.

During the time she was away from the house, my Aunt Nasab made predictions: 'Taj al-Arus must be staying at one of her sisters' houses now. Or perhaps her mother is still

alive . . . ' while I blamed myself because I hadn't stood up to
Rashid when he forbade me to go with her, then took comfort when my aunt laughed and remarked, 'Taj is sure to be
lying to them, and pretending she's a Sultana!' I pictured my
mother's bewilderment at being alone for the first time in
forty years.

When Taj al-Arus came back after a week, she handed out
boxes of Turkish Delight to us with an expressionless face,
and refused to say anything about her trip.

She had known, as soon as she arrived in Bursa, that she
would never reach her village. Even the ornate and plentiful
minarets, which she was told were hundreds of years old,
looked strange to her. She was taken to a number of villages,
and in the village squares the people gathered around her, old
and young, men and women, wearing clothes very different
from how she'd remembered them. She could no longer see
the pathways which she'd seen in her dreams, nor the trees,
nor the houses which she'd remembered stone by stone, and
she didn't go running up to her own house. When the guide
told them her story, in case any of the old people remembered
the Sultan's visit and the cars parked in the village field and
the dogs which had barked and followed the train for miles, it
was passed around from ear to ear. The crowd took several
paces forward to see at close quarters the woman whom the
Sultan of that far off land beyond the railway line had
married. When this happened she gathered herself in and
pulled her abaya more closely round her. Her heart beat
fiercely and she took refuge in silence, praying fervently. She
found an opening for one eye to see through the blackness,
and looked at the inquisitive faces. One man introduced
himself to her and said that she was his aunt, and took her to
his strange house.

As she studied his strange face, she couldn't smell the
springs, and when she asked him about them she realized that
he'd been lying. All the same she kept waiting for something
unexpected to happen. As soon as he found out from the

women clustered around her that there was no gold in her bag he handed her back to the guide.

She didn't despair, except once when she was sitting in a village square under a spreading tree surrounded by men and women and children, and she started to think. There were birds twittering right overhead and they didn't stop singing even though small children were pelting them with stones. Like every other time she felt embarrassed; but this time that embarrassment was mixed with disappointment and sorrow, perhaps because the children were unconcerned by her presence as they threw stones at the birds, and the grown-ups said nothing when the stones landed all around her and one of them hit her on the hand; and perhaps because she was starting to get bird droppings on her abaya. She found herself thinking for the first time, 'Why? Why?' She pictured her father bending happily to kiss the Sultan's hand, the whole village lined up to watch Taj al-Arus leaving to become a queen, and only the dogs chasing after her.

Suzanne

1

I moved the packets and jars out of the way and took down the slender bottle. Although I could hear Maaz joking with Ringo, his loud laughter like the chattering of monkeys, I went to the door of the kitchen to make sure, then hurried back and poured Scotch and water into the glass, took the lid off the narrow bottle and brought it close to the glass. How was it going to be possible to add just two drops? I was at a loss, and afraid that Ringo and Maaz would come in while I was holding the bottle. But all the same I began to tilt it slowly towards the glass as if I was squeezing the breath out of it: one drop, two, or twenty? This time I hid the bottle in a cooking pot and picked up the glass, but I didn't leave the kitchen. Had I put in three drops or twenty? Perhaps he'd be poisoned, die even. I went towards the sink to pour it away, but then drew back. This was my last chance and I had to risk it. I encouraged myself with the thought that if anything terrible happened nobody would realize the cause. They'd blame the Scotch and bundle the case out of sight, just as they'd bundle him away if he died. I found I was shaking my head, revolted by my own thoughts. Was I trying to calm myself down because I was scared, or had I really grown that hard?

When Ringo saw me coming with the glass in my hand, he rose to his feet announcing that he would begin by cleaning the rooms on the top floor. I gave the glass to Maaz, hoping that he wouldn't notice my hand shaking. I looked at Ringo and pointed to my mouth and my cheek. He nodded and went upstairs and came down a few moments later with my make-up bag. I sat down facing Maaz, trying to appear indifferent, although my heart had begun to beat violently and my mouth was twisted to one side with the force of my agitation.

Each time his mouth went down to the glass and he drank, I felt a throbbing pulse in my neck; when he'd finished he handed me the empty glass and said, 'More iced tea, Suzie. Why aren't you drinking with me?'

I stood up holding the glass, trying to control my twitching mouth. With a forced coquettishness, I pronounced, 'You can't live without Scotch, and I can't live without you.'

Maaz laughed his loud laugh and put his hand to his heart: 'Our hearts are our witnesses, Suzie.'

I went into the kitchen and put on lipstick and powder, using the glass door of the oven as a mirror. I told myself solemnly that I'd hear his body crashing to the floor any moment now. As I poured more Scotch and water into his glass a voice of guilt whispered inside me, blotting out everything else, 'Sita said I had to mix the drops with tea or coffee, and here I am adding them to Scotch,' But then I pushed away the idea that something would happen to him, offering myself the justification that Sita would never have heard of Scotch and wouldn't know what it was.

I was still shaking and I blamed Suha for ever taking me to Sita. Irritably I thought to myself that in spite of her clothes and her excellent English, she was like Sita and the rest of them whom I saw walking around the streets like sacks of coal. I found myself wishing I'd responded more positively to Ringo's scheme and seen it right through instead of using this potion of Sita's.

I'd woken up that morning, or rather I'd left my bed, still more or less asleep. A whole month had gone by since we'd come back from our trip together and I hadn't seen him. I'd heard his love talk and his voice trembling with emotion on the phone every week or so, and he'd brought me a gazelle that he'd caught out hunting, and then not waited to see me when I came out of the bath. My longing for him was unbearable, and yet I couldn't manage to have him in my grasp although I telephoned him and went to his house and sent Ringo to his office.

That morning I'd shouted at my husband, and then sat crying loudly. This craving was agony; it opened up a chasm in my body which the blood couldn't reach. For the first time I'd thought about playing with myself; I'd controlled the hand hovering over my stomach the night before and put it back by my side, vowing that I would try to get Maaz back and marry him, whatever the cost.

Ringo had patted me on the shoulder soothingly and told me he'd get Maaz to come that same morning. When I shook my head disbelievingly, he insisted that I'd see him sitting on that very chair, pointing to a chair untidy with newspapers and James's clothes; probably he was thinking as I was that he'd begun to neglect the housework because I'd stopped giving him orders and distracted him from what he was supposed to be doing. He bent down to gather up everything that was on the chair, and repeated, 'Maaz will sit on this chair today.' Then he began to explain his plan to me, taking out the pin which he usually kept stuck in his shirt pocket. He lit a match and held it to the point of the pin until it turned red as a glowing coal, then black, and I thought Maaz would rise up out of it. At the same time Sita's bottle gleamed in my head and I began to laugh. Ringo handed me the pin and told me to prick my finger a few times until I had some drops of blood on my hand. I did as he said, and when a few drops of blood were just appearing he mixed coffee with tincture of iodine and sprinkled it on a bandage which he bound around my right wrist. Then he made me sit down on the sofa, and brought a jar with the remains of some cream in it which he rubbed all over my face, and I burst out laughing again. When my pallor still wasn't convincing enough for him he went to fetch the saffron used for colouring the rice and dissolved some in water and began massaging my face with it. All this time, I was holding a mirror and trying to see what was happening to my face. Then he asked me how to say, 'She's killed herself,' in Arabic. I got up to phone Suha, although I didn't think there would be an equivalent expression in Arabic. I couldn't imagine anyone taking their own life in this country: there was no need for it. In her usual fashion, Suha had forgotten our recent rapprochement and our visit to Sita a few days before, and replied tersely that she was busy and hung up. I rang again, cursing her inwardly, and told her that I was about to give Maaz Sita's drops. When I sensed her enthusiasm returning, I asked my question, and she asked me sarcastically if I was planning to kill myself. Then she asked me to let her know what happened to Maaz.

I repeated the expression over and over again until Ringo had mastered it; this was the whole sentence: 'Uncle Maaz, Madame Suzanne has killed herself.' Then he ordered me not to open my eyes and not to answer Maaz except when he swore that he would never split up with me again.

'No,' I added involuntarily. 'He has to marry me. He asked me to, or have you forgotten?'

'How could I forget?' said Ringo, going over to the door. 'He chased you like a wasp shamed by its own buzzing.'

Ringo's words made me feel happier, even though I didn't understand the comparison. I wasn't stretched out on the couch for long, or it could be that I didn't notice the time passing because I was going over and over the same subject: I wanted to get him back, and to marry him even if I had to be the second wife.

If I'd stood and repeated this to myself in the mirror a few months before, I would most likely have thought there's a woman who's gone beyond the nervous breakdown stage and is well and truly mad — Maaz al-Siddiq's second wife?

When I heard the car roaring to a halt, I closed my eyes. I heard Maaz's voice before I heard the door: 'You heathen! You don't believe in God. You'll go to hell.' When he added in English, 'You crazy, you suicide,' I was overcome by a desire to laugh. He shook me and I couldn't stop my eyes opening. I began to cry but instead of being cut by my tears, he told me reproachfully that anyone who tried to take their own life without waiting for God's will to be fulfilled went to hell. The minute he showed signs of pity for me because I'd be going to hell, Ringo came up and took hold of my hand, gesturing to Maaz and shaking his head sorrowfully.

Maaz obediently took my hand from Ringo and I seized the opportunity and flung my arms round him, crying violently and pressing my breast against him with every convulsive sob; I hissed like a snake in his ear that I couldn't live without him, why had he left me, and where had his love for me gone? The strength of my resolve convinced him, and created just the effect I'd imagined, and did it quickly, because he turned to Ringo laughing and said, 'God damn you! Bring me some iced tea!' But as Ringo went towards the door of the kitchen, warning bells rang in my mind. I pictured what was going to happen between us, maybe standing up, maybe for no more than a few moments, then like someone who'd relieved himself of a burden, he'd be off. At this, the picture of the Indian woman on Sita's bottle, holding up her long hair, flashed into my mind and I recalled her words: 'Even if it doesn't do any good, it won't do any harm.'

I couldn't hear a sound; he must have guessed from the taste of it: perhaps Fatima had resorted to Sita and her potions and that was why he didn't want to leave her even though she put oil on her hair and had yellow teeth. But he was strolling around the sitting-room and he stopped by a model aeroplane which David had made. As soon as he saw me he reached out to take the glass from me. 'God, I need this, Suzie,' he said. 'Tell me, where did you buy this plane? It must be the biggest you can get. Has David been into the desert to fly it yet?' 'I've told you a hundred times,' I answered irritably as usual, 'David didn't buy it. He just bought the motor, and you know he goes into the desert to fly it every Friday.'

I forced a laugh, annoyed at myself for answering him in this way, and aware that the days of the proud pleased assurance which his love had brought to me were gone.

He stretched out his hand to my breast and said, 'It's been ages since we ate pomegranates.' When I asked him what they were he began to explain, and I nodded my head without really understanding: a pomegranate was a fruit like a pearl, he said, and if one of its seeds dropped on the ground, God wouldn't let us enter Paradise. He went to put both hands on my breasts and I stopped him, making the excuse that David would be home soon. At this he looked so put out that I asked him why he hadn't been in touch with me if he felt so passionate.

The image of Sita's bottle gleamed brightly, and I remembered her promise that a few hours or a night after a man took these drops 'his body would be ablaze as if he had peppercorns up his backside'.

'Don't lie, Suzanne,' he yelled at me. 'Lying's a sin. David doesn't come back at noon.' I found myself swearing in God's name, just like him, that when Ringo had saved me from cutting my wrists he'd sent for David too and when he hadn't been able to find him, he'd left a message.

Only then did I suddenly remember that my attempted suicide was supposed to have been the main topic of the morning, to the exclusion of all else, and I realized that because I knew it wasn't real I'd forgotten all about it.

'I want more iced tea, Suzanne,' he said. 'Since there are no pomegranates, I'll drink tea.'

Why didn't he try again? Or didn't he love me any longer? I went up to him and embraced him and clung to him and told him how I'd missed him. When he pulled me closer, I knew that he still wanted me, whether Sita's drops got to his brain or not, and that what had happened between us during our trip abroad didn't matter. And because he could squeeze me and pull me to him for a few minutes and feel happy, I pulled away like a fish slipping out of the net and said provocatively, 'I'll go and get the Scotch.' I'd dreamt for so long of being in his arms and of the pleasure he gave me, and yet I didn't feel any longing or desire at this moment; could my

passion have been no more than the result of his abandoning
me?

He sat drinking. Then he asked, 'Why this long separation,
Suzie?' Before I could answer, he stretched out his arm to
show me his new wrist-watch.

I wouldn't have believed that he could be so sly as to turn
the question round like that. But he jumped to his feet
suddenly, and seized hold of me, pulling me up off the couch.
'Suzie, I can't wait. Come on, let's go upstairs. We can go into
the bathroom, or do it standing up behind the door.' Pushing
him off, I said, 'How did you wait for a whole month?'

He struck one palm against the other, then one palm
against his forehead and said, 'Maaz, you bastard! It's been a
month since you were blessed by Suzanne's fragrant aroma!
Suzie — I went to the bedouin to see my mother. She wasn't
well at all, nor was my father. And I went on a trip hunting
gazelles with some of my relations.' Perhaps he was telling
the truth; perhaps he did go to his mother's for ten days.
When I didn't make any comment, he must have imagined
that I'd agree after a while and we'd go to the top floor, into
the bathroom, or stand up behind the door, because he
added, as if exonerating himself further, 'When I got back,
we had people from the oasis coming to stay with us.'

My eyes bored into his, trying to find out the truth.

'Where are they? In your house?'

'What do you think? Would they be sleeping in the street? '

I raised a hand to silence him.

He sipped a third glass of Scotch, then turned to me: 'What
was your answer, Suzie? Are we going upstairs?' I heard the
shrieking of children in the garden and answered, 'No. Why
don't we go in the garden?'

He began to laugh: 'God, like the Imam of Yemen's apes.
His house has been turned into a museum and when we went
to visit it, I saw apes in the garden one on top of the other,
just like human beings, not paying the slightest attention to
anybody round them.'

I said nastily, 'I saw the guests. One day I went to visit Fatima and I saw them.'

With complete lack of affectation he said, 'I swear Fatima didn't tell me, Suzanne. She must have forgotten. She's got the children and their problems, and the little one worries her to death. He's still eating earth, and it'll kill him.'

I lost faith in Sita's drops. If they'd changed anything in him, they'd made him more balanced. Laughing, he asked me, 'You've seen Aisha, you know how beautiful she is? Three men want to marry her and she refused them all because she wants to marry a man from the town, not a bedouin.'

My heart missed a beat but I nodded my head, while he went on, 'She drives a tractor and a landrover. When the desert guard told her that it was forbidden for women to drive, she said, "Try and stop me. I'd like to see you bringing drums of water in by camel, and winter supplies." She comes in to town every three months.'

I sensed that the way he talked about Aisha was out of the ordinary; I began to understand Maaz. 'Does Aisha want to marry you? ' I asked.

He started to laugh, slapping one palm against the other, until his eyes disappeared into his head, and his teeth showed white like pearls. 'Fatima must have told you?' he said, questioningly. 'I swear she's joking, Sheikha Suzanne. Aisha's father is a nomad and a real bedouin. He lashes people with the cord of his headcloth and they say one of his strokes is enough to take your fingers off. He decided to marry Suad, relying mainly on God to help him, but also on me. He told me that Suad, who's a nurse, had fallen passionately in love with him when he was a patient in the government hospital here. Aisha asked him how he knew that Suad loved him and he regaled us with stories of how she'd washed his face for him, changed his sheets, brought him hot food and even helped him to eat, and not been disgusted by him; when she took his temperature she'd always rubbed the thermometer on an apron tied around her waist so that a trace of him stayed with her. It was while he was still in hospital that he'd told Aisha he wanted to marry the nurse and Aisha, the wicked girl, had said, "There's nothing to stop you." Then she went off and told Suad, who was Lebanese, and the two became close friends and laughed together over the old man. When he was better and they took him back to the oasis, he couldn't get Suad out of his mind, and began saying to his sons and daughters, "It's not right. The girl Suad's waiting for me. I must keep my promise. Take me to the town, or bring her here to the desert." Aisha assured him that Suad was preparing herself for the wedding, and so the father began dictating poems to a bedouin who'd learnt to read and write, then he folded some money inside the poems and gave them to Aisha: "The money's for winter clothes for Suad," he said, "because I can see one cloud chasing another, and the cold winds will start to blow at any moment." '

I realized what was awaiting me, and cried out, 'And you love Aisha, and she loves you?'

Maaz was unconcerned by my accusation and went on, 'Listen! I told Aisha not to play tricks on her father, because one day he might crack up over Suad and it would kill him. Or he might try and go to the town and wander off into the desert and lose his way . . . Every day he says to her, "Take me. Suad's waiting for me." '

Again I asked him, 'Are you and Aisha in love?'

He laughed and said, 'Let's go upstairs, and I'll tell you.'

'I'm tired,' I replied. He didn't look disappointed. He'd begun to know me very well and he came over to me and pulled me up. Although I usually submitted at the first touch, sometimes at a glance, I found myself feeling remote from him, thinking that desire too was just an idea in the head. I felt how strong I was now, and how he needed me.

He whispered, 'Never mind. Let's go up. You know what I want.'

I went in front of him to the door, rejoicing that I still held the key to our relationship, and said, 'Go now. Tomorrow I'll be waiting for you.' He made for the Scotch bottle and began sipping from it. I pulled it away from his mouth and asked him maliciously how his cousin Muhammad was. (The doctor had implanted a small instrument in his body to help him give up drinking.) Maaz replied laughing that Muhammad's body had adapted to the instrument and even to the sensation of nausea which it produced, and continued to swallow a tumbler of Scotch as if it were water.

He asked if he could use the bathroom. I knew he wanted to be by himself, as usual when he was drunk or had been looking at pictures of women in magazines, and I wouldn't let him, claiming that my son was about to come home. I went with him to the door, moved out of reach and his kisses, said goodbye and closed the door behind him.

In spite of my sense of victory, I thought sadly that there must be some way that I could marry him, and yet it appeared that the chance had passed me by. Maaz was no longer that ripe fruit hanging on a tree in the middle of the path. He'd changed and even seemed able to behave tolerably when he was drunk. In the past would he ever have left so meekly when he was in that state?

Alcohol used to make him crazy, and put me in a state of shock at the effect it had on him. Once he'd crumpled up on the sand and fallen asleep. I'd been terrified of the darkness and silence of the open countryside and when I tried to wake him up he opened his eyes and didn't know where he was. It was as if he couldn't see me properly or had forgotten who I was; he threw his empty bottle at me and then ran after me and I crept behind the car to hide. I heard him calling me an Israeli spy and asking me how I'd learnt Arabic so quickly, then he collapsed on to the sand again and I heard him snoring. I looked around me, frightened even of the moon and the stars. I was certain that the moving lights I could make out in the distance were a caravan of camels, but it was only a car because I heard the roar of its engine. I began to use it and other lights to guide me up on to the main road. Only then did I discover that blood was dripping from my forehead and that I'd left my shoes behind on the way. I stopped a truck by shouting and waving my hands about; the driver must have thought I was a stray camel from a distance because when he saw me and heard me saying 'Please, home, please,' his mouth dropped open, and he mumbled, 'In the name of God the Compassionate, the Merciful,' and looked around him. When he made no attempt to open the door, I said pleadingly, 'You open door?' and when he still didn't move, I went round and opened it and got in. He went on looking at me as if I wasn't real. I don't know if he noticed if I was barefoot or not. I found myself repeating, 'Thanks, brother,' and this sentence of mine put him in a state of utter confusion because my blue eyes and blond hair didn't go with my Arabic and my desert accent. When at last he started up the truck I relaxed, but only for a moment, because one hand was on the steering wheel and the other resting on his thigh and his glances travelled between my face and my body. I'd felt something hurting me on my forehead ever since Maaz had thrown the bottle at me but I'd ignored it. As a precaution against what I feared might happen, I put my hand to my forehead and when I saw a smear of blood on it I gasped, pretending to be frightened, and then became engrossed in wiping off the sand which was sticking to my face and hair. It wasn't long before my fears that he had only one idea in his mind were confirmed: he stared at me, then, reducing speed, he moved his hand from his thigh to put it beside me; I cried out 'God is great! God is great!' looking at the blood on my hand and then striking myself on the face just as I'd seen Arab women doing when they were lamenting because someone had died. I kept saying, 'God is great! God is great! ' then 'Thank you, thank you,' as I directed him to the street where I lived, using my hand and the word 'left' or 'right', until I called out, 'Just here, brother,' and opened the door and climbed down, leaving him stunned. I saw him in our street

again every day for a while, alone or with others, driving
slowly around in his truck as if he were looking for me;
sometimes he seemed frantic, as if blaming himself for missing his chance.

2

Maaz came back sooner than I expected. I'd spent the whole
afternoon in a state of nervous apprehension, thinking that
he would surely have hit a tree or a telegraph pole and now
be locked up in jail for being drunk. He stood facing me, and
every cell, every drop of his blood, all his bones and the pores
of his skin, his inhalations and exhalations, had abandoned
their proper place and landed here in a mass which hadn't
properly gelled. It was as if he hadn't known how to find the
way to my house. He was bellowing at me, then kissing my
feet, trying to eat the varnish off my toenails and when it
wouldn't come off he bit it and said it tasted red, then he
pulled my hair and muttered to himself, 'I don't understand
her scent. It's not perfume, or incense, or sandalwood.' He
called me Suzie, Susu, Sinsin, Suad. This time I wasn't aware
of his body in spite of my longing for the pleasure of sex. I
was waiting for the right moment to whisper to him that I
was his wife and that we must get married. As if I'd actually
told him what I wanted to say he began shouting at me,
swearing to me that he was going to marry me and that I was
his woman, the Suzanne of a lifetime, that without me he was
camel dung, he was a toothpick; without me he was a
eunuch; he told me that he'd seen me naked passing by his
office door, and how as he'd pulled up in his car he'd seen my

breasts undulating before him. He wouldn't be quiet, and I left him shouting out his feelings while I went into the bathroom; I did my hair looking in the mirror, unable to believe what was happening; I put on fresh lipstick, powdered my face and neck, and splashed perfume everywhere, even on my thighs. 'Long live Sita and herbal medicine, or magic,' I thought. Then into my head there floated a vision of rows of bottles bearing my name and a picture of me in the main stores in America, and I saw myself talking on television about the time I'd spent going between desert and village and from tribe to tribe to collect prescriptions that could be classified under the heading 'Love'. Then I saw myself in my own private clinic, wearing a white overall, with medicines and lotions all around me like Sita had, but mine would be in containers looking like bottles of French perfume. I'd be just like the foreign women who collected old silver jewellery and bedouin clothes and produced books with their pictures on the cover.

I heard a knocking on the door and went out but I couldn't find him anywhere in the room. He was hiding behind the door and he snatched the towel off me and began looking all over the room: how should he start and where? On the bed, on the floor; he opened the curtains and closed them again; in the clothes cupboard, standing up, sitting down. The black pupils of his eyes darted about like a falcon's eyes, pursuing his thoughts and stopping motionless at the impossibility of what he was thinking. I was flying through space, except I had one eye on my watch to see when it was time for Jimmy to come home from school. I became an instrument in his hands, the willing subject of his fantasy, and he didn't leave me until sleep overcame him. Then I kept watch, not letting any noise infiltrate the room where he was sleeping, while Jimmy, delighted that Maaz had come back to visit us, sat trying to count his snores. I felt like a bedouin woman sitting with her son in her lap, waving the flies away from him, and giving him her breast day and night so that he'd stay young and be satisfied within the bounds of her breast and her lap.

My self-confidence returned and I no longer needed constantly to turn for comfort to the memories of the first few times with Maaz to feel confident and to make myself believe that he'd have to come back to me; this had been a short-lived confidence in any case, rapidly turning to dejection. I'd always begun by remembering the falcon which he left in the office on its wooden perch. Its wary, frightened eyes moved whenever I moved or hit a key on the typewriter. From time to time it spread its great wings, then fixed its eyes on my face again. The office was empty; even my boss Ahmad had gone off with the falcon's owner. I couldn't bear the bird looking at me any longer and I began to swear at it and tried to think of some way I could get out to go home. I gathered my courage and stood up and took one step; the bird moved, fluttering its wings, as if it wanted to fly. The noise of them was shockingly loud, and I clung to the wall again, even though the falcon remained chained to its perch, and stayed where I was until its owner returned. He laughed when I begged him to rescue me. I found his name hard to remember but I couldn't forget his black eyes which were like the eyes of his falcon and watched me all through his visit to our office and began to amuse me after a while: I hadn't known before that a man like that could exist in real life and not just on the cinema screen.

He smiled constantly and sat in front of me like a faithful dog; as soon as my hand reached for the cigarette packet, he lit a match and fetched the ashtray, having first rubbed it with his fingers to make sure it was clean. He brought in a thermos flask of coffee which had cardamom in it. He took my cup in his hands and whenever I put it down on the table he held it against his heart and raised his eyes to the ceiling. When I laughed he presented the cup to me, mumbling something, and when I asked what he was doing he answered in broken English that he was bewitching the cup so that I would exchange feelings with him. Each time I reached the end of a piece of typing and heaved a sigh he came across and bent over me and asked if he should fetch a doctor. It was the way he kept on insisting that he would drive me home which really annoyed me: I was afraid that he'd make it difficult for Ahmad and me to be alone together, and answered him irritably. He pretended to be angry and disappeared, but when I went home I found he'd preceded me to the house.

Three days after I first saw him in the office he began to visit us regularly, never coming without presents. He brought a bottle of monstrously expensive cologne for Jimmy, who was no more than eight, a lamb and a gazelle, then a tortoise, a snakeskin, a basket of dates and leather slippers. We clustered around him and his presents, not believing what we saw. He brought a lizard and as he tried to extricate his hand from between its teeth, he struggled with it and spoke to it as if it was human; he asked us if we'd like to eat it if he slaughtered it and cooked it. He left his sandals at the door and wandered round our house barefoot and happy, touching everything and asking what you did with things, anything from my son's toys to the automatic egg whisk. I would find him standing entranced by the rumble of the dishwasher, asking how it cleaned the plates, scoured the dirt off them and dried them; and how the oven cooked the chicken while I was away and stopped of its own accord.

After a while we began to be aware of the fact that we weren't friendly with him just because of the presents he brought or the magazines, banned for their politics or the amount of bare female flesh in them, which he could get because of the work he did. It was more as if he was the unfamiliar desert land come into our midst. Jimmy grew accustomed to him and considered him a necessity in our life because we were here, just as Ringo was a necessity in the house. Meanwhile he admired our way of life and our possessions, and my knowledge and worldly wisdom: I read out to him the instructions accompanying medications; I sprinkled something from a bottle on a stain on his clothes and it disappeared; I could type a line in a flash without looking at the keys; I knew how to find my way around and what the street names were in Arabic; I loved Arab food and dipped my morsels of bread and rice into the meat juices the way that they did. I knew how to adjust the television, change a light bulb, paint a wall, read books, drive a truck.

For our part, we grew accustomed to eating the rice and meat which he prepared, to the way he ate with his hand, gathering the rice into a little ball and throwing it into his mouth, and the way he drank water straight from the water bottle but never touching it with his lips; the way he drank Scotch at our house, then got drunk and sang songs, the way he circled around me and the numerous questions which his curiosity provoked; his incomprehensible English, the way he kept saying my name; on one occasion this led me to answer exasperatedly, 'Suzanne yourself', and perhaps he hadn't seen my expression because he immediately bent and kissed my hand repeating, 'Suzanne yourself: that means you and I are one person.' Then he said that he loved me very much, with a love that was as vast as the sand and the sky. He was bouncing around me and I extricated myself, laughing despite my embarrassment. He followed me into the kitchen, insisting that I visit his wife, Fatima, and when I refused he said that he wanted my opinion on installing an American kitchen just like mine in his house. I knew he was thinking up excuses, and I said to him, 'I'll give you the name of my kitchen and you can order it from the States.' The sentence was hardly out when an idea flashed into my head: why didn't I order a kitchen for him from the States and benefit financially, be a trading link between the desert and America?

I began to calculate in my imagination how much I'd make, and agreed to go; in any case I was anxious to see his wife: one day he'd telephoned her from my house, and tried to hand me the receiver so that I could talk to her, saying in English, in a tone of voice that was almost an order, 'Speak to

Fatima.' At first I'd refused, uncertain what I should say, then I gave in when I saw the disappointment in Maaz's eyes; Jimmy, disillusioned with me, had already decided to have a go and had snatched the receiver out of Maaz's hand and shrieked down it in Arabic, 'Hallo. Hallo, darling.' When I spoke I said in Arabic, 'Hallo, Fatima, how are you?' and her voice came down the line to me like the speaking clock or the recorded information services, 'Hallo. Hallo. Hallo,' then silence, then laughter, then again, 'Hallo. Hallo. Hallo.'

I think I understood the reasons why Maaz was attached to us from the moment I first entered his house, but I couldn't fathom his wife's attitude to me. She was young with a shy smile. When I held out my hand to shake hers, she embraced me and kissed me three times on alternate cheeks, and kissed my son, then ran into the kitchen. The house had a particular smell, and after a while I came to know that it was the smell of incense and basmati rice and heat all mixed together and that it was in all the Arab houses I visited, except Suha's. I cast my eyes around the house. There was only basic furniture: a rug in deep colours, sombre sofas, dust over everything, and heat, because not every room had an air-conditioner in it. Maaz wandered between the kitchen and the room where we were sitting, just as he did in my house, carrying plates and cups of tea and fruit. I turned to Fatima and said, 'Maaz's doing the housework.' She smiled and covered her teeth with her hand and turned to look at him: 'Just today. For you.' I thought, this house hasn't seen a blond hair before today, and Maaz doesn't trust his wife to do her duty towards the guests. Gradually I began to comprehend that they saw me as an important guest from Nixon's land, the land of the oven that cleaned itself without spilling any water. My sense of my own importance began to increase, as if my yellow hair which hung lifelessly round my face had turned into shining gold, and my speech into pearls, for his children's eyes were fixed on me and my son, and the neighbours' children poured in to greet us and sat asking

Maaz for an explanation of every word I said, then giving me
smiles of admiration and encouragement. I thought to myself
that at home in my own country I had never been spoken to
or even looked at admiringly like this.

Fatima sat facing me, bending forward as if she was sitting
on a sofa for the first time, her long dress covering the floor
at her feet; she wore a headshawl, a veil over her eyes, and
her hands and feet were stained with henna. We conversed
with fleeting smiles, and I found that I was laughing and
smiling without reason; I felt as if I were years younger than
her, and like a spoilt child. Maaz interrupted, urging her to
bring me more biscuits, since my son had swooped down on
the plates like a flock of pigeons. Maaz's two daughters had
withdrawn into a corner and stood looking at me in astonishment. Only his little boy was unaware of my presence and
cried continuously because his father had shut the door, and
he still had the habit of eating earth in the garden. Maaz
dominated the gathering with his movements and way of
talking, as he did when he came to visit me; he didn't care
who was there when he told me in English that his love for
me was vast as the sands and the sky, while Fatima smiled,
then held out her hand as if apologizing to me for her
husband's behaviour; she didn't understand what he said but
perhaps she guessed because I did no more in reply to him
than look arch and say, 'Stop it!'

She seemed happy and told Maaz that having me to visit
was more fun than watching television or going for a drive in
the car. I smiled at her, trying to appear especially grateful
because I'd noticed that she was hiding something in the folds
of her dress. Perhaps like Maaz she liked to give presents,
either as a social obligation or because it made her feel happy.
My curiosity grew and I followed the movement of her hand
intently to try and see what she was hiding but only succeeded because her little son wanted her to pick him up. I saw
a packet which in disbelief I made out to be jelly. Maaz began
to sing in Arabic, pointing to his heart, his eyes dancing, till I

ordered him to stop, smiling at Fatima who was happy and at ease with the company; the jelly packet must just be a wrapping for something else: in the women's market I'd seen them putting gold in milk tins and silver in empty soap-powder boxes. Maaz's little son threw the jelly packet and Maaz caught it and said to me, 'Fatima wants you to teach her how to make jelly but she's shy of you.' I stood up inpatiently, trying to hide my disappointment, and Maaz took me to the kitchen with Fatima following slowly behind. I strutted proudly along in a new way, indifferent to my surroundings, pulling in the muscles in my bottom to make it look slimmer and more shapely. I tried to explain to her, but she only smiled and didn't look at what I was doing, didn't even seem to be listening to me, but just nodded and covered her mouth with her hand.

In the car Maaz tried to persuade me and Jimmy to go with him to a small village to see a newborn camel on a farm belonging to a friend of his. I didn't raise any objections; his interest in me and his amorous behaviour amused me, and the monotony of these days needed some such novelty, especially since I no longer saw Ahmad.

When Maaz took off his headcloth and cord to try them on me, I saw his head, his hair, his forehead – and I saw a man, and as he reached out his hand to take the headcloth back I felt a fierce heat touching me. He returned his hand to the steering wheel and I longed to feel the heat again, and turned to Jimmy in the back of the car, smiling at him as if to excuse this urge in me, then turned back to look at Maaz's brown hands which were covered in little black hairs. I caught sight of his white underpants through his loose robe and looked away, staring out of the window; his attempts to reach me had eventually succeeded: I'd previously been convinced that the whole idea was absurd, because I'd been sure that he knew all about my relationship with Ahmad from the first day he'd come into the office with the falcon.

So I asked him casually if he could find me a job as Ahmad

no longer sent me anything to type. He answered that the pressure against women working was increasing and he didn't think that I ought to work. It wasn't this pressure which had forced Ahmad to do without me, but the arrival of his family from Egypt. I was about to ask Maaz when Ahmad's family was leaving, but I stopped and asked him instead if he'd seen Ahmad. 'Ahmad's taken up with his wife and children,' he answered, and I understood from this that Maaz only saw him in his office since there was no mixed visiting. Then suddenly Maaz asked me if I'd like to go abroad with him. I stared hard at him but he was asking in all innocence, and when I asked why, he replied, 'I've never seen anything but sand and sea.' He went on, 'Perhaps the best thing would be when you go to America on holiday, I could visit you and you could show me around. You in the daytime and David in the evening.' All I could do was wonder fruitlessly how he could make amorous advances to me and at the same time visit us and talk to David, indeed establish a firm friendship with him, and take me to see his wife, and how she could welcome me royally even though she knew how he frequented our house and spent many long evenings with us. Were the two of them more liberated than me and David? And I didn't answer him, although it struck me that we'd planted in him a germ of curiosity about a world which he'd never previously given a thought to.

I found myself wishing I could be alone with him at that moment; since I'd stopped seeing Ahmad, the rooms in the house had grown cramped, the shouting of the children in the compound louder, and Jimmy's requirements more preposterous. I began to feel the need to go out of the house and talk to anyone I happened to meet, my neighbour opposite for example, or to get into the car and ask the driver to take us for a drive around; we would go to the store to buy what Jimmy wanted, and what my greed prompted me to buy, much of it, especially the American products which I didn't need, without regard to the inflated prices. I felt that money here had no value. I didn't think of visiting the other women here and I didn't find things to complain about like they did, because unlike them I didn't mind the voice of the muezzin in the early hours of the morning or the fact that the shops closed during the daytime prayers.

Nevertheless my life here was different, and had been since my third night in the desert when I'd opened my eyes in alarm at a sound, neither a song nor a sermon, proceeding from a microphone: I found myself naked in a garden surrounded by a high wall. I looked frantically around me for my clothes and when I found them in a heap near me I began to wonder about my husband; I covered my stomach with one hand and pulled on my clothes with the other. What had happened to me? Where was David? When I stood up with some difficulty I remembered that I'd had a lot to drink. I could only move slowly in spite of my anxiety to find out what had happened to David. I went into the house and saw the owner of the firm fast asleep on the sofa, and traces of the previous night's dinner, glasses and the remains of food and cigarette ends, and cassettes scattered here and there. I remembered the blue movie and how I'd refused to watch it at first, then laughed and demanded to see it. I'd been happy, hardly able to believe in the interest that was being shown in me, the dishes covering the table, the respectful behaviour of the two servants bringing us drinks, the firm's owner telling the driver to go and fetch a video of 'Dallas' from a friend's house simply because I'd asked him whether he'd seen the last episode. I couldn't remember if this had happened before or after David had left the party to check on Jimmy. Had he come back and seen me watching the movie and gone angrily away again? I sat down, pushing ashtrays and plates around in the hope of waking up the sleeping man on the couch. Dawn was beginning to break. I looked out of the window but could see only the high wall. The man was still asleep. I went to the front door and unlocked it and saw his car. Leaving the door open, I went down to the outer door and opened it and looked out.

A few houses were all that I could see and the light made my eyes smart; I went back into the room, closing the door noisily behind me. At this the man sat up; he didn't seem surprised to see me, and smiled at me. Feeling embarrassed, I asked about my husband and he replied simply, 'David went home.' I was on the point of asking more questions but felt confused and said nothing. He stood up, searching for the car keys which were hanging on the door latch. Then he bent and took my hand and kissed it, then he kissed my neck and I felt a faint quivering in my thighs. I moved backwards, but in spite of my nervousness I couldn't help being aware of the warmth of his brown skin. I let him kiss me, put his hands on me, and when I surrendered my body to his I felt a great happiness flooding through me in spite of my disordered thoughts. I tried to recall his name and couldn't. He wouldn't agree to write it on a piece of paper for me, but he taught me to remember it: Ahmad. We'd met him for the first time that morning when I'd gone with my husband to stock up with food and buy second-hand furniture from him. When he invited us to dinner we'd wondered whether we were dreaming, and thought how lucky we were to have been posted to a country where people were more concerned about others than they were where we came from.

Jimmy asked me if he could touch the baby camel. Maaz answered for me and told him that the camel's mother was tired and might bite him if he went too close. He bit his own hand to make his words more impressive. I didn't care about the baby camel or its mother, or Maaz's friend or the women who were watching us through cracks in the door in spite of the veils which covered their heads and hung down the sides of their faces. Even eating dates and drinking tea out of a glass was dull. Maaz's agitated longing for me had been obvious from the moment I got into the car with him. It reminded me of the incomparably happy times I'd spent with Ahmad and made me long for them again now. On the return journey he drove at a crazy pace as if with the speed he came closer to me and touched me; when we reached home I invited him in for a cup of tea. I noticed that the veins in his hand were standing out and he was pressing one leg down on the other. When I put the tea down in front of him I deliberately brought my face and breast level with him. He asked me if I had an aspirin and I knew he wanted to follow me into the kitchen even though there was a danger that someone might come in and find us there. He held my breasts and rubbed his face against them and held me close for a second and seemed happy. I felt irritated and wondered what I'd been expecting, seeing that we were in the kitchen.

As I opened my legs for the first time I didn't think about what he made of my relationship with my husband and why he was always winking at me and laughing as he asked me to marry him. Instead, I watched him closing his eyes, letting his body go loose, murmuring that now he would welcome the Angel of Death. I didn't understand and he explained that he wanted nothing more from life after this. At the start I was convinced that he was acting: when he saw me without my clothes on he gasped and struck his head with the palm of his hand, exclaiming bitterly, 'Why did God create foreign women different?' When I asked him what his wife's body was like he didn't answer me, but passed his hand over my flesh saying, 'It's like silk. Pure silk.' When he let out a noise like a bull roaring I nearly laughed. He said I was like one of the houris whom God had prepared for true believers when they entered Paradise. He even grabbed my foot and smelt it, muttering, 'More fragrant than sandalwood or incense.' I started to laugh out loud then. I was relaxed. The curtains were drawn and a gentle gloom enveloped the room. It was eleven in the morning and the house would stay quiet until three o'clock.

I kept on laughing even though he pleaded with me to stop. I couldn't help myself in the face of what he was doing with my body. He was like a man worshipping at a pagan shrine, uttering incantations, most of them incomprehensible to me.

I couldn't understand why he wanted to restrict me: he refused to let me move about or get off the bed or even cover myself up.

Suddenly he was on his feet, shouting at me. Although the veins were visible on his face I went on smiling. As his anger mounted and I watched the expressions following one another across his face and his hands shaking, I thought to myself that he must have seen a lot of silent films: his black eyes almost made holes in the screen, or in my face. I had no idea of the reasons for his outburst of emotion until, nearly in tears, he asked me why I was laughing. I didn't tell him that it was his melodramatic admiration of my body and his manner of loving that I found so funny; I made do with saying that there was no need for him to talk and behave as he had been doing because I was quite happy with him. Later I realized that he wasn't acting and that he really meant it when he called me the Marilyn Monroe of the desert. If I gestured, sat still, walked along, I was exciting; if I spoke, there was someone picking up my words as if they were kisses. He wanted me on the sand, in an empty house, in the open desert, at an oasis, waiting till midnight and keeping a big stick near him in case anyone surprised us. He wanted me in a camel hair tent, even at his mother's after he'd drunk some camel's milk and his mother had fallen asleep; in my house, in the bathroom or in bed. I abandoned myself to glorying in my plumpness, not caring about the blue veins in my legs and thighs; I no longer wore a girdle: Maaz took hold of the folds of flesh as if he were snatching up gold in Ali Baba's cave. Only my stomach worried me still and I devised various schemes to prevent him seeing it in daylight. I always pushed his hand off it or covered it with a sheet until eventually, like an explorer, he began to enjoy what he'd already discovered, whereas before his concern had been to find out where further advances would lead. He began to notice what I was doing and one day he asked me if it was not done in America for him to see my navel. I forced a laugh but kept my hand over my stomach. Then he asked, 'Do you think there might be a baby in there?' Laughing, I shook my head and all at once he pushed my hand away over my thigh, using his two feet. When he only saw bare flesh he seemed surprised, and I too was surprised that he didn't remark on the wrinkled skin or on the broad white lines and the deep brown ones or on the ridge of flesh around the navel. He wasn't interested in listening to me as I told him how embarrassed I was about my stomach since I'd had my second daughter, and bent over to kiss it. Gathering the flesh to one side so that my stomach looked smooth as if I was a young girl, I told him I was going to have surgery for it. Maaz took a renewed interest in the subject of my stomach and with a look of revulsion on his face he gasped, 'God forbid. You should be grateful your stomach's healthy.' Then he kissed it again greedily, in an exaggerated attempt to convince me of its flawless beauty. My mind wandered and the idea that David's lack of interest in me was related to my stomach or to my plumpness in general seemed more remote, as it certainly hadn't the slightest effect on the harmony of my relations with Maaz. Although at the beginning I used to keep control of my body like a Playboy bunny who has to think herself into the part, his way of behaving made me feel that I really was a bunny and I wanted to be intoxicated with passion. I never once envied him when he abandoned himself to his own passion as I used to do sometimes with David or in a fleeting affair I'd had with a distant relation, or with Ahmad; and I never once faked it with him and opened one eye, as I had done with the others, to make sure that they were noticing me shudder. With him I was silent in my ecstasy, confident that he wasn't going to leave me unsatisfied, because he always wanted me again and for a long time.

3

Two days had passed since Maaz had come back to me and Sita's drops had exploded noisily in his head. When he got up he called me Maryam and said from now on my name was Maryam not Suzanne. 'Like the Virgin Mary or Mary Magdalene?' I asked, pretending to be gentle and at ease. 'Maryam. The wife of Maaz al-Siddiq. And if anyone calls you Maryam the American woman I'll break his neck.' I didn't ask him when our wedding was going to be or say what about David, and Fatima, afraid that he might withdraw his offer, and he merely repeated, 'Your name's Maryam, and if anyone calls you Maryam the blonde he'll be my enemy for all time.'

I stood up, full of delight at being the only woman he wanted in the wasteland of the desert. I didn't feel the same as before when he asked me to marry him. In the early weeks of our relationship it was because he wanted to own me, exactly as he wanted an American kitchen; this time it was the result of a relationship between a man and a woman, and it meant, as well, that he must have grown accustomed to the idea that I and his wife belonged to the same sex, even if there was a vast difference between us.

I draped the bed cover over my head and let it hang down around me just like an abaya. I smiled, wishing I could get used to an abaya and cover my face with a black handkerchief and become like the others, wrapped up because I was precious and easily damaged and had to move about from place to place. A second wife. It didn't matter, on condition that I didn't live with Fatima. Of course I would never live with her for one reason – the children – unless there could be some acceptable arrangement like the one I'd seen between the bedouin woman and her husband's new young wife.

I'd gone with Suha to visit her bedouin neighbour because

the bleating of one of the woman's nanny goats had disturbed her son's sleep for several nights. We stood in the doorway with Umar and my son, and Suha asked her why the goats bleated day and night. The woman laughed, showing her gold teeth, and struck one palm against the other and insisted that we come in. She tried to shoo away the nanny goat, addressing it as if it were a child, while Umar stood face to face with the little creature he was so used to hearing, and it continued to bleat. We followed the woman and left our shoes at the door, as she did, and went in to see a young woman with fair skin and long hair sitting on a rush mat painting her toenails. When she saw us, she rose quickly, excusing herself and welcoming Suha with a pleased smile. We were astonished. What was she doing here, this young woman? Her nail varnish, her short dress, her fair hair and her accent were all alien to the surroundings. She insisted that we should go into the sitting-room to sit on sofas, then disappeared and returned in a flash with dishes of fruit and cake and green almonds. 'Fresh from Syria,' she announced. At this, Suha asked her if she came from Syria and the young woman answered, 'Of course I do. Do I look as if I come from this country?' Then she added that she was the second wife and we could only stare in amazement. Looking towards the door as if to indicate the other wife, and as if she had understood our surprise, she said, 'She's like my mother, and I love her. She does the housework. She cooks. She washes my clothes for me. When I get angry with my husband she brings us back together. As long as no one interferes with the goats, everything's fine.' When Suha asked if her husband was old, the Syrian woman smiled, gathering her blond hair to one side, and said, 'Not at all. He just married young. Imagine how much he must have loved me. He would have done anything to make me marry him, but he didn't want to divorce her. He said she was the mother of his children — they're grown up now. He said to me, try it, and I tried it and now I really love her.' Then she winked at us and whispered,

'There are times when I can't believe she's his wife, poor thing.'

I wanted to ask her a lot of questions, but Umar came rushing in excitedly to tell his mother about the goat, while my son stood by looking bewildered because he didn't know what Umar was saying. The first wife was standing in the doorway with the goat close beside her; she stuck her head into the room and said, 'Excuse me. This goat won't let me talk to a soul.' Then she bent down and picked it up and came into the room, looking at her husband's Syrian wife: 'Don't worry. I'll take care that she doesn't make a mess.' She sat down. The leather of her face veil had faded and looked like an extension of the skin on her face. She nursed the goat like a child in her lap, stroking it gently, never taking her hand away from its face. When Suha asked her if the story of the goat was true, looking at Umar, she answered, 'It's quite true. God bless him, he understood perfectly. He asked me one question after another like a bubbling spring. God bless him. I told him about the goat's mother who died, God rest her, while she was giving birth.' She pointed to the lower part of her stomach. 'If I hadn't pulled hard on the little one's legs she would have smothered in the mother's stomach. God decreed that she should live, and I began giving her milk from a bottle. She grew accustomed to me, and because I was always in black she thought I was her mother. She follows me wherever I go. She doesn't like going out in the street with the other goats. She wants me near her, lying beside her. Whenever I go out and bang the door behind me, she begins to cry out like mad; a couple of days ago I went away to see my sister and the poor little thing missed me.' She raised the goat's chin and addressed it: 'You were missing your mother, weren't you? ' Then she stood up, still holding the goat, took some nuts and returned to her place, eating one and giving another to the goat who was waiting expectantly.

I thought of Fatima's smile and her thinness, and banished the thought from my mind: I was older than Fatima, and the second wife was always the younger one. I dropped the cover on the ground and sat at the typewriter, banging out all my thoughts on the subject of arrangements regarding the children and divorcing David. I had this habit of writing everything down in order to arrange my thoughts, and consequently my feelings. Sometimes I had more than ten lists on the go at a time: lists of what food to buy, of people I had to write to, of people I should visit, of what I ought to say to Maaz, of the gold jewellery I owned, and of the gold I thought I should acquire.

I sat there just as I had done before we left Texas to come here, when I was getting ready to let the house, and finding boarding-schools for our three daughters. The difference between me then and me now was a difference in the way I felt. The world beyond the desert seemed far away. I seemed to be a different Suzanne now, and I found myself speaking my name: 'Suzanne. Susan.' Then in a louder voice: 'Suzanne. Suzanne,' until I heard Ringo asking if I was calling him. I was calling myself, asking if I was the same Suzanne or Susan who'd sat in Texas, a woman in a house like any other house, or an ant in a garden like any other garden.

Here, because I sat at a typewriter, people looked at me with surprise and admiration on their faces. I passed through the minds of everybody in the houses round about, just as they passed through mine, and those people who went by my door, if they didn't long to come in, at least they thought about me. This knowledge stole all through me and made me feel calm and secure.

I'd been an ordinary American housewife in the past, washing my children's nappies and enjoying folding them up neatly, switching off the lights in their rooms every evening with a feeling of real happiness because they'd eaten and washed and gone to sleep. I would pick their clothes up off the floor and be delighted when I saw dirt on them because it saved me the trouble of deciding whether to wash them or not; seeing the family eating sandwiches without asking where the cooked food was pleased me too as I calculated to myself that they could eat the roast which I'd prepared for that evening the next night. I sat in front of the television from the early morning following the soaps. I read romances and detective novels and drank Pepsi continually. I couldn't find any real reason why my relationship with David was lukewarm; we never quarrelled and I was sure that it was what happened to married couples, even after a passionate love at the start. Even though I was relatively young, I can't have been in touch with any lively circles of people. I never gave a thought to other countries or even to neighbouring states, until I talked to Barbara. Barbara was the owner of a gallery, which I'd never entered in my life although it was near my home. She caught my attention because she dressed like the magazines and television commercials in cotton and silk, clothes by designers whose names I'd heard of and thought were for a special sort of woman, like Jackie Kennedy and foreign princesses. I don't remember ever seeing her in polyester trousers or with her hair tied up out of the way; her hair was always clean and newly done, the gold bangles jangled on her wrist and the chains and necklaces round her neck. Barbara stopped me, just as she stopped everyone else she saw and asked them to visit her. I knew that her interest in me was instrumental, since it was inconceivable that my mundane personality could have attracted her; I was a potential customer and she wanted me to see her gallery. But I was wrong, for after a short time things which I'd never seen in my life before like engraved wood, copper and brass, paintings on silk, appeared less interesting to me than her conversation. She talked a lot about her life in India where she'd been a teacher, and her two train journeys round the subcontinent, on one of which she'd surprised a gang trying to smuggle stolen jewels in her luggage and got to know her husband who was one of the passengers who'd jumped up to help her. At this, I stared at her necklace, so she took it off and dropped it into my hands, telling me that it was made of precious stones. I felt embarrassed by my red hands and my nails next to her long painted ones. She went on to explain how she'd won over the Indian jewel merchant and begun buying a single stone from him every now and then. At last she asked, 'What about you?' and fell silent. I smiled at her and reached for an ashtray, cheaper than most of the other things, and refrained from telling her that my life had been uneventful except for a burglary at our house some years before.

I remembered the strange feeling that came over me when I took that brass ashtray out of its bag and put it on the table at home. For the first time I was unable to sit indolently, my mind undisturbed by anything but the most obvious domestic duties; I began to think about Barbara and her way of life and her liveliness, and was curious to see her again. This feeling led me to another feeling which I can't describe but it was as if I'd lost something, or as if I was watching an isolated episode from a television series.

I visited Barbara again the moment David told me that he'd been offered a job in an Arab country in the desert. It seemed that at last my chance had come to tell her with pride that our life too was interesting. She gave me great encouragement to go there and said that we'd live like characters in *A Thousand and One Nights*. I smiled in polite acquiescence, although I'd never heard of the book, then she began to tell me about the riches, the palaces, the jewel-studded fabrics, while I looked at the gold she had and thought happily how I would surely be able to buy similar things in the Arab country since David's salary would be double what he earned here. She said that Omar Sharif came from the same country, also the Empress Soraya. I was at a loss to know whom to believe: my father told us to watch out for fleas and lice, and my aunt warned us against scorpion stings and said they loved blondes' blood.

The feeling that had come over me when I was looking at the brass ashtray, an article that had no connection at all with the rest of the furniture in the house, came over me again the night we landed at the desert airport, and I was sure that something which would be quite unfamiliar to me was about to happen. The black eyes stared at me often, and I stared at the white cloths on the men's heads. My son pointed at them and asked if they were the shepherds who'd come to see Jesus in the manger. I laughed. When I laughed, the black eyes smiled. The man who stamped my passport looked at my photo then at my face then back to the photo. He passed a finger over his lips and sighed, and I realized that the bold eyes were admiring and pleading at the same time.

When David came home, I'd organized on paper and in my mind what was to be done. I told him that Maaz and I were going to get married. With great deliberation, and continuing to spread butter on his toast, he asked, 'When?' This reaction should have put me at ease but I burned with anger. He went on crunching his toast and I didn't answer that we'd have to be divorced first. Perhaps he'd forgotten that we were still married. I felt a strong desire to tear the toast out of his hands and rub it into his face. 'You seem pleased,' I said, and then I began to scream at him, accusing him of being without feeling, self-centred, weak. In a loud voice I remarked that I wondered how he'd been able to land this job of his. Then I answered my own question with sarcasm, still talking loudly: 'You must have deceived the evil spirits themselves.' 'I'm pleased,' he answered, 'because it's what you want, a divorce from me, because you're unhappy with me, and naturally I want your happiness.'

'The children stay with me,' I shouted, 'and Maaz will be their father, and you won't see them at all.' 'As you wish,' he replied amid the crackling of toast in his mouth. 'You're mad!' I cried. 'Do you think I'm going to pay for them? You're their father, and you can be responsible for them.'

This time his only response was a sigh, a shake of the head, as if to say, 'Give me strength.' I stood up, pushing the plate and the bread and butter and honey away from him to the other end of the table but trying to make my voice sound normal, as if it were unconnected with my actions: 'Jimmy will stay with me, and the three girls will stay where they are and we can share them in the holdiays.' 'Fine,' he replied, and I went on provocatively, 'Of course I'll convert to Islam and bring up Jimmy as a Muslim.'

'As you wish,' came the answer.

I pictured Jimmy trying to read the Qur'an in a Muslim school, and the teacher scolding him for his ignorance, and I shouted, 'You're the same as you always were and you'll never change: cold and selfish, interested in nobody but yourself; you don't care what happens to your children.'

It was obvious that I'd tried his patience as far as he was prepared to allow me, for he began as he usually did on such occasions to tell me that I was mad, talking in his normal voice as if debating a point with me.

I responded by saying he was the one who'd reduced me to this state, and I meant what I said. I accused him of being cold, of feeling pleasure only when he was flying his model areoplanes, and suggested that he preferred sex with other men, and was having a relationship with Ringo. When he remained with his head bowed over the table, I screamed at him that he must have taken money from Ahmad, otherwise why would he have left me alone that first night with all the men, and here he was now giving his blessing to my relationship with Maaz.

At this point he could no longer control his agitation, perhaps because Ringo was in the kitchen. He got up, but instead of coming towards me he made for the door and went out.

I opened it and shouted after him, 'I'll be in touch with our lawyer.' 'I was in touch with him several weeks back,' he replied. 'He's doing the paper work for the divorce.'

Only then was I forced to confront my fears: two days went by without Maaz contacting me. On the third day I thought I could feel the beads of sweat seeping through the faint hairs on my upper lip. I wiped them away with my hand, and leapt up to dial his number. Fatima answered with a laugh, and said, 'Maaz's at work.' I dialled his office number, and a colleague of his drawled, 'Darling. Honey,' when he heard my voice. I shouted back, 'Can you get Maaz, please,' but he knew that I was Suzanne. The whole town must have known about my affair with Maaz. Then I heard Maaz saying in his usual way, 'Darling. Honey. Ooh darling, I miss you.' I wasn't reassured. These were the words he always used, even in the days when he'd stopped coming to see me. 'When will you come today?' I asked him, talking fast. He asked me if Ringo was at home, which surprised me, because he didn't usually bother. 'That doesn't matter,' I replied tersely. I heard him talking to his colleague and interrupted irritably, 'Hallo, Maaz.' 'Darling,' came the reply, 'I've got some brochures for Sri Lanka.' As if I hadn't heard properly, I repeated, 'Brochures for who?' 'Sri Lanka,' he said quickly. 'Tell that son of a gun Ringo to wait there till I come.' I held my tongue, not wanting to argue with him or question him. I was anxious that no animosity should develop since he'd come back to me.

I hovered about, thinking that I couldn't wait for Maaz without doing something to take my mind off my feelings of hatred for David, which were growing with every breath I took. I thought about taking down the Afghan rug from the wall, and gathering together everything which I'd bought or Maaz had given me. I picked up the stuffed lizard with a snake in its mouth, and put it beside the brass coffee pots, and the skin of some animal I didn't know. I couldn't think where to begin, and what to do with all this stuff, or where we would get married, and where we would live. I threw myself down on the sofa in a state of collapse and instead of thinking about myself and Maaz I began thinking about David, and clenched my teeth as if I were about to enter the ring with him.

Fifteen years I'd been with him. Fifteen years and I didn't

know him, even though I knew the number of hairs on his shoulders. After a few years of marriage his interest in me had begun to grow less bit by bit. If I'd read about this in the problem pages of women's magazines I wouldn't have believed it. It was a feeling that led to madness, and after a while to recklessness and then to frustration. Gradually he cut down on the time he spent talking to me, then on how often he slept with me. I assumed he must have another woman. I tried to catch him out, and I kept an eye on his mail, stood waiting at a discreet distance opposite the building of the company he worked for, and eavesdropped on his telephone conversations. I discovered nothing, except that he was no longer interested in me. If ever I tried to put my arms round him when we were watching television, he pushed me away saying that he'd rather wait till the sports programme had ended; it seemed that he was genuinely fanatical about sport on TV, and that it absorbed all his attention. In bed I would approach him and he would move me off, saying that he didn't like me to be the one to start. When I waited for him to make the first move, he turned on his side away from me, wishing me good night. But I didn't know the full extent of his indifference to me until that morning when I'd found myself naked in Ahmad's garden.

I remember that when Ahmad brought me home in his car and dropped me in front of the house and disappeared, I stood for a few minutes at the door, not daring to knock. When I knew that I couldn't bring myself to knock, I gave the door a push to prove to myself that I was capable of some action, and to my amazement it wasn't locked. I took off my shoes and picked them up, and went into Jimmy's room, then into our room. David was fast asleep. I crept quietly into bed and held my breath, waiting. In spite of my fear I couldn't help thinking about how much I'd seemed to mean to the men I'd spent the evening with, especially Ahmad, and how I didn't mean anything to David. In his looks, his ways of behaving and the amount of respect he showed me, he didn't compare with Ahmad. For the first time I criticized David's heavy body and large stomach to myself.

The next morning David got up and said good morning to me in a normal tone. Then he asked me if I'd got on all right with the Sri Lankan servant. I nodded my head and remained silent for a while, not knowing what to say. In the end I asked him if he'd enjoyed himself last night. 'Nice people,' he replied, tying up his shoelaces. 'Shall I send the car round for you?' I didn't answer. I was astonished at his behaviour, and didn't get out of bed for some hours.

4

Maaz arrived carrying tourist brochures and a number of fashion magazines. I wasn't interested in the magazines or the fashions, although I pretended to take them with some enthusiasm so that he'd feel useful. I begged my ears to let me hear what I wanted to hear from him, but I despaired and my ears grew numb with waiting.

I began to blame myself for not marrying him the day he'd come back to me, when he'd lost his equanimity and shouted that I was his wife. Here I was now listening to details about travel, hotels, cash, the sights to be seen. I found myself gripping the edge of the sofa, afraid to let slip a single word in case I said that the most distant place I wished to go to was well within the confines of the desert; but then instead of just listening as I'd promised myself that I would, I interrupted: 'We don't need to take planes and travel abroad. We can marry at your mother's.' 'Aren't you getting divorced first?' he asked. 'It'll only be a short time before my divorce comes through,' I replied.

He put up his hand as if to wave a fly away from his face. 'It'll work out fine, God willing, Suzanne.' Then he turned back to Ringo, all eager to hear about Sri Lanka.

Every time I began to think that there would be no harm in going abroad with him now, a light flashed in my head, warning me that he was planning to make the trip alone. I sat there, trying to put this notion out of my mind, and actually covered my mouth with my hand to stop myself saying anything: I didn't want to give him even the slightest impression that I had any doubts about whether I was meant to accompany him.

I began to compare the preparation for our previous trip abroad with what was happening now. He hadn't believed that I was really going to go with him. He'd paced around me with his ticket in his hand, wanting to make sure that the date of the flight was written on it, and his name, comparing his ticket with mine to see that we were travelling on the same day. This was because he'd bought his own ticket, but given me the money to buy mine myself since he'd begun to be scared about our relationship. It was Suha who'd made me understand that Maaz was genuinely afraid, when I recounted to her how he sneaked into our house, how he wore a different headcloth every day – white, striped, blue, red, brown – how sometimes he'd hide his eyes behind dark glasses, and sometimes he'd wear spectacles borrowed from a colleague at work even though they made him trip up; how he began to come empty-handed, without his confiscated goods; and how when he started to jump up and hide under the bed, imagining that he'd seen something move or heard a noise, I could no longer restrain myself from laughing uncontrollably. It had always seemed to me that he was putting it on, for I'd never before seen him at all concerned at the prospect of being caught. Around the same period, I grew weary of him accusing me of not loving him each time he asked me to marry him and I refused, ostensibly because of

Fatima and David and my children and his children. So all in all I had welcomed the idea of a trip abroad with him, the more so because the hotel where he'd made reservations was like the luxury hotels I'd seen in advertisements, and this was a unique opportunity to visit Europe. I avoided looking at him when we were at the airport although he wasn't looking in my direction; he was comforting his son who'd been hit in the face by the bag hanging from his shoulder in the crush of people saying goodbye to him, kissing him on the nose and forehead as if he were about to embark on a journey from which there was no return. He looked like a stranger to me, dressed in a suit and shoes which seemed to make it difficult for him to walk.

Although we sat side by side we didn't move close to one another or speak until the aircraft had taken off and the noise of the engines was drowned by the passengers who broke into applause to express their joy at the freedom and the drink. Maaz began to order one glass after another, and to joke with the stewardess, and with the other passengers round about him. Then he stood up and began distributing dollars to them, insisting that they accept them, while some laughed at him and others joined in the game. I was embarrassed and sank down in my seat, pretending to be asleep. He talked and drank and guffawed all the way, and to my surprise when the plane landed, he took the names and addresses of several of his fellow passengers and promised to be in touch with them. I decided to myself that we wouldn't go out much in order to avoid the embarrassing situations which arose all the time with him. But he wasn't content, as I'd thought he would be, to draw the curtains and stay in our hotel room: I didn't know that he and I had other means of communication besides our bodies.

Maaz grew tired of staying in our room. He wanted to walk about, and go into the shops, and watch television. He wanted to remain constantly at the heart of the roar and clamour, just as on our first day he'd stood on the pavement, holding my arm and trying to take in the noise and the cars and the people and the different way of life. He saw women and breathed, 'Praise God.' As well as staring at breasts and bottoms, he began to take in the trees and the water and to lie in the park watching the girls stretched out on the green grass, their dresses raised high, revealing white thighs which changed to a pinkish hue as they lay there. He even stopped and stared at armless mannequins in shop windows waiting to be fitted with new clothes, and said laughing and pointing to their breasts and bottoms, 'Fantastic! My God!' He was thunderstruck at the sight of men in tight trousers. 'Where are you, Ringo?' he asked, 'You should be here. It would blow your mind.' Then he went on, 'I tell you, if that man walked along Nafoura Street, even a newly-married man would jump him.' He wanted to run along behind the pigeons, and he paused for some time before a dog who was wearing a coat, shaking his head in wonder. He wanted to touch everything he saw in the department stores, pick the roses in the gardens, and wash his face in the pond where ducks were swimming. When we went to a striptease show he began to laugh and asked me why they had bits of spangly material the size of lentils covering their nipples. He exclaimed at the shapes and colours of the spectacle, then seemed to forget that the women were naked because they were putting on a show, and asked if they were mad, and began comparing them to the animals we'd seen in the morning. We'd been to the zoo, and he'd watched the apes and monkeys and played games with them, knocked on the glass of the reptile house, swearing at the snakes, and stood for a long time by the falcons, telling them about his own falcon, who'd been poisoned to death. Then he turned to me and asked me why I wasn't smiling, and I replied that I was bored with the animals, and that going in and out of stores fingering the merchandise, or buying a Mickey Mouse telephone and a machine to make popcorn wasn't my idea of fun. I wanted to say that I would have preferred to buy jewellery for me, or a leather coat like the ones I'd seen in the windows, but I kept quiet. Deep down, I knew what was annoying me: I'd begun to notice how fat my legs were, how fat I was all over, and was sure that this was the reason why he didn't say passionate things to me and want me like he did in the desert. The fact that I wasn't enjoying myself showed on my face: round about us adults and children alike were urging one another to buy packets of seeds and so Maaz joined in and bought some himself and began trying to bite on them; I said nothing, but just sat there at the edge of the fountain, aware of a man and a boy laughing at him. When he realized that the seeds were for the pigeons, he laughed back at the two without a trace of embarrassment. I wouldn't agree to take a photograph of him standing next to a beefeater resplendent in his uniform. I found I had not an atom of patience left in me, and that night when we got back to our hotel, I sighed and said I was fed up with the crowds and the noise. I didn't know how much I missed the desert until I talked to David and my son that evening and their voices came to me serene and carefree down the telephone. I stood with my face to the window, seeing the car lights flashing by, and pictured the calm of the house in the desert. When the telephone rang there it seemed to ring slowly, the voice on the other end of the line was always calm, even Maaz's loud voice. I realized that I'd grown used to the routine of my life there, far from the hurly-burly of humanity and its inventions. Even finding a taxi here seemed to be a serious business, and I began to see why I was in a bad mood and felt ill at ease, and it went beyond missing the monotony of the desert. I watched the women here, hurrying along with their bags of shopping, bent over with the weight of them, leaning to one side as they waited at bus stops. I saw a toy bear propped up in a window opposite the hotel and thought of the mother who'd be scrubbing the clothes or doing the ironing, and my mind wandered, comparing myself with her, then comparing my life in the States with my life in the desert. I was a different woman, unrelated

to the one who bit her nails every time she remembered
something she'd forgotten to buy; I was a woman living in
luxury and I could ask the driver to go and fetch me as trivial
a thing as a box of matches, and Ringo to wash even my
hairbrush. Food stuffs were delivered, clothes from the dry-
cleaners, money from the bank. I no longer even had to sit
down and write cheques to the newsagent, or cheques to pay
for the electricity and the phone. I didn't drive my son to
school in the early morning, or wait in the afternoon with the
other mothers, our lips turning blue with cold. The sun shone
brightly all the time; even the cold weather in the desert was
like springtime.

Wanting to bring some joy to Maaz's heart, I said to him
that I preferred the desert to this place and to America. He
rotated his hand and pointed to his head, indicating his view
of my mental state, although he did say afterwards that he
missed the desert too.

I stretched out on the bed, happy to hear the chink of the
ice in the glass as Maaz poured Scotch over it. We'd come
back to our room because I'd succeeded in exciting his interest while we were out shopping. Before that he'd insisted on
giving a gold pen to a salesgirl who'd been nice to him and
laughed at his jokes, and I hadn't intervened until he'd put his
hand to his stomach and said that he was hungry, and began
asking if there was a good restaurant with rice on the menu
nearby, as if he was about to invite her to eat with us.

The first time we made love, I couldn't get into a rhythm
with him because I could hear voices in the corridor and I was
distracted by the noise of the lift. It didn't bother me, and I
stopped trying because I knew there was always a second
time. But suddenly I thought that perhaps there wasn't going
to be a second time and as he lay on top of me limp and
relaxed, I fidgeted and gripped the small of his back with
both hands. Then I moved, not caring that he was stiff and
unresponsive, and took his hand and put it on me and raised
myself up so that I was clinging to him and he couldn't

escape. Although I felt his body resisting me and refusing to submit to me, I kept moving, the sweat pouring off me. To my surprise Maaz jumped up off the bed before I had grown still, in a manner which made me forget my pleasure of a moment before. 'In the Name of God the Compassionate, the Merciful!' he cried out. I closed my eyes. 'Damn your race!' he shouted again. 'You're a devil! God preserve me!' I didn't take any notice. He always behaved in an exaggerated way after he'd made love to me. Sometimes he banged his head against the wall and sometimes he covered my body with kisses, beginning with my painted toe nails, and sighing that I'd always be in his heart, that he wished he could have my name tattooed on him. I wanted to sleep, and I wondered if he'd had a lot to drink that night. When I woke up at noon he was already dressed. I spoke to him and he answered curtly so I asked what was wrong, but he didn't reply. As I got out of bed, I deliberately showed my thighs as usual, and I didn't hitch up the straps of my nightdress which had slipped down over my shoulders. But he lowered his eyes and certain now that something was wrong I asked him what was the matter with him. He seemed to regret me not pressing him and after a bit he asked why it was that God created foreign women out of the same clay as men, or at any rate not out of the same clay as normal women. I didn't understand what he was getting at – much of what he said I didn't comment on. Then I washed my hair and sat drying it with the hair dryer, at which he said he was off to have a haircut at the hotel barber's.

When he didn't come back after an hour I felt uneasy. I went out and bought several nightdresses and some novels. For the first time I felt confident and pleased with myself as I chose what I wanted and paid for it, and even as I walked along the street. After some time I returned to the hotel, but I didn't find him there. I wanted to teach him a lesson. I marched off into the city as if I was on a military exercise, and didn't stop until I came to a bridge. I was experiencing a

sensation which was new to me: for the first time I was alone,
and there was no place for me in the whole world if I didn't
go back to the hotel now. Deliberately I thought about
David, and realized that he meant nothing to me, for he
didn't act as a safety net and he definitely wasn't a friend.
When I'd had an awful tearing pain in my guts one day, he'd
carried on sleeping, oblivious to my cries of pain. It hadn't
surprised me: he dealt with his illnesses alone. And my
children? My children were my children, wherever I was and
wherever they were. Nobody could take that away, but all
the same I felt lonely. I thought of Maaz and felt less lonely;
perhaps there was a place in the world for me after all. He
must have lost his way, and I started back to the hotel once
more. When he didn't open the door, I told myself that he
must have come in really drunk. I went back down to the
desk to ask for a key and was handed it along with a
telephone message: 'Jimmy says hello.' When I opened the
door he wasn't in the room and, perplexed, I tried to think
where he might have gone. I couldn't believe that he would be
alone because he wasn't confident of his English without me
– the only person, it appeared, who could understand him. I
went out to look for him in the hotel restaurant and café, in
the sauna and the swimming-pool, and then returned to our
room. My eye fell on the message again: 'Jimmy says hello.'
An hour passed. I was sure he must be lost. I turned on the
television and flicked it from one channel to another in case
there was any news of him. Then I phoned the desk to ask if
they'd heard or seen anything of him. I occupied myself
picking his clothes up off the floor, then it was as if I tried to
clutch on to him and ease the pull I felt towards him by
gripping the clothes in my hands. The shirt was silk, likewise
the socks, yet he'd dropped them on the floor just as he used
to his white robe. When he was buying them it hadn't
occurred to him to convert the price to desert currency. Every
time I hesitated over something, he would buy it, although I
knew he wasn't as wealthy as all that. Since I'd first visited

Fatima I'd been amazed at their generosity and their lack of
greed for material things. Before that, I'd imagined that his
presents to my family were because of me. I remembered one
day when Ringo had pains in his stomach and Maaz heard
David and me deliberating whether we'd be the ones who'd
have to pay the doctor's fee: he'd put his hand in the pocket
of his robe and given Ringo all the money he had on him,
laughing and saying, 'I hope they find a snake inside you.'
Then there were the fountain pens he handed out here, even
to the waiter in the restaurant, and the tips he insisted on
paying, even to the shop assistant in the jeweller's. Maaz
went about catching people's attention with his laughing face
and the atmosphere of easy familiarity which he transmitted
to everyone we met. People weren't attracted to him because
of his tips or his presents, but for his simplicity and charm. I'd
begun to feel important when I was with him, and to have a
sense of security which wasn't only the result of the affection
which he lavished on me. I found myself learning from him,
and grew accustomed to never hurrying to keep an appointment. If the train had gone, there was sure to be another. If it
meant the end of the trip, there was no need to get in a state.
It didn't matter, there was plenty to do here; we could even
be quite happy strolling around the station. I put his clothes
on the chair, and the Mickey Mouse telephone which he'd
bought for his family back in its wrapping, and smiled. I
began to think of him in a different way, almost jealous of his
quick perceptions and secure tradition, his grasp of what was
happening round about him as if it was already there in his
memory and he just had to dredge it up. I clasped his clothes
to me again, to feel close to him. When another hour went by,
I felt a heat encircle my head. I opened the door and stood
looking up and down the long empty corridor for a few
moments, then went back in. I contacted the casualty depart-
ments of the local hospitals and when the woman at the desk
stopped answering, I called the police, who asked me to wait
a few hours and call back. I leaned back on the sofa, my fears

for him growing with every sound I heard, although I couldn't hear much beyond my own breathing. I wondered whom I should contact, and dismissed the idea of getting in touch with his embassy. The fear of our relationship being discovered was as great as my fears for him. I went over to his suitcase and took out his passport and turned over the pages. They were all blank, except for the one with the stamps of his country and the country where we were now. Then I opened my handbag and made sure that my passport and the airline tickets with our names on them were still there. I wondered if he'd told anybody that I was going away with him, and I'd just decided to ask to be put through to David, when I heard a movement at the door and the sound of Maaz's voice and someone else's. He must have been lost. But when I opened the door I knew that the woman standing there with him hadn't been showing him the way, and that he hadn't been lost at all. I stood there calmly, despite the sensation of heat enveloping my head once more. But what he said made the volcano inside me erupt. He'd forgotten her name and he pointed to her: 'This is a nice woman who likes Arabs. Susan, honestly, I've been away and come back again like a homing pigeon.' The woman was standing in the face of the volcano moments before it spewed out its lava, and she only increased the ferocity of its explosion as she spoke, bending over towards him. The smell of Scotch filled the place. I screamed at them, pushed them out of the room as if they were two pieces of dough, and slammed the door violently. What had finally made me snap was the woman's tone of voice, which made her sound as if she were talking affectionately to a little boy. He was like a bird whose mother had fed him from her beak constantly, and then when the time had come for him to spread his wings he'd learnt from a stranger and flown off with her. Besides feeling angry, I was depressed as I seemed to see the nice things I'd been thinking before he arrived torn to shreds by millions of hostile fangs; I was frightened that the tenderness and concern which he'd bestowed on me alone were figments of my imagination, and when I heard shuffling and laughter, as if the two on the other side of the door were joined by fate, I flung the door open, pulled Maaz in by his arm and pushed the shouting woman away.

In spite of other doors opening, voices being raised in protest, and the intervention of the man from the desk trying to be civilized, the woman continued to bang on the door and call out threats and demand to be paid. I turned to Maaz, who was lying on the bed fully clothed, and told him to give her some money. As usual his hand went down to his trouser pocket, then to his other pocket, then to his jacket and he gave me everything he had on him. I took some of it and bent down and pushed it under the door. I didn't wait to hear her taking the money and going away, but turned to Maaz, thinking how beautiful the woman was, and wondering about the coat she was wearing. My curiosity grew to the point where I had to ask him why he'd brought her back with him, why I was no longer Suzie, and Sand-and-Sky; but Maaz just laughed, and his laughter caught at my throat. I'd lost my stronghold. In my frenzy I found myself shaking him, and that night I didn't sleep beside him; I sat up on the couch and he only called me once. I prepared myself to hear him calling a second time and to find out why he'd brought the woman and why I was no longer Sand-and-Sky. Before I'd made up my mind to ask him myself, he said to me as if he wasn't saying anything in particular, 'Suzanne, that woman was nice. And she liked Arabs. Honestly, I don't understand why you insulted her like that.' Then, in all seriousness, 'God forgive you.' I realized that he had no idea why I was angry and jealous. He must have thought I was Fatima who didn't feel either emotion, and I heard myself saying scornfully, 'She liked money.' 'Poor thing,' he answered, 'Perhaps she wasn't married and didn't have any family.' Then he asked me confidently, and as if I were a friend, 'Did you think she was pretty, Suzanne? ' I pretended not to be interested, although I knew he hadn't meant to provoke an outburst from me. I'd calmed myself with the thought that in a couple of days we'd be going back to the desert, and what had happened today would fade into memory. I tried to control my irritation and changed the subject. I asked him how he'd known his way around the streets. A mixture of interest and pleasure appeared on his face. He got up and, using his hands and his eyes, he told me how, as he'd left the room, he'd been making himself remember everything he saw: the flowers growing in a pot, the mirror, the room numbers, so that he'd remember where our room was. Then he asked the name and address of the hotel from the man at the desk. When the man gave him a card with everything he'd asked written down on it he knew that his English must have been comprehensible, and his self-confidence returned. But as soon as he'd stepped outside the hotel into the narrow street, he began to feel scared of the main street which ran parallel to it. It was as if he were seeing the crowds, the cars and the lights for the first time. He kept reaching into his pockets for his piece of paper and his money. He felt that he was in a strange, odd country, where the cigarettes with cats on the packets were called Craven A. In the desert the names on the packets corresponded to the pictures: the ones in the packet with a camel on it were called Camel, and the ones in a packet with a gipsy dancer, Gitanes. He didn't know why he felt a sudden sadness. It seemed that he didn't know how to walk along pavements, or how to look at people, or how to decide when to stop walking. He tried to give himself encouragement, reminding himself that he'd always wanted to travel and see the world – the countries which produced everything that came to the desert. He wanted to go back, but he knew in his heart of hearts that he did really know how to go about things (here he mentioned that he'd learnt from me the right way to stroll around the streets). He went along until he came to a news stand where he saw some Arabic magazines and newspapers. When the man at the stand counted out the money and handed him the change Maaz, full of pride, said 'Thank you' in English, and began to walk with a more confident step. Enthusiastically, he went into a restaurant, and as he wasn't hungry he ordered a Scotch. He paid for it and when he heard the 'thank you' coming back at him he relaxed. He went on his way again and didn't stop until he saw the word 'Bar'. Inside, it looked like he'd known for a long time that it would, low lights, high stools, just like on the videos. He was pleased at his discovery and smiled to himself. On his right a woman sat drinking. When he turned in her direction she smiled welcomingly at him. He felt as if he was flying through the air with joy. He couldn't understand what she was saying, but she understood him and asked where he came from, and what he was doing here. When he told her, she asked him if he was a sheikh, and he felt like nodding his head. Then his eyes fell on the bottles in their dozens behind the man pouring the Scotch. Laughing and talking to himself, he said out loud, 'I could take them and smash them like I have to at home.' The Scotch had affected his head. He couldn't help thinking that what he did in the desert was ridiculous, and he seized the magazine he'd bought and went through it, pretending to censor parts of it. The woman didn't understand, and a picture of himself sitting at his table at work went round in his mind: he saw himself swooping down on the magazines, turning the pages and enjoying looking at the women's bodies, with the thick black pen motionless in his fingers; then he would go to the bathroom and play with himself, and return to the woman who was blonde, dark, thin, a foreign star, an Arab star, depending on which magazine she was in. When he visited friends of his who worked in embassies they used to show him the small black and white photographs on visa appli- cation forms, which also triggered off their desire, so much so that they went to the lengths of stealing the photographs of all the pretty women and copying them and enlarging them and swapping them with one another; eventually the authori- ties had introduced a regulation to the effect that a form would be refused if the accompanying photograph showed any part of the woman below her neck or if a seductive expression could be detected in her eyes.

Then, recalling the high point of his adventure, he clapped his hands and turned to face me to be sure of having my full attention: 'Listen, Suzanne, if it hadn't been that woman, when I was in the underground city, I would have – O God, it was all twisting passages as if you were inside an ear – I would have been lost and starving, I could have died down there and nobody would have known. How would I have got up again?' 'An underground city? Like an ear?' I repeated, losing patience.

'Yes. The woman took me in a tram, and she began walking from one underground tunnel to another. It was like being in the land of the jinn. She'd go up a level and down a level, with me clinging to her hand and clutching my heart, terrified that she'd leave me . . .'

When I heard him snoring, I jumped up, but instead of shaking him by the shoulders I switched on the light and went to fetch a glass of water. I sat on the edge of the bed and called his name. When he opened his eyes, he said, 'God bless you. What's wrong?'

I handed him the glass of water, acting cool and calm, and said that I'd decided to accept his offer of marriage. To my surprise he didn't answer, but closed his eyes again and said, 'God willing.' For a moment it was as if I'd gone back to being the Suzanne who sat in front of the television in the suburbs in Texas with my hair tied back and nothing in my life but sentimental soap operas. Miserably, I wondered how he had dared to bring home a woman, and why I was no longer Suzie and Suzanne and Sand-and-Sky. I went to wake him again, and shook him, not realizing how violent I was being until my arms and shoulders began to hurt. I was full of anger because I'd agreed to marry him and he'd refused me. As usual when I wanted the truth from him, I made him swear by his children before he said anything. He sat up in bed, and to my surprise he announced that he'd been afraid of me the previous day and felt disgusted by me. My thoughts strayed back and I couldn't think of any reason. Was it because I'd bought another piece of jewellery, or told him that I preferred life in the desert to life here? 'Why? Why?' I asked him, irritable in my curiosity to find out what sin I'd committed. He answered that I'd done things for my own pleasure like a man. When again I sifted through what had happened the day before and still couldn't guess what he meant, I shook my head questioningly, and he said calmly and gravely, 'God created you to bear children, and to give pleasure to a man, and that's all.' I didn't understand. Perhaps I hadn't understood his English? Naturally I'd had children, and naturally a man enjoyed me just as I enjoyed him. Wide awake by this time, Maaz repeated seriously, 'God created woman to make children, like a factory. That's the exact word, Suzanne. She's a factory, she produces enjoyment for the man, not for herself.' I laughed, and replied quickly, 'If God doesn't want her to enjoy it, then how and why do I enjoy it?' He looked confused and, not finding a ready answer to my question, he shouted, 'Yesterday you were like a she-devil.' Then he mumbled, 'I swear, in God's name, I was disgusted by you, and by your whole race. You seemed like a man to me, when you were crying out. I said, Maaz, this woman's a hermaphrodite. She's both a man and a woman.' Then he added, 'You enjoy it because you're a hermaphrodite.' Although I felt embarrassed when I remembered my unstoppable wave of desire of the day before, I began to laugh. I thought of the grave way he had spoken, the pain he'd expressed, and I laughed. No doubt my laughter confirmed to him that I was indeed a devil, for he began looking at me with distaste. 'And what about Fatima,' I asked, tears of laughter running down my cheeks, 'is she a devil too?' 'Foreign women must be made out of different clay from ordinary women,' he replied. I didn't find it strange about Fatima, and her lack of pleasure and desire; when I was in America, I'd stopped having sex with David or doing it by myself, and I was no longer conscious of my body and sexual enjoyment, except occasionally when I was asleep and I dreamt that I had it with the local policeman, or my children's teacher, or the edge of the table or the bath water, and I'd thought at the time that it was my body fulfilling one of its functions in spite of me.

I moved closer to him and, in an attempt to reawaken his desire, asked him if he'd brought the woman back here to sleep with her. 'Poor woman. You insulted her,' was his only reply. 'I thought that I'd introduce her to you because she was nice.' I tried again, playfully: 'Does this mean no more Suzanne? Ever, ever?'

When he went on staring at the ceiling, I was sure that he'd made up his mind not to give in to me, even though he wanted to, but suddenly he shouted, 'Now I understand why you've never got pregnant by me . . .'

Serious now, and eager to understand his way of reasoning, I exclaimed, 'For God's sake, why?'

Before I'd finished, he interrupted, 'I know you're not a man, but you're not a woman either otherwise I would have made you pregnant.'

Laughing again, I told him that after Jimmy was born I'd had an operation to seal off my tubes. At this he brought his palms sharply together, then rubbed his eyes and said, 'God forbid! You heathen.' Then with spiteful glee: 'I see, God's punished you, so now you're a hermaphrodite.'

My thoughts strayed to the occasion he'd first seen me naked, and how he'd said something which I hadn't understood then, but now I did. I found it strange that he'd been amazed at the sight of my pubic hair, and felt sure at the time that it was because he'd never seen a completely naked woman before me.

I would have liked to reply to him, but I heard his breathing growing louder, and turned over to try and sleep myself. I concluded that I'd been protected all this time by his *naïveté* and ignorance, and wondered why I wasn't annoyed by what he'd said, or hadn't taken him more seriously. I vaguely tried to think what my reaction would be if David thought about me in the same way, and automatically clenched my fist. But I looked at Maaz and smiled, captivated by his sincerity and spontaneity, which put me on a level with Marilyn Monroe. I felt safe at his side and vowed to myself that I would always sleep beside him like this, with his money, his gold watch and his possessions on the floor the other side of him.

Only as I packed my bags, delighted with the clothes I'd bought for my daughters and the gold jewellery Maaz had bought for me, and delighted to be going home, did I think how much this trip had changed Maaz, and our relationship. But I didn't doubt that he would keep coming to see me, until we were back at the desert airport and I saw how he behaved with the friends who'd come to meet him, and how they looked at me, and then how he went off with them, without even bothering to find out if David was waiting for me outside.

I continued to sit there, resting my cheek on my hand, while Maaz and Ringo pored over the dozens of brochures about Sri Lanka, talking in English and Arabic and using their hands. Ringo was encouraging Maaz to go to Sri Lanka as if it were the only place in the world worth visiting, and when he felt that his description might not be conveying a true picture he would purse his lips into a whistle of admiration. I couldn't stand it any longer. I didn't want to shout at Maaz, so I attacked Ringo instead and asked him why he didn't go back to his own country if he liked it so much and thought it was the most beautiful country in the world. Ringo didn't understand the reason for my outburst and said hesitantly, pushing a lock of hair off his face, 'I'm happy here.' Mockingly, Maaz took his hand and pointed to the gold bracelet with his name on it and the gold ring, then stood up to pull the chain with a gold heart on the end of it from around Ringo's neck, and said, 'How could he get all this gold in Sri

Lanka? He'd only be given tin there!'

5

Sita's bottle stayed where it was, and I was still in my house
in the desert. I no longer saw Maaz. From time to time it was
again as if I were the only woman who existed, almost a rare
specimen. I wasn't under a misapprehension about this, and
it wasn't difficult to find men. The men in their white robes
searched for women among the freezers and foodstuffs in the
supermarkets. They tailed foreigners and car passengers who
weren't wearing veils. As they walked along the street they
stole glances at the gates of houses just in case a woman going
in behind the high walls gave them a smile: telephone and
electricity workers and private gardeners were the worst
offenders. The first time I was hesitant; I pushed my trolley
around the supermarket, and concentrated on reading what
was written on the packets and tins, not looking at the man
who was looking at me and going through a charade of
coughing and spitting to attract my attention, nor at another
who tried to test whether I was really there to shop by
moving his lips and moistening them with his tongue. I
pushed the trolley along at speed, paid the man at the cash
desk and rushed to the car. But on the second occasion, in the
bookshop this time, I found myself making an approach to a
man who I'd heard talking in English, whose American
accent and good looks gave me encouragement. For some
reason I said to him, 'Since you speak English, perhaps we
could talk together and you could help me understand the
nature of the males in your country.' I began to tell him about

Maaz and how he'd left me, although I knew that these things weren't relevant while I was with this man. He looked at me in astonishment, obviously thinking that I was crazy, and didn't reply, but went on turning the pages of a magazine, then looked around for the foreigner he'd been talking to before. I told him that I wasn't mad and seriously wanted to understand the personality of the Arab male. The man looked to one side then the other, before feeling in his pocket and taking out a card which he left on top of a magazine at the edge of the table. Then he vanished. I snatched up the card, covering it with my hand, and stuffed it into my bag with a sigh of relief. I dialled his number day and night until one day he answered and said that he'd been at his engineering project in the heart of the desert. I had to meet him: his voice gave me a strange feeling of warmth. The boredom I'd felt since returning from my trip abroad evaporated, and I rested my hand on my heart, afraid that he'd try to avoid meeting me. A long time passed before he did arrange to meet me. He asked me to come and visit him at his project, and agreed a time with me and described the car which would be waiting to take me at the entrance to the store.

The other man was the one who had come from the department of health because of a dog which used to come to my neighbour's doorstep at dawn every day with a cat or a large rat in its mouth. The man didn't even want to look at the dog which we'd shut up in my neighbour's garden. Instead his gaze shifted between me and my neighbour, and he told me later that he knew from the way I'd spoken to him on the phone that it was him I was interested in, not the dog.

I didn't think about Maaz again until a tall man knocked on the door of my house one morning. Ringo opened it, smiling, thinking that he'd come to see him. The man ignored Ringo's smile and as I stood behind the kitchen door listening, I heard him asking if this was Mr David's house. Then he asked about me. I hesitated before coming forward. 'I can't say anything until I've consulted my lawyer,' I told him. The man looked startled; he said quickly that he was a friend of Maaz's and had come with a request from him. Maaz had begun to pester me in various ways, hanging around my friends, phoning me and then putting the receiver down or hanging on without speaking; once he'd come to drink Scotch at our place, accompanied by an Indonesian nurse. Why had this man mentioned my husband's name, and how could he permit himself to come in and sit down on the couch and help himself to a cigarette? I thought the time must have finally arrived when they were going to make me leave the desert. Who was behind this tall Arab? Maaz? The engineer I'd met in the bookshop? Someone from the telephone exchange? The owner of the bookshop? The owner of the drugstore? The man lit his cigarette and said that Maaz had told him where my house was and sent me his best wishes. He was lying, but I regained my composure and said nothing. I stood listening and wondering whether I should contact David, chase him away, phone Maaz, or believe what he said. Then I heard him coolly stating that he preferred them between the ages of sixteen and twenty and that he was ready to pay from three hundred to five hundred dollars provided that the meeting took place in my house. He fell silent while he extinguished his cigarette and I stood before him in amazement. 'They must be going to force me to leave,' I thought, 'and they need evidence against me.'

I told him I didn't understand what he was talking about. He laughed and struck his hand against his thigh, and I noticed the clean whiteness of his robe, the gold watch, the expensive ring. With another affected laugh, he said, 'You understand quite well. When will you be in touch?' He stood up, put his hand in his pocket, and took out a card. I hesitated and then fear made me take it. Under his name I read the title of his official post. This time his laughter was genuine and, adjusting his headcloth, he said, 'Government officials are men too . . . and you know the situation here.' 'They've spoken against me,' I thought, confusedly. The neighbours, Maaz, the engineer whom I no longer saw, the owner of the bookshop, the pharmacist. The man went calmly over to the door. He turned to me and reached out his hand to shake mine. 'Don't forget. I'll be waiting.' Although he spoke in a low voice, his tone was commanding. I held out my hand and he immobilized it between his and said, 'Maaz's very lucky.' Then he thanked me for the coffee and my kind hospitality. I almost leapt back into the sitting-room. I didn't see the coffee cups but pictured myself packing my bags and cast my eyes around me, taking in everything at a single glance. Mad with anger, I stamped my foot, vowing that I would never leave this place. My thoughts were in a turmoil and I no longer knew how I should act. I called Ringo and told him what had happened, pacing around the table and not paying attention to him telling me in a soothing voice that he was sure the man had genuinely come in search of a woman. I knew there was nothing for it but to enlist Maaz's help, but he hadn't been to the house since I'd refused to let him in late one night.

When I couldn't find him at his office I made my way to his house. Fatima opened the door and seemed astonished to see me. She looked at the telephone as if she couldn't believe that I'd really phoned her minutes before and here I was now in front of her. Although I begged her not to go away because I could only stay a few minutes, she rushed off into the kitchen. I sat there smelling the same old smell, which I'd never liked. How the house had changed since they'd known me! Everything my eyes fell on was pleasingly familiar: the horn fish, the picture of Mecca worked in white metal, the shaggy mustard-coloured moquette rugs, the artificial flowers which we'd bought together.

Fatima appeared with a big bowl of fruit and a broad smile. She pointed to her stomach and said, 'I'm having a baby.' I smiled back at her, as if it didn't concern me, which it didn't. All I wanted now was to seek help from Maaz so that I could stay in this country. When I asked Fatima where he was she shrugged her shoulders. 'Son of a bitch,' I said in English. 'Thank you, Madame Suzanne,' replied Fatima, smiling delightedly at her English. She pointed at the dish of fruit, then at me, wanting to know why I wasn't having anything. When I started towards the door, she stood in my way seizing me by the hand and dragging me towards the fruit. She held out the bowl to me then took a banana and apple from it herself and pushed them into my hand.

I went back to the car. I must be imagining things. This wasn't the way to drive me away from here. Maaz must come and visit us again like before. He was a lifeline: his regular visits to us had given me a sense of security and I was beginning to miss it on occasions, like today for example. Or the man may have been genuinely after a woman and known Maaz. He must surely have heard about my daughters' visit from the States: perhaps he'd followed us and conducted his own investigations, or perhaps he knew about me from friends of Ringo's. Ringo's desert admirers were on the increase and he accepted every invitation, claiming that in this way he stood the chance of meeting one suitable person and then he would break off his numerous relationships and settle down. It wasn't that easy: the desert was full of people like him; European firms had begun to favour appointing gays to desert posts for both practical and financial reasons. They spared them the expenditure on large houses, family travel, children's schooling, and problems with wives who had too much time on their hands. There was no desperate longing for a woman, no sexual frustration leading to lack of concentration at work and an inability to tolerate the desert, and requests for transfers back home or continual holidays.

It could have been the engineer whom I hadn't wanted to meet again after I'd visited his scheme in the desert. Although he phoned frequently and circled the house in his car, he was the one man I couldn't even bear to remember. The journey had been long, two hours' drive into the heart of the desert with nothing to see except black crows against the changing hues of the great expanses of sand. The Filipino driver had met me at the door of the store as I'd agreed with the engineer, and all the time he looked at me in the driving mirror which he'd trained on me for the purpose. He played one tape after another until we reached an outpost of human existence dotted about with tools and machinery and workers with their heads and faces swathed in cloth as an armour against the stinging sand.

It wasn't easy to recognize the engineer when he was dressed in trousers and a shirt. To my surprise he began to take me on a tour of the place, explaining to me seriously how the machines worked and what the men were doing. The sun grew hotter by the moment as we walked to the furthest point of the scheme and he took me into a trench, talking and explaining non-stop, redoubling his efforts when he saw that the men were watching us. I asked him where he'd got his American accent from, to shift things on to a more personal level. 'New York State University,' he replied, walking a few steps ahead of me. I despaired and caught up with him and we arrived back at his office, a concrete room smelling of cigarettes and wet cement. He sat down at the table and asked me about my Arab friend, but before I opened my mouth he stood up and opened the door for me saying, 'The air-conditioner isn't working in the office,' and took me back into the sun. Disappointed, I felt that I'd been wrong to come, and was angry at myself and sick with exhaustion and the heat. He went up to one of the workers and the man handed him a bundle of photographs. He began giving me one after the other, pictures of steel foundations and trench-digging equipment. I told him irritably that I was thirsty. His features didn't change. Retaining his solemn expression he led me over to the car and opened the door for me. As soon as I got in I wished I was still in the sun. It was boiling inside the car. I swallowed down a scream. My thighs were almost on fire from the plastic of the seat. I wiped sweat off myself with my hand, thinking that I was no longer of an age to be able to handle these tiresome escapades. He stopped the car in front of a small building and I followed him out; I'd begun to understand his behaviour: he was afraid and on edge. The coolness spreading through my body in the little cafeteria, which was fragrant with the smell of curry and rice, made me forget the outside. He spoke constantly to the workers who were seated at tables round about us, then he showed me the photographs again and stood up. I was scared of the burning car and wished I could stay in the restaurant or go back home straightaway. So I said that I had to be getting back. He nodded, as if this request of mine had made him feel easier. He said that he wanted to go in the car to fetch some papers and although I didn't understand my connection with these papers, I nodded and followed him out again. Without waiting for the air-conditioner to take effect, I opened the car window and stuck my head out. We only went a short distance. When he got out, I stayed in the car, but he signalled to me to get out too. I did so hesitantly, telling myself that I'd soon be free of him. There was a secretary typing there. He introduced me to him, then led me into another room. The moment he'd closed the door he took hold of me and we stood there right by the door. He felt my breasts, then opened his flies at speed, as if he was receiving orders from somewhere. He brought me close to him, and I was forced to cling to the wall to keep my balance. Then he turned away, closing his flies and straightening his shirt. He picked up an envelope off the table and began talking to me again about engineering terms. There were signs of annoyance and impatience on his face now. He was hurrying me and didn't wait even while I reached for my bag. Still talking in technical jargon that only another engineer would have understood, he went out ahead of me. Then he gave me the envelope which he'd been holding. 'Say that this is for the firm,' he instructed me, and I was left completely at a loss.

It was inconceivable that any of these men would have

reported me, I told myself confidently. I stood up and, on Ringo's advice, I called the man who'd come to the house the next day but he wasn't there. After I'd tried for several days in a row, I was told that he'd gone away. When I'd had numerous conversations and the voice at the other end had started to get flirtatious, although I wasn't sure whether it was the man himself or another man in his office, I felt reassured. My fear evaporated altogether when I saw him by chance in the street with a veiled woman, and he hid his face in fright.

6

I returned home one day and Ringo rushed to meet me saying that Maaz had called dozens of times. Instead of going to the phone I went to the fridge to look for something to drink, Ringo started to tell me that Maaz had been shouting in a way that wasn't like him, and he'd scarcely finished speaking when the telephone rang. I rushed to pick up the receiver not expecting it to be Maaz again so soon. His voice came weakly and thinly down the line. He asked me to visit him; he was ill, he said. He must have thought I'd refuse because I was angry with him since the day he'd come to ask about Sri Lanka and gone off there without me. He went on urging me to come and I made the excuse that there wasn't a driver around. 'What about Ringo?' he asked. Then I heard him cursing in a loud voice: 'God damn the yellow bastard. He can bring you.' It usually made me laugh when he cursed Ringo, but not this time. 'Tomorrow,' I replied. 'I'm tired.' And I put the receiver down. I'd scarcely flung my head back on the couch when the phone rang again. It was Maaz and he was pleading with me. I got up in spite of myself. I thought I knew exactly why he was so insistent, and it was as if just for a moment I missed our times together. I asked him why he didn't come here; I was tired. Lunch with the owner of the drugstore and his family had been a heavy meal and the drink had flowed in abundance, but he persisted to a degree that was uncharacteristic of him.

When Fatima opened the door to me, I knew that something was wrong in spite of the broad smile and her kisses on my cheek. 'Maaz's ill,' she said, clasping her hands together then pointing to her head and inclining it to one side. I followed her, still beset by feelings of tiredness. The smell of incense seemed extra powerful that day. We passed through the sitting-room and I couldn't help noticing the new things: there was a picture on the wall looking like a television screen, depicting slowly changing images. I remembered the present which he'd been promising me since he returned from Sri Lanka. Maaz was in bed in the room which I'd thought would one day become part of my daily life. There was nothing in it but the bed against the wall, a pile of mattresses against the facing wall and a chest. Smoke from the incense rose into the air.

Maaz was thin, his face was pale, there were mauve circles under his eyes, and his hair was on end. Inclining his head to one side, he accosted me with words that I couldn't understand. He talked about electricity, lights flashing on and off in his face, a dirty house. Then he spread out his hands in front of me, and made them shake. I was struck by how bad his English was and wondered how I'd understood him before. I must have helped him to express himself and here he was now unable to do it, even with the help of Arabic words and sign language.

I found myself turning to address Fatima who stood there looking at him and talking about him as if he were a stranger, not her husband. 'He doesn't eat. Doesn't drink coffee, tea.

The poor thing has a few crumbs at each meal, and a drop of water to get them down.'

He seemed like another person to me, unrelated to the Maaz I'd watched in a storm of emotion as he talked to Ringo about the trip to Sri Lanka, while I sat making plans to marry him; the man whom I'd thought of following to the airport, indifferent to the shame, and then even accompanying against his will, when I'd heard that he was travelling without me. Now he was asking me for help, just as he had done when the washing machine didn't spin the clothes and when the oven didn't work, only to have me discover that they hadn't pushed the right button or the electricity was cut off that day. 'Has Maaz seen the doctor?' I asked Fatima, whose stomach had swollen visibly. She held up two fingers: 'Twice,' she replied. Then she disappeared and I asked Maaz, 'What do you feel, and where does it hurt?' He didn't bother to answer but sat up in bed and moved his head about restlessly. When I repeated the question, he answered, 'Ask Ringo. God damn the yellow bastards. Gog and Magog. They don't fear God. They're devils. God preserve me!' At this point Fatima came back in. All the time she'd been away I'd heard her scolding her youngest child, the boy, in the kitchen. He must have been eating from the dishes she'd got ready for me and wanted to place before me untouched: dishes of pistachio nuts and fruit. I tried to find out what the doctor had said to Maaz, but he was talking again about the light which went off and on, about his face, his head and especially his spine, about the dirty house where there was a big rat, and about the funny-tasting Scotch. Then he stretched out his trembling hands so that I could see the veins protruding on them, put them up to his eyes and began crying like a child. I couldn't bear to see him crying, and it was made worse by his two daughters crying in the hall and Fatima trying to calm the little boy and to finish what she'd started to say: 'I swear to God, I said to him don't go abroad on your own. Take the Qur'an and put it under your pillow. He

didn't listen to me . . . God forgive him.' I noticed that the
small veins in his temples were standing out and I rose to my
feet, saying to Fatima, 'He must have a doctor.' Together,
Fatima and I helped him up. I noticed a large gold ring on his
finger, set with a wine-red stone. To my amazement Maaz
couldn't stand. He leant on my shoulder for a moment, then
sank back on to the bed. I asked the name of his doctor and
turned to Fatima, saying that I'd contact him. Maaz held out
both hands in protest, then bowed his head and kicked out at
me with his feet. I couldn't understand why he was objecting
and said to him reassuringly that the doctor would have to
come if I spoke to him. But Maaz stopped shouting and said
some words which sounded like gibberish to me. Fatima
explained, 'He wants the doctor from your husband's firm.
An American doctor.' Only then did I realize why he'd asked
me to help. I spoke to David, then the doctor, then Ringo,
who promised to bring the doctor here. I sat drinking coffee,
feeling proud of myself. Nothing was hard for me in this
country; it was as if I owned it. To date I'd sold five kitchens;
telephone cables led up to our house in three different spots,
over other houses and across the desert, because storms had
brought them down. The road leading to our house had been
surfaced with asphalt where before there had been sand. I got
what I wanted either by making telephone calls or by con-
fronting people in person, or through friends. Maaz wiped
away his tears with the sleeve of his robe. I noticed his
luxurious leather sandals and the suitcase on top of the chest,
looking out of place in this room. The doctor came and
opened up Maaz's eyes and peered at the whites. The first
thing he asked him was if he was taking any medicaments. I
asked Fatima and she hurried away and came back with a
little bottle. She gave it to me and stayed outside the room
while I went in to give it to the doctor. The bottle contained
tranquillizers and the doctor asked Maaz what dose he was
on. Fatima replied from outside, 'Four or five.' She may have
heard me gasping, for she went on, 'It was him

who said he wanted more, so that he'd get better quicker.' When I translated for the doctor he laughed and said tht he'd had a patient who'd refused an injection in his thigh, saying that the pain and the swelling were in his eye, not his thigh. I left when the doctor said he wanted to examine him, and when Fatima and I went back in later, she remarked, 'Thank God he's repented. No more trips abroad.'

The doctor said he hadn't found anything wrong with Maaz, except that his nerves were upset; he was to stop taking the tranquillizers and meanwhile the doctor would have some tests carried out on the specimens of blood and urine which he'd taken. Maaz wanted me to stay and I could only leave by slipping out of the room when his attention wandered.

At dawn the next day the telephone rang again and it was Maaz asking me to fetch the doctor. I told him to wait for the results of the tests and he began to shout at me. He came to me in the afternoon because I hadn't been to see him, accompanied by one of his neighbours. As I went through the motions of contacting the doctor, I could see Ringo urging Maaz to sit down and the neighbour devouring me with his eyes. Then I heard him telling Maaz that he ought to register with the nearby clinic: everybody returning from the Far East had to be examined, and their wives as well. Maaz held out a hand to silence him: 'What do you know about it? I've got this burning light in my eyes.' He went on talking, saying things which I couldn't understand. I couldn't bear his shouting, the movements he made, the sound of his voice: was he crying, laughing or ranting unintelligibly? I found myself phoning Suha. Agitatedly I asked her to come round, not giving her any scope to invent excuses. When she asked me what was going on, I screamed at her, 'Please. I can't explain. Please just come.' I went into the kitchen and asked Ringo to go and sit with the visitors, and I could hear a renewed burst of shouting from Maaz and the same old cry: 'Yellow bastards. Gog and Magog.'

I stayed in the kitchen until I heard the door bell. I'd refused to go in with Scotch for Maaz or for his friend although both Maaz and Ringo were calling out to me, and Ringo had begun to repeat to Maaz that since he'd stopped visiting us the Scotch supplies had been cut off. He was lying: Scotch, gold chains, Persian rugs were all in greater abundance than ever.

I didn't understand why Suha was annoyed when she saw Maaz and his friend, even though I explained to her that he was ill. She wouldn't agree to sit with them and let him tell her what was wrong. She came into the kitchen looking at her watch and saying that she had to contact her husband so that he could send Said for her. But when we heard Maaz calling, we stopped and listened; his calling turned into shouting and I saw Suha laugh. I laughed too and we collapsed together in helpless floods of laughter. His tone was more one of laughter and weeping mixed than of protest. Was he acting? 'The light shining in my eyes, aah . . . I put up my hands to my eyes. They pulled them away. The light was like a fire and it shot down my spine, burning me. I cried out, and I heard them laughing. I said, "Forgive me, Lord. Cast the devil out of me as you cast him out of Paradise." And her black mole. If the whore's uncle had got rid of the mole, none of this would ever have happened.' I was waiting for just a sign from Suha and then I thought we'd both begin to laugh again, but this time she ignored me and rose quickly and went into the sitting-room. I heard her asking boldly, 'Who was she, Maaz? Who was this woman?' Maaz tried to stand up to greet her but he sank back down again. 'Madame Suha. There's a light shining in my eyes. A burning light. It never goes away, even for a second. Aaah. The rat was as big as a chicken. It strutted around and stared me straight in the eyes. I should have guessed from the story of the black mole and escaped with my manhood. But I bought her a diamond like the one in the picture; she talked a lot, pointing to the diamonds and then to her mole. Every time I met her she talked about diamonds and the mole, and she cried, and I didn't understand. Bit by bit the group she was with made me understand that she wasn't married yet because of the big mole on her cheek. They said that the family who'd come to betroth her to their son had seen the mole and changed their minds. It was near her eyes and so the tears would flow over it when she cried; they took this as an omen and said that if she married, her husband might die. Her uncle bored into the mole with the thorn and blood came in its place, then a scab which healed up and fell off, leaving the mole where it had always been. And they told me that she wanted to cover it up with a diamond stud so that she could get married. I said I'd marry her and I wasn't afraid of the mole. On the contrary, I told them, where I came from it was considered a sign of beauty.'

It was many days before Maaz began to show signs of recovering. I didn't go back to see him, being content to ask after him on the phone from time to time, until one day Fatima invited me and Suha to lunch: she'd slaughtered a sheep to celebrate Maaz's return to health. Suha agreed to come and arrived with her son, carrying a box of chocolates. I couldn't stop myself asking her in a challenging manner how she'd found the time to have lunch with Maaz and Fatima when she'd completely given up visiting her friends because she was getting ready to leave the country. She laughed and said, 'I was bored with everybody. But hearing Maaz tell the story of his illness is quite amusing.' We went with Said who came into the building with us at Maaz's request. He took him off into another room, and Suha looked at me and smiled. For the first time Fatima took off her face veil, after Suha had told her that one of her daughters was like Maaz. Fatima looked young, with an innocent expression in her eyes and a beautiful smile, yellow teeth notwithstanding. Her thick black hair hung loose but was sticky with all the oil she put on it. She wore a gold chain around her neck with King George gold sovereigns hanging from it.

I noticed Suha's eyes roving over the house. She picked up

a red plastic mug, then put it back on the plastic table, which was the colour of a pomegranate. 'The same colour,' she commented. Then she asked Fatima about the bunches of grapes made of interlocking metal rings, which were hanging on the partition. Fatima smiled and brought some bunches of plastic grapes and insisted that Suha should take them. I thought she liked them even though she refused them. But when Umar grabbed them and ran off with them, I heard her telling him in English to put the horrible things down. He didn't stop pestering Suha until she let him ride the huge stuffed camel which had hair like a hedgehog's spikes and eyes that were two green pearls, and a brown tongue and brown lips. Umar fell off repeatedly, so Fatima brought the two boys a damp wooden stool from the bathroom. They climbed up on it and hurled themselves on the bunches of grapes on the partition, fighting to pull them down; Fatima hung them up somewhere else, and seemed delighted at the uproar, even though Suha and I were scolding our sons vigorously.

When Maaz came into the room where we were after the meal, it was as if he banished the spectre of drowsy boredom which had begun to steal in on the three of us and especially Suha, who at once asked him where Said was. 'He's on an errand. He'll be back in half an hour,' answered Maaz. Then he said, 'Come and see what I brought from Sri Lanka.' At his bidding, Fatima bent down and pulled out a wooden box from under the bed and opened it. It was lined with red velvety material, and contained prayer beads and rings set with semi-precious stones – mauve, dark blue, pink – and with pink and red coral. I picked out a ring which appeared to have more gold in it than the others. 'This is beautiful,' I remarked, hoping fervently that he'd say to me as usual, 'Please have it,' and he did, quite happily: 'Please have it, Suzie.' He took out a necklace and put it in my hand, then proffered the case to Suha who'd remained standing. 'Please, Madame Suha. You're my sister, I swear to God.' Suha refused, as I thought she would. Although Maaz pleaded and insisted that she should take anything she wanted, she wouldn't and eventually she asked Fatima for a glass of water and followed her into the kitchen.

My eyes became riveted to the box again and I said playfully, 'So you went away without me?' 'It was a mistake, I swear, Suzanne,' he replied, laughing. 'See how it's drained my strength and health and left me with hallucinations. After the land of God and Magog, God's decreed a new life for me.'

I wanted to bring him back to the main issue: I reached for a ring set with a pearl and a red stone and slipped it on my finger. 'Fatima's lucky,' I sighed. 'Fatima doesn't like Sri Lankan work,' he answered, 'nor Italian. She says the gold's poor quality. I promised her a chain from Bahrain.' I pretended that the ring wouldn't come off my finger and he said, getting to his feet, 'Leave it there, Suzanne.' Suha came back in, asking when we were going to leave. I smiled at her. I'd put everything that Maaz had given me in my handbag, afraid of what she would think. She turned to Maaz challengingly. 'You didn't finish the story,' she said. 'What happened to the woman with the mole?' I didn't feel like hearing the story again. I was pleased with the jewellery and I wanted to take it home and look at it properly. I stood up: 'We must go.' But Maaz gestured to me to sit down again and turned to Suha, appearing happy at her interest in him. I'd sensed for a while that he was anxious to talk to her. 'In the hotel they told me to make the trip home and be with my family when I died. They looked for my papers and then contacted the embassy. A man came to show me how to get to the airport and he stayed with me right up till I boarded the plane, God bless him. I told him everything that had happened to me, and he said, 'You're very lucky.' And it's true, I am. If I'd died in Sri Lanka I would have died unclean, without the prayer or the creed.'

I had no idea what he was talking about, but Suha asked him, 'What caused it? You haven't told us what caused it.'

Maaz paid no attention to Fatima who came in carrying a stainless steel coffee pot, and answered, 'The woman with the mole cried and said nobody would marry her, and she wanted to hide the mole with a diamond. I told her that I'd help her escape from them and take her to my country and marry her. The following day I went to the casino. She didn't turn up. Some of her group were there, and they took me away and tortured me with fire and with lights that hurt my eyes and made me confused. Maybe they put sleeping pills and pills to make me crazy in the drinks they gave me. I didn't know why they were doing it, and every time I asked about her they tortured me some more. When I understood what was wrong, I told them that I was married already, and I'd said the things I'd said for a joke.'

I smiled at Fatima, and so did Suha. Fatima returned our smiles, raised her hand as if she was throwing something over her shoulder, and repeated, 'God guide you, Maaz.' Without sitting down, she began pouring coffee into the cups. She stood up nearly all the time we were eating. Whenever Suha invited her to sit with us, she poised for a few moments, pretended to eat something, then stood up again, listening out for Maaz to call to her. She sat down again to fill my plate and Suha's with rice and meat which she broke up with her fingers, although we tried to stop her. When Suha stood up, I did the same, and with difficulty we prised Umar and James off the camel. We shook hands with Maaz, then with Fatima; she held out a bottle of cologne and shook a few drops from it over our hands and on the ground. Meanwhile Maaz went to fetch an aerosol; 'Haven't you sprayed any incense over them?' he asked, spraying it at Suha's face, while I moved out of reach. A smell of incense spilled into the room, sickly sweet like sugar, mixing instantly with the smell of the cologne. Fatima said in embarrassment, 'Really, I only like to burn sticks of incense. They cheat us by selling us these aerosols instead of proper incense, and you can't see smoke coming from it or anything.'

In the car Suha told me that Fatima didn't believe that Maaz and I were having an affair, then she began to laugh. She wouldn't tell me the reason until she'd made me promise that I wouldn't be angry whatever she said; but she couldn't stop laughing. Fast losing my patience I said that if she didn't tell me I really would be angry. So she told me and I didn't understand why she'd laughed such a lot: Fatima had said that the blue of my eyes was like glass, my skin was the colour of a red fish, and my bottom was like a sheep's buttocks.

Eventually she told me the rest of the conversation: Fatima didn't believe what the neighbours said about my relationship with Maaz because I was married and had children; I taught him English in exchange for Arabic lessons as I and my husband wanted to start a business; Maaz took us to visit villages so that we could get to know the country, and he'd become a real friend to us. Then Suha laughed again, and told me at last after more hesitation all of what Fatima had said, that she presumed I left my pubic hair unshaven like a forest, and since this was unclean, and Maaz was a good Muslim, he wouldn't have risked invalidating his prayers. I found myself sharing Suha's laughter, and I recounted what Maaz had discovered when we went away together, and how he'd moved away from me as if I were a leper.

7

I knocked on Maaz's door again – it wasn't passion, or the memory, or boredom – but his door remained silent. I saw an eye looking through its newly installed spy-hole and began to bang with the flat of my hand, as I thought of the return to the States coming closer all the time. I paused, then started up again when I heard his daughter's voice, and then his son crying. I couldn't make myself move away from the door: it was as if I had to see it opening now or it would turn into an aircraft door. At the thought of this I kicked it. There was a rattling noise from inside but the door remained closed.

I leaned my head against my hand which still rested on the door, and wondered who I could turn to for help. Maaz was the only one lodged in my mind and I returned to him instinctively as the sole person I felt I had any power over. It was as if I was still contining to exact payment from him for his relationship with me which had shown him another life beyond it and allowed him to escape out into the world. I'd contacted all the men I knew; they were the ones with young frustrated bodies always wanting me. Through them I found out that Maaz's frenzied infatuation and jealousy were both quite normal: most of them, especially those who'd never been abroad, pursued me day and night. More than Maaz, they made the fantasy of *A Thousand and One Nights* come true for me. They held parties for my benefit and had caviare and salmon flown in. They procured the latest videos straight from the studios, and I probably used to find out what happened to Sue Ellen before the television companies. When I'd begun to get in touch with them one by one about my problem, and asked them if they could think of a solution, I felt that I was becoming more aware of their delicate situation for the first time. The man who replied seriously to my requests was not the same man whom I'd seen dancing, drinking glass after glass to forget some woman or other. All of them avoided the issue of my wanting to stay here and tried to talk about something else. The company David worked for had been declared bankrupt, closed its offices, and named the day on which its employees were to leave the country, but I was desperately anxious to prolong our stay so that perhaps David would find another job and we wouldn't lose our residence permits for ever. As I knocked on the door these ideas were on the tip of my tongue and I only needed to come face to face with Maaz to put them into words.

Suddenly I heard his voice. 'What's wrong with you, Suzanne? We were asleep.'

Quickly I replied, 'Open the door. You must.'

He was silent, then he said, 'I'm not well. Perhaps we can talk on the phone . . .'

Without letting him finish his sentence, I replied like a stubborn child, 'You must open the door. Just for a minute.'

When he didn't, I thought about what was going on, and could hardly believe how crazy relationships were which came about as a result of a desperate need. In the past he'd knelt humbly at my feet. Now he wouldn't open the door to me. I let my mind wander, remembering the time I'd gone away with David to another part of the country to spend the day with his boss. When we opened the door on our return we were met by a horrible smell. Ringo wasn't at home and there were glasses all over the place, empty Scotch bottles, vomit, cushions strewn about. I realized that Maaz hadn't left the house since saying goodbye to us that morning; he'd turned up with a bottle of Scotch, asking if we minded him drinking a glass there because Fatima would tell the neighbours if he drunk it at their house. I found him lying on the floor with the curtains drawn. I took hold of his face and shook him awake. Then I went into the kitchen to get him a glass of water. When he'd drunk it, David left me with him and went pointedly upstairs. Maaz wept and said that he'd missed me and hadn't wanted to leave my house; he'd lain on my bed and smelt my clothes and kissed them, even kissed my shoes. I helped him to his feet, afraid of the burden of his attachment to me. And David who'd made me run away with him so that we could be married and who'd cried to see my suffering at the birth of our first child stopped taking me in his arms. As I remembered, my sadness changed to anger. I swallowed it back with my spittle as I drew breath, then drummed on the door in a subdued manner and said, 'David hasn't got a job any more. We have to leave and I want to stay here.' His reply came back fast: 'Never mind. You go, and I'll come and visit you in the States soon I hope.' 'No. I'm not going,' I shouted. 'You have to fix my passport and David's, or mine anyway.' 'I can't. I'm not well, Suzanne. You go back home with your husband. He's a good man: at least he didn't kill either of us.'

With all my strength I pounded on the door. 'You've got to let me in,' I cried, my feet planted resolutely on the ground like an animal about to be led to the slaughter.

When the only response was a movement behind the door, which remained firmly closed, I felt as if a power secret as the wind had stripped me of everything which I'd put my trust in as I moved about the rooms of my house deep in the desert. I was like a deposed beauty queen: the jury had turned on me and replaced me with a new queen, dragging off the crown, robe and shoes, wiping away the make-up and taking the sceptre from my hand, tearing the smile off my lips and even the memory of the past happiness out of my heart. I felt like a fortune-teller who'd seen her own future in her crystal ball and then made it go wrong. Nobody would ever understand that I was scared of going back because the roar of cities destroyed people and I was scared of being destroyed. Going back to America was going back to being a speck among the millions, while here I felt aware of my importance every minute of the day; if I just said good morning in Arabic everybody praised me. What does a woman in her forties do in a country swarming with others like her when she's been used to being the one and only? Who'd look at a fat woman in her forties with a lisp which made her hard to understand? Who'd call her on the phone except someone who'd dialled a wrong number? In my mind was an image of my telephone ringing all the time irrespective of the hour, transmitting their crazy longing to me. I was an oasis, green and sparkling in this great drought. I'd become like Barbara, jangling with gold bracelets and confidence and security, even spiritual and material security for years still to come. I could picture exactly what was going to become of me: in the car on the way to the airport I would revert to being a woman with rather a round face, hair hanging on a podgy neck, two fat arms, slack breasts and a stomach protruding over two short fat legs.

In a final desperate attempt I knocked so ferociously that my gold bracelets hurt me. I touched them one by one and although this comforted me the thought of Barbara pained me. Was I going to go home with only these bracelets and a few pieces of jewellery? What had happened to my dreams of doing business and growing rich, my dreams of the man with whom I was going to spend the rest of my life? This time I shouted, 'Fatima! Fatima!' I heard a commotion, followed by another burst of noise, then the key was turned in the lock and the door opened. I didn't recognize the person standing there for a moment, although he bore a resemblance to Maaz. I gasped. It was Maaz, his legs weak and emaciated, his face yellow, with white sores on the lips. When he came to offer his hand to me, I saw red sores on the fingers. Behind him was Fatima looking thin, with a beautiful smile on her face. I noticed that her stomach had disappeared. I was still in a state of shock at the sight of Maaz but I asked her straight out, as if everything was normal, 'Was it a boy or a girl?' She answered me hesitantly, looking at Maaz, 'A boy. But he's not very well.' I found myself wondering if I ought to take the gold chain, with 'Allah' in ornamental calligraphy hanging from it, from around my neck and give it to the new baby like the women did here. 'Where is he?' I asked. Maaz tried to mumble something but it was Fatima who led me into the bedroom. 'Poor thing. He's not well,' she said. The baby was lying in the middle of the bed with some white powder on his face. When I went closer I saw white sores on his hands and face, even on his eyes. I said nothing. I put my hand up to the chain around my neck then let it drop, feeling sick. I tried not to, but I couldn't help looking back at his eyes, where the syphilis showed so clearly. I noticed that the baby was wearing the clothes which I'd ordered for Fatima from the States, and then I don't know why, but when I saw the brightly-coloured cover which Maaz's mother must have woven in her tent, the thought came to me that it was I and the oven which cleaned itself and the aeroplanes which had caused the syphilis in Maaz and his newborn child. Why hadn't Fatima been treated? Why hadn't the doctor given her an abortion, knowing that her baby would be born with syphilis? Then my thoughts trailed away: Maaz must have hidden it from her, ashamed to tell. I considered asking what his name was and a lot of other things, but I just smiled as if I hadn't seen anything or thought anything. A vision of the doorway of the private clinic, jammed with people newly returned from the Far East, flashed into my mind. Only then did I know for sure that Maaz couldn't help me.

I went back to the car, trying to chase away my thoughts, the pangs of conscience, the self-reproach, but they moved back in again little by little, chasing after one another, weaving the syphilis into the story of Maaz's trip to Sri Lanka: this was the first time I'd encountered the disease in real life and not just at second hand in books and pictures. I thought how lucky I was that I hadn't caught it, and moreover I wasn't living with him as I'd so often pictured I would be. This realization made me more cheerful. As I rode through the streets, protected from the burning sun outside, Maaz's house began to seem a continent away. I sensed the slow regular pulse of life, which was apparent even from the men and goats resting in the shade, and found that I loved this reality. I forgot the baby bit by bit and vowed not to leave here whatever happened. This resolve made ideas come tumbling into my head, including fantastic ones. I could say I'd converted to Islam and ask to stay on as a children's nanny, or sign my divorce papers and go through a formal marriage with Ringo, whose residence permit didn't expire for a least a month. I found myself counting on my fingers: I had five days left.

Nur

1

Everything was tranquil, the water in the swimming-pool, the gazelles' house. If Saleh's robe and his white headcloth hadn't been lying on the floor, I wouldn't have believed that I'd really been wearing them. I was lucky to be safely back in bed, although I could still see myself panting along the street. I hadn't taken account of the moon and it had been full, shining down on me and lighting the way so that Suha's house looked as if it was lit up.

Standing before the outside door of the house, I had noticed that my uncharacteristic feelings of agitation were growing, and that the excuse I'd thought of using to her and her husband had suddenly evaporated. But when I looked back along the street I couldn't imagine going home, and I felt a renewed burst of courage at the thought of Suha being inside these walls. The wooden garden door opened easily. I pushed her son's toys out of the way and stood up on the table to open the small window of the bathroom. I'd meant to sneak quickly through it like her son did, but Saleh's clothes held me up and I had to lower myself in gradually until my foot touched the edge of the bath. When the whole of me was inside the bathroom I stood listening: the house was still and the air-conditioners roared noisily. I confronted myself in the mirror in men's clothes and tiptoed out of the bathroom past the canary's cage, which was covered up for the night, wondering whether to scream for help and wake up everyone in the house; I could say one of the servants had tried to come into my room, or a driver had abducted me, so that I'd had to fling open the car door, roll out on to the ground and rush to their house; or should I say my heart was pounding, my breathing constricted, and I needed their Lebanese doctor friend to examine me?

I dismissed all these ideas as I pictured how Suha would

look at me, and slipped quietly out of the door leaving it open behind me. I went back along the empty street, cursing her at first then feeling annoyed with myself for not waking the driver up to bring me; he must have noticed my relationship with Suha, and with the Italian woman who'd come to the desert at my mother's request to design a garden of artificial trees and flowers. I quickened my pace along a street that I'd never been in before on foot even in the daytime, and pulled the headcloth tight around my face, ready to talk in a deep rough voice if I met anyone. With every hurried step I took my dislike of Suha grew. What if I was discovered now? I'd be in disgrace and people would think I was meeting a man.

For the first time I was glad to see the wall of my house in the distance, to take refuge in my room, but as soon as I'd forgotten about the fear which had taken hold of me out in the street, Suha started to dominate my thoughts again. Plenty of people had occupied that place before her, men and women, but only for a short time, and before I got to know them well. Suha was the exception: I'd been crazy about her all the time, perhaps because she'd lost interest in me moments after we met in the swimming-pool. Her thoughts were always somewhere else, and when they weren't, she complained and grew irritable. Even when she began to come round to my house it was because I insisted and phoned her continually and persistently. Only once did I feel that she envied me, and that wasn't for my clothes or jewellery but just for the swimming-pool, when she said that she wished it was in her garden, then took it back and said she'd prefer the merest drop of water away from the desert to this swimming-pool of mine.

At first I thought she was putting on her indifferent attitude, because I'd never met anyone who wasn't attracted by my personality and my way of life, or just my hair, or my house and all the entertaining things in it. She even began to criticize the number of servants that I had and the noise of the video and the general anarchy; she said the gazelles had no life in their eyes, no beauty, none of the magic that gazelles were famous for. Looking at my clothes one day she asked where I was going, and laughed scathingly at me when I said, 'I'm staying at home.' I only realized the full extent of her pride when she refused a present I'd tried to give her, even when I sent it back to her with the driver. When I spoke for too long on the telephone in her presence she left and at that I decided to have no more to do with her, reminding myself of all the people who were only too anxious for my company; but I discovered that I preferred to spend my whole time desperately trying to reach her and dominate her. Being turned down by her had a magic similar to the feeling I had when I was chasing my cat to pick her up and cuddle her: when I finally succeeded in catching hold of her I was always overwhelmed by a desire to give her a lesson she wouldn't forget.

I wished Suha would come to me at that moment, or to be honest, I longed for any human being who would hold me until the first ray of sunlight stretched down through the darkness, but the silence deepened.

I dialled her number and let it ring and didn't put the receiver down even when I heard her husband repeating, 'Hallo. Hallo.' I wanted to hear a human voice; dawn was still a long way off, I was scared of being alone, and the voice repeating, 'Hallo. Hallo,' restored life to me in spite of its dry tone. I got out of bed and took a tablet from a packet in the drawer among my lipsticks and eye make-up. I noticed it was grubby and began looking for a clean one but they were all the same. Without giving it time to work I swung back the mirror near my bed and pulled out a white phone; the existence of this phone was known only to me and a telephone engineer who'd demanded a large sum of money to install it secretly. I dialled a number and heard the voice that I remembered so clearly. He sounded drowsy this time but as soon as he heard my voice, he answered excitedly, 'It can't be . . .' I hadn't contacted him for days because the line had been out of order and I hadn't dared risk using either of the other two. His excitement was obvious, because subconsciously he'd promised himself that he was going to get something out of this call. Every time I spoke to him I wanted more, and as I'd expected I heard the heat in his voice down the receiver and I began to talk to him. I'd learnt his habits, which video films he liked best, and from my knowledge of the details of his life I'd built up a picture of him in my imagination.

'Where have you been all this time? I've melted down my fingertips trying to hit on the right number for you. You must give me your number for emergencies.'

'I was away,' I answered, and thought to myself that the poor man really had no idea who I was. All he knew was that I liked Warda al-Jazairiyya because he'd heard her singing in the background when I was talking to him; since I didn't like being alone I used to beg him not to say goodnight to me even after an hour, but just to carry on talking, even though my eyes were closing and he'd stopped answering. As usual our conversation got on to passion and love and I began to pretend that his voice was penetrating my senses and spoke more caressingly, letting him hear my moans of pleasure. I didn't stop until I heard his voice shaking, as if it was being squeezed out of him. At this point I wished him good night and returned the phone to its place like someone under a spell. Even though I enjoyed myself and wanted this relationship, I never failed to be amazed when I thought about where my voice was going to, and how his voice held my interest and left me waiting for the next day.

My daughter came into my room in the afternoon, dropped her books and black abaya on the floor, and rushed over to me. I was still stretched out in bed where I'd been since the night before. She burst into tears: 'The teacher was cross with me. . .' 'Never mind,' I answered. She seemed to notice my indifferent tone because she began to shake me and carried on speaking while I nodded my head pretending to show interest, until in the end I shouted irritably at her, 'I heard you! I heard you!'

Ghada ran out. I thought of going after her but stayed where I was. I thought about sending for someone to bring me a drink but then found myself phoning Suha. When she answered and I whispered 'Suha?' she slammed the phone down on me. Then I phoned Suzanne, her American friend, and asked her if she had any water melons or cakes. When she finally understood what I was saying, she made her excuses. The general hubbub throughout the house rose above the sound of the video, which mingled with the strains of Filipino music. The servants had just woken from their afternoon siesta, and I didn't take my hand off the bell until my coffee arrived. Drinking it, I thought 'What can I do for the rest of today and tonight?' I went over to Ghada whose staring eyes and audible breathing seemed to make her one with Michael Jackson's hissing dead. She was addicted to the 'Thriller' video and had watched it at least ten times, each time more avidly than the last. She reminded me of myself when I was little and used to sit alone with my Somali nanny watching Arabic and foreign films one after the other. In those days there was no video, just a screen on the wall and a projector. It was operated for us by a tailor whom my mother had had brought over from the Philippines too. These films must have aroused something in the tailor and the nanny because when I got up and wandered about the house one night, unable to sleep, I saw them on the kitchen floor. I remembered that I stood and watched them without feeling embarrassment or any other emotion. I was used to seeing kissing and men and women together on the films and in our house. A day rarely went by when I didn't hear whispering, and see two bodies clinging together in the darkness, or in daylight, behind the door, in corners of our large house: the servants with one another; my brothers with the servant girls and my girl cousins: a man and a friend of my mother's whom I could recognize from her red shoes poking out from under her abaya, as her face was veiled too. I used to be able to work out who was pregnant in our house because I'd seen if so often and knew the symptoms by heart. A woman who was pregnant would sleep most of the time, and rush to the bathroom and throw up, claiming to have a stomach upset. Then she would boil up cumin and other plants from Sudan and India, herbs and spices which had a wonderful smell, and drink these concoctions constantly. The ceiling fans would be switched off and she would cover herself with rugs and sheepskins to make herself sweat and stay in her room for two days. At this point she seemed to become more weary and sick and she would take aspirins and other medicaments. After a few days I would hear a shrieking louder than I'd ever heard on the films and would race to see the new baby. But the door was always closed. Only when Mother Kaukab came out did I go in to the room, and I would see the servant girl writhing on the bed, and no baby.

Mother Kaukab was a relation of my mother or my father, I don't know which. I became aware of her visiting us on special occasions, when a servant girl was pregnant or someone was ill, or at weddings: she was there when the bride-to-be was decorated with henna, trilling for joy at the ceremony when the girl's body hair was all removed, shouting at her to silence her if she gasped and cried out in pain, telling her, 'You have to be strong to be beautiful.' And she was there for the preparation of the special food which was buried in the sand and for the slaughter of the lambs. Even my mother used to call her Mother Kaukab, and she was the only one who dared to go into my mother's room. Then when I got my own house at the age of thirteen, Mother Kaukab moved in with me. My mother and father had promised me a house of my own when I was seventeen, but I couldn't wait and they were tired of my insistent demands. Whenever my father hugged me he would say, 'I'm building you a really special house,' and I would glow with pride and ask him, 'Like my brother Jalal's house and my brother Hamid's?'

'Of course,' he would answer. 'I don't have daughters and sons. All my children are as good as each other.' There was a vast amount of land around our house and on it my father had built a house for the male servants, a house for his mother, one for each of my brothers, and one for my sister who was married and lived in another part of the country, for her to stay in when she visited us.

Then he would add, 'You know the big date palm? Right next to it.' I don't know why, I would have liked to tell him that it was too close to their house, and that if only it were further away I could be properly alone. My mother would say, 'I'll furnish the house for you, Nur, with everything in it, just as it should be.' She was always spoiling me and her affection was at its most lavish when she was making me try on the clothes which she bought me locally or on her trips abroad; whenever she noticed the length of my hair, which reached right down to my thighs, she whispered in my ear, pointing to her stomach, 'Look what came out of there. The most beautiful girl in the world.' My mother was one of the first women to go abroad and discover life beyond the desert, and she would return bringing back with her everything which these other countries produced. I got used to her not being at home, or rather to not seeing her there, for if she wasn't abroad or visiting one of her friends, she would be asleep or talking on the telephone. From when I was small, I'd been aware of her criticizing my father for staying out late with his friends, and sometimes talking about him in a depressed sort of way and crying in front of Mother Kaukab. But when I saw them together I knew she would smile and be loving and call him 'my soul' and 'my darling'.

I remember that the glimmer of joy I felt at having a house of my own disappeared rapidly after a few days or weeks. I wearied of the red hearts which matched the bedcover, and the pillow that was shaped like a single big red heart; even the chairs were patterned with red hearts, not to mention the curtains. My father had sent for a European designer to do these red hearts everywhere. My pleasure at having her there outlasted any pleasure the hearts gave me, and I believed that she was going to live with me for ever. I remembered once when she'd been with my brother into the desert, she came back to the house as if she'd gone crazy. Distraught, she began packing her bags, crying all the time. Mother Kaukab guessed what had happened and I heard her saying to my brother, who wasn't even thirteen at the time, 'You had an old woman? But you're a young man strong as a brass pestle, God bless you!' and he answered, and he was laughing too, 'She was the one who wanted to go and see the desert at night.'

When I heard them I rushed to her, pleading with her as she picked up the receiver and asked for my parents' number. Only when she saw my tears did she give in and put it down. I wasn't thinking of the hearts on the wall which she hadn't finished yet, but of the fun I had just from her being in the house. I no longer found the Somali woman or Kaukab amusing company, and I'd stopped listening to their stories. Recently I'd begun to keep up with life outside the desert, in Cairo or Paris, and through my travels with my family or the presents my mother brought back from her own travels I learnt about the latest clothes and films and singers and songs, and the men and women who were famous in international circles. Not satisfied with just knowing about them I began to look for ways of bringing them to where I was. We would wait for occasions like family weddings and then nag the grown-ups to hire famous performers from Cairo. When they agreed to come we all rushed to arrange parties for them and give them presents. We followed them around all the time hoping for a word or a touch or a kiss, and then we discovered that the aura surrounding them grew gradually less powerful and finally disappeared altogether as they began to chase after us, or at any rate the presents we gave them. I remember the actress who borrowed some diamond ear-rings and didn't give them back. When Mother Kaukab asked her for them she pretended to look for them in fear and trembling and offered Mother Kaukab all her own jewels. But those little details didn't stand in the way of us inviting famous people we hadn't met before. Even writers and poets aroused our curiosity and I remember one writer who always hailed us with the same phrase: 'How are you? I've missed you,' and he promised all of us girls that he would write stories about us. I'd never read any of his celebrated novels although I'd seen films of them. I wasn't much good at reading. I went to school but I didn't seem capable of attending regularly. I and my Somali nanny both slept heavily perhaps because we stayed up until the early hours of the morning. The alarm clock didn't waken us and even if I managed to get up at the right time I was slow choosing what to wear and what to eat and looking for my books. It was as if I thought time ought to be subject to my will. On some occasions when I was ready in time I couldn't find the driver, and when the nanny called him he came after a while, barefooted, hurrying, rubbing the sleep from his eyes, and drove the car at breakneck speed. Then one of my mother's friends arranged for a Lebanese teacher at the school to help me after school hours so that I could catch up with my class. I was delighted with her and began to have great fun with her, because sometimes instead of teaching me she was happy to come for a bicycle ride with me – on our land of course – and she started plaiting my hair for me like in the magazines. She only stopped coming when she'd tried without success to see my mother for months on end, and on several occasions she had to wait for ages before the outside doors were opened for her.

I was pleased. In the end she'd started interfering in my affairs and giving me lectures about the shortcomings of my upbringing, and she'd let me know the meaning of the word 'frivolous'. She began to criticize the anarchy of our household and shake her head regretfully at everything, even the kitchen equipment – which she admired and said was like what you'd find in a luxury hotel: she told us we were spoiling it and ended up trying to explain to the cook and the other servants how to use it properly. She advised me to go back and live with my family and told me I didn't need a personal driver or a cook or Mother Kaukab, but my mother and father and brothers and sisters. When we didn't pay her on time she wouldn't leave the house until she had the money, saying it was a matter of principle not money. She used to make me wait with her until Mother Kaukab woke up, or until the driver had gone to my father's office to pick up some money. Once she even insisted on contacting my mother, although I'd often told her that my mother didn't like being woken from her afternoon nap. The teacher's exasperation grew when she found that my mother had unplugged the telephone and locked the door on the inside, and angrily she expostulated that my mother wouldn't know if something dreadful happened to me or my brothers and sisters. It didn't seem to occur to the teacher that we could have knocked on the door, although none of us had ever dared to do it, and she began calling my mother selfish and ignorant.

In response to my request I was sent by my father to a private girls' college in Cairo like a lot of other girls from the desert. There I discovered that the freedom which I'd thought I would gain by moving out by myself into the desert was nothing compared to my freedom in Cairo. Just walking down the street on my own two feet was freedom, so walking without an abaya was out of this world. Freedom no longer consisted of dialling a telephone number and giggling and whispering love down the line, or making the driver follow the other cars, or eyeing the shopkeepers; even kissing and sometimes other things in cars – which seldom happened anyway – weren't freedom compared to Cairo with her wide-open arms reaching out beyond the horizon.

2

I began to think about marriage after I came back from Cairo, even though I'd always said before that I wouldn't think of it until I was in my twenties. Mother Kaukab had married when she was twelve, and my own mother when she was fourteen. I wanted to have a husband and a wedding and then I would become my own mistress. Not that I wasn't that already, but I was still having to ask permission to go abroad. Then my mother would forget that she had promised to take me with her and leave when I was fast asleep in my house, or take me with a group of her friends and I would tire of being abroad for such a long time because our trip would be taken up with eating in restaurants, buying clothes and giggling. I wanted to get to know lots of the sort of people who went to parties at night, although I didn't dare to go to them without my mother and father. When I was there I became all eyes and ears and stared at the men, wondering who would suit me. When I saw Samer I knew that I had to marry him. He was three years older than me. I was seventeen. He'd heard about the motorcycle which I'd ordered and which I used to ride between my house and my parents' and my brothers'. These houses and their gardens were all surrounded by high walls over which only the tops of palm trees were visible. Samer came with my brother to see the motorbike when I decided to sell it. I was wearing a leather jacket and trousers and dark glasses. I knew by the way he rode bikes and by his wristwatch and the type of bracelet it had that he would suit me. I took it as given that he would like me, because I was beautiful: the blackness and great length of my hair and the permanent pallor of my complexion were oriental, and my clothes and everything around me were western. I found myself looking at him in a way that embarrassed him and I wanted to ask him to marry me, but I made myself wait and spoke to him and pursued him on the telephone until we'd decided to get married. He was a male Nur. He loved the latest fashions and everything conjured up by modern civilization: the newest models of cars, skiing equipment, a stainless steel model of Ali Ibn Abi Talib's sword made in Japan, an Aubusson chair, a type of honey found high in the mountains of Tibet, a handbag made of ostrich skin. He was inventive in his dress even when he was wearing a plain white robe, but he also wore blue, grey, and pistachio green, and when we travelled abroad he wore the most beautiful suits and the weirdest ties. There was always a lot going on in our house as we had friends round every night. We knew nurses, nannies, even married women, from various countries, and we danced and sang and ate and watched films until dawn and slept till the afternoon. We didn't begin our night's entertainment before eleven in the evening, then we swam or went out into the desert, and he would ride the motorcycle and try and jump obstacles on it, little natural hillocks or ones that his friend Waleed constructed for him. I was so used to Waleed being around that we seemed incomplete without him. The fame of these nights of ours spread until everybody who felt they shared our way of thinking and could entertain us or enjoy themselves with us found a friend who was coming and came along too. We soon found that the desert was crowded with people wanting to entertain and be entertained. There was a man who liked imitating famous actors, another with a guitar who pretended to be Elvis Presley, a third who acted out a pantomime of a woman giving birth, behaving conquettishly if it was a boy, and telling the other women what an awful time she'd had and how she'd passed out with the pain if it was a girl. When we were tired of these mimes, friends would bring along people they knew with mild deformities, like the man who stammered, or the simple-minded one who was funny when he was provoked. Someone brought a monkey who liked drink and we stood around it pouring whisky down its throat and watching it caper and scream in its cage.

I didn't know that Samer liked his own sex as well until in the course of one of our trips abroad he chose to stay in the hotel rather than come sightseeing with me, and when I met him for lunch Waleed wasn't with him and I sensed the tension in him. I asked him if someone from home had been in touch with him; even abroad we sought the company of show business people and night club society and we were always scared that word of our wild nights would get back to the desert. He didn't answer. I asked him where Waleed was and saw his jawbone moving as he clenched his teeth. When Waleed appeared and sat down apologizing, my husband gave him a look which was meant to be between the two of them, but I understood what it meant, as I understood the inquiries, the riddles, the jealousy which followed. He tried to hide his feelings but his face and his nerves gave him away, and gradually I realized how artificial his desire was when he slept with me as it was always connected with his fantasies and most times it subsided half-way through.

Waleed was quite attractive. I sometimes wished he would press himself against me when we were dancing together. As well as being handsome he was nice, quick-witted, with a never-ending flow of stories and information and jokes about his home country, Morocco. When I found out what was going on between him and Samer, I laughed as I thought of all the women who'd flirted with him or made approaches to him directly, or through me; I wondered if he was like my husband and liked both sexes, and planned to find out.

I wouldn't have thought of divorce if Samer hadn't sent someone to inform me that he'd already divorced me. He was on a naval training course in Belgium and Waleed was with him. Apart from the driver who gave me the certificate of divorce, nobody knew about it, and I was able to take advantage of others' ignorance by behaving for a time as if I was a married woman and my own mistress.

I was still thinking about who would come asking to marry

me, when I met Saleh's sister at a wedding. The moment I saw
her I reproached myself for letting my thoughts stray so far
from Saleh. Apart from the fact that there was an aura of
magic surrounding him because of his lifestyle and his constant travel abroad for his work, he was good-looking and an
important person in society. I'd begun to realize that I
wouldn't meet anyone else like him. Civilized young men no
longer wanted to marry young, nor on the other hand did
they abstain. They travelled abroad and went out with girls
who were very beautiful and very young, often little more
than minors, while the ones who preferred their own sex
married and had children for the sake of society, like Samer. I
found myself talking to Saleh's sister most of the time. The
happiness on her face was plain to see because I was paying
her so much attention. Like the other girls she was curious to
get to know me face to face because my flaunting of conven-
tions was much talked about. I wore a green and red abaya,
and sometimes covered my face with a heavy black veil and
stuck a diamond pin at nose level. When the wedding was
over I stopped off at my parents' house, went straight into my
mother's room and told her that if I didn't marry Saleh I
would never marry at all. I knew how much they wanted me
to marry because they couldn't bear my impetuous behaviour
any longer, my artful adaptations of abayas, the night-time
gatherings I held, which were attended, it was rumoured, by
my brothers' friends. My mother asked me if his mother or
sister had broached the subject with me. I didn't answer. I
began phoning his sister at every opportunity just as I had
done with other girls whose brothers I wanted to get to
know, in case the brother happened to answer. Saleh never
answered and I discovered that he had a place of his own
separate from his family so, claiming to be his sister, I called
him at work in the Ministry. When I told him my name, he
gave me his private number so that I was able to talk to him
every day. Eventually we agreed to meet at the home of his
married sister; she'd been at the wedding and had looked on

discouragingly as I talked to her younger sister.

I knew that Saleh wanted to marry me. As he said to me one day, I was the bride he'd been searching for: beautiful and educated at the same time. I knew there was more that he didn't tell me: I was the daughter of a man whose millions grew every time he drew breath. Although there were many like my father, my breeding and ancestry were better established than those of many girls. As I sat opposite him his white robe and headcloth and the rosary between his fingers seemed to give off a cool breeze of freedom, not at all like the stale draught from the air-conditioners, and as it brushed my face I felt invigorated and no longer thought beyond the four walls that contained us. I felt as I watched the brown fingers that life flowed through them and that I ought to cling on to them. They were like the fingers of a giant who held the land about him in thrall. I even felt the power bursting from his car keys when he jingled them in his fingers, as if they were capable of knocking down whole walls and opening buildings up to the outside world. At the same time I began to feel a great longing to move closer to him and take his hand and bury my head against his chest, and I wondered at myself because only moments before I had thought of marriage as a way of being free and gaining access to others.

There was no question of him taking my hand. He began to talk, telling me that I had to help him. I didn't understand what he meant; he wasn't rich like my father but he was a wealthy man all the same. Rather than naming a figure, as I'd expected, he said that like me and other girls here he too lived in a state of frustration, and that the pressure exercised by the society and its traditions was great, but this was our country and we had to put up with it, despite the immense riches which allowed us to wander about the world, to go to countries where there were trees and lakes and where I could wear a low cut dress and walk freely in the street. But was it right to take wealth from one country when your eyes and heart were set on another?

I shook my head, but as if I was telling him to be quiet. I wanted him to hold me close, or to move closer to him myself. I passed a finger over my lips which had parted in anticipation of his lips touching them, but he went on talking while my urgent desire for him to hold me and kiss me distracted me and I didn't listen to what he was saying. Eventually he asked me if I was listening and I nodded my head and tried to force myself to, despite my irritation. He reached out a hand towards my neck and I rejoiced, but then he said, 'That necklace – if your father and generations of your family before him hadn't struggled against the heat and hunger of the desert you wouldn't be wearing it now.' Trying to reassure myself, I answered, 'But you travel a lot.' 'I know,' he laughed. 'I'm just trying to explain what I'm like to you, so that you can understand me and help me – when you learn to understand this country of yours and appreciate what it means to live here.'

3

The difference between Saleh and me which had drawn me to him began to annoy me and make me on edge, and I became as unyielding as stone. Since our meetings in his sister's house, before we were married, I had been aware of it, as it became clear that we were there for different reasons: I was waiting for him to take my face in his hands and kiss me and whisper words of love and admiration in my ear; while for him the purpose of our encounters was that we should understand each other's natures so that we shouldn't repeat the mistakes of our fathers and grandfathers.

His sister only agreed grudgingly to our meetings, fearful that they would cause a scandal, whether we eventually married or not. I used to phone him constantly as well, something he was unused to, and was never going to grow used to. When I asked him why he was so short on the phone he made a joke of it and said he wasn't alone in the room; and when he asked me in turn why I so much enjoyed telephone conversations I didn't know what to reply because it was true that I loved talking on the phone, and every time our conversations seemed to be tailing off I tried to inject new life into them, even inventing bits of news to reawaken his curiosity, or provoking jealousy in him by the way I talked. I remember especially when a famous Italian designer came to make my wedding dress; this man lost patience with me because I couldn't keep appointments however hard I tried, and once, pretending to make a joke of it, he remarked that perhaps the weight of the diamonds in my watch had made it stop. The version I told Saleh later was that the designer had suggested that I shouldn't wear my diamond choker in case its sparkle distracted attention from the beauty of my breasts. Instead of being jealous, Saleh upbraided me for letting the designer speak so uninhibitedly to me. When I suggested that he was reacting this way out of jealousy he denied it and said nothing more, as if he wanted the subject to be closed.

Less than a month after our wedding I began to feel restless. The happiness and the hustle and bustle seemed to vanish upon our return to the desert, and Saleh began to get up at nine in the morning and wanted me to get up with him so that we could have breakfast together. I did it once but the following day I protested that I was tired and stayed in bed. That night Saleh didn't want us to stay up after midnight but I wouldn't sleep. He reminded me of how tired I'd been that morning, and I joked that he would make me forget that I was from a family of Draculas. Despite my efforts I never managed to get up till noon or a little afterwards, when he came back from work to have lunch. He continued to insist that I must get up in the morning and when I asked him what the urgency was, he replied, 'What about the house?' and I laughed and said sarcastically, 'What about the servants?' 'What's the use of a crew if the ship has no captain?' he returned.

On one particular evening our visitors departed early because Saleh had said a pointed farewell to them even while I was begging them to stay. Boiling with rage I went back into the room: 'How can you drive them out like that?' I shouted at him. Without looking up from his book, he answered that they were spongers, a flock of sheep moving from house to house to be fed, held in submission by the videos and funny stories. 'I thought you enjoyed yourself with them,' I said challengingly. He marked his place with a bookmark and shut the book. I found myself thinking that the division between us really was vast, not because I didn't read books but because it would never occur to me to use a bookmark. Then he said in an affectionate tone, 'Nur. Come here. I want to talk to you.' Putting an arm round me he told me he loved staying up with them once or twice a week, but said that we shouldn't use them to fill up our spare time. 'How should we spend our evenings then?' I demanded. 'With one another, or are you bored with me?' Then he added, 'With one another, or with normal people.' 'With one another?' I thought to myself. 'That means him reading or watching films that I don't like, or practising tennis or training on his exercise machines. And normal people means businessmen and embassy staff and their wives.' However hard I tried, I could never think of anything to say to their wives.

Then Saleh began asking me like a school teacher if I'd read the newspapers and whether I'd liked the books he'd brought me to read. He began urging me to continue my education and enrol in a university, or even do a correspondence course. Anything rather than wasting my time sleeping or talking to friends whom he described as unfortunate because of their lack of intelligence.

I didn't show the faintest desire to listen to what he was saying, and at midnight he went to bed, while I began pleading with a servant or a guest or a relation to stay up with me into the small hours.

These differences vanished during the holidays. He no longer said my English was awful because I'd picked it up haphazardly from foreign nannies and acquaintances, or criticized me because my only interest, according to him, was a single-minded study of the goods produced by modern industry for the consumption of the rich, such as yachts and sun beds. Instead he seemed proud of me as we moved around together in our yacht or our private plane between the chalet in Switzerland, the Paris flat and the house in a London suburb. We spent the time sailing the yacht and lying on beaches which we had almost to ourselves, and in winter wore skiing clothes, although I didn't keep up with my lessons because it was always nearly sunset by the time I was ready. Still the weather and the people and their talk and laughter aroused a mood of happiness and enjoyment in me wherever we were. I quickly forgot that I'd been annoyed with him for trying to make me learn to read the compass while the white yacht ploughed through the Mediterranean; or for urging me to learn to ski and get out in the open and move at speed over the great expanses of whiteness. As soon as the holidays ended and we returned to the desert the old resentment returned too. When I asked him why we only came close to one another on holiday he answered that he liked life without work or responsibility for a while but my problem was that I wanted it to be like that all the time; of course he traced the causes back to my upbringing, as he did with all my behaviour. His continual criticism of me, even over stupid things, surprised me more and more. I remember how upset he seemed that I didn't call back as soon as I heard that someone had called me. When I blamed the servants he said it was my fault because I didn't encourage them to tell me.

One day Sally the American, the daughter of a friend of my father's, came to the desert to attend my brother's wedding. She tried to phone me more than twenty times, and as usual I knew about some of the calls and didn't pay much attention. Then Saleh happened to answer and she was on the other end apologizing because she was leaving the next day and hadn't seen me. Looking at me angrily he told her that he'd come and pick her up straightaway, and with one more furious glance at me he was off. His behaviour didn't surprise me and although I was jealous I felt relieved that he was the same as all the rest, and wanted to get to know foreign women. Sally came back with him apologizing, as if she was quite sure that I couldn't have known about her calls. I replied coldly that Mother Kaukab didn't understand English, and Sally said in some confusion that she'd asked the servants at my parents' house – where she was staying – to make the calls.

Then she turned to talk to Saleh about the time she and I had spent together in the United States when my father had left me with her and her family and they'd taken me over most of California, from Disneyland to Universal Studios. She talked enthusiastically and seemed to have captivated Saleh, as if my dress and the way my hair was done no longer mattered. Then their conversation took off beyond the table where the three of us were sitting and away from anything that I knew about or was interested in. She began to talk about her work: she was one of the people who wrote speeches for the American president; then she switched to talking about her father's club and I pricked up my ears and thought that here was my chance to make them listen to me and look in my direction since I knew most of the internationally famous clubs. But a cloud of dullness descended on the conversation once more when I heard that the club was only for men and that their activities didn't go beyond delivering speeches. Then he asked what university she'd graduated from and when she told him the name of some university he laughed and asked if she knew Candice F. She didn't, but she'd heard of her because she was president of one of the graduate societies. He hesitated a little, put his hand on mine and said, 'With Nur's permission,' then proceeded to tell us that he'd promised to marry Candice when he'd said goodbye to her after his graduation. But as soon as he'd arrived back in the desert he'd found that he couldn't begin to imagine her wandering about the house, or sitting at his side in the car or talking in sign language to the other women; the thought of her light-coloured hair, her unrestrained way of talking without regard to time or place, seemed absurd in this setting.

Sally remarked laughing that she couldn't envisage a girl like Candice here for a moment. Saleh listened to her and he pressed my hand when I tried to draw it out from under his hand; it seemed to me that his talk of Candice was to make Sally understand that his being married to me didn't mean that he was like me, or was even meant to justify his mistake. Then he began talking again in that enthusiastic voice which perhaps meant nothing when he used it to me or to people he found in our house; contradicting her, he said, 'Sally, Candice is intelligent. She could even manage to live *here*. She might have a hard time because she'd be forced to lead a double life. Take me and Nur for example: when I came back here I found that the ideas which I'd been convinced were right when I was in the States seemed ridiculous here, like the contents of my suitcase. But I made a firm decision that Saleh who wore a white robe and sandals and tore meat apart with his fingers should also be a man of the twentieth century discussing Margaret Thatcher's politics and standing to applaud dancers in a club.' Then he turned to me and said, 'Nur wears an abaya when she's here in her country but abroad she walks around in a cocktail dress. Of course she feels hard done by, but this is where she was born.'

When we took her back to my parents' house, it was the first time I'd given someone a lift to where they wanted to go; I'd always been on the receiving end of such treatment, and only contacted people when *I* needed them. Saleh got out of the car to shake her hand, then the two of them stood for a moment looking towards me. When I made do with a desultory wave, Saleh came back to the car and got in heaving a protracted sigh. He didn't speak until I asked him what was wrong with him and then he shouted at me, 'Even the Queen dismounts to say goodbye to people.' Then he muttered, 'Sorry. You're more important than the Queen.' I found myself saying that I hadn't wanted anyone from the house to see me. He stopped the car and turned to face me: 'And what would have happened if someone had seen you? Wouldn't it have been more normal to go in and visit your family? Or are they at the round table solving the world's problems?' To himself he added, 'I don't understand your family. I don't understand the stuff they're made out of. None of them are normal.' At this point I screamed at him, 'Is all this fuss because I didn't get out and shake hands with the American woman?'

Thumping his hand down on the steering wheel, he shouted back, 'How can I make you understand that it's not a question of an isolated incident? It's to do with your view of the world, your understanding of life. Is it reasonable that Sally should be with your family for a week and you don't get in touch with her? Instead you spend you time fooling about with empty-headed women and the nannies. From what I've heard, you only had to mention somewhere in the States and Sally would take you to see it. What about the telegram she sent us when we got married, and the present that would still be in its paper if I hadn't opened it? You don't only have this careless attitude towards people – you have it towards things as well. There was that orchid that was thrown to one side in the kitchen, and died still in its cellophane paper. And the plants left to wilt in their pots. Do you know the cost of orchids even before they reach the desert! Your problem is that you weren't born into one of the ruling families.'

4

When I found out that I was pregnant, and the doctor said my feelings of nausea and tiredness were normal I told him that I couldn't stand it, as if he were the one responsible for my condition. As well as feeling sluggish and sick, I began to swell up like a sponge and became convinced that I'd never go back to my old shape. Perhaps the state I was in began to bore my visitors because I no longer had people around me every minute of the day, and I grew lonely. I found that this isolation was something I didn't have the strength to endure, and one day when I was barely awake I began to scream and shout; I tore my clothes; I bit the hands reaching out to restrain me, and then I rushed out of the house; Mother Kaukab caught up with me and contacted my mother and I called Saleh at the office and told him I wanted an abortion. The main reason I could think of was that the clothes I'd had made to wear this season were such beautiful and unusual styles that they would never be fashionable again. Although he was kind and showed some understanding of what I was suffering, he tried to convince me that I would become fulfilled as a woman if I had a child and that there were maternity clothes which were as unusual as ordinary clothes. When I gave in he began pestering me to stop smoking. My reply was that the doctor had said to me that if I stopped it would make me tense, so it was better if I didn't.

When I gave birth to my daughter, jewels were showered upon me, too bright to believe in and almost too unbearably beautiful to touch; and flowers the like of which, I was told, the desert had never seen before. The day I had the baby I said I wanted to rest and wouldn't pick her up, and the same that night, but on the following day the English nurse insisted that I should hold her so that she and I could get to know each other. After a few minutes she began to cry and I pressed the bell and gave her back to the nurse. I tried the trick of feigning sleep every time I sensed the two of them in the room until the nurse gave up in despair and took her away. When one time she came in to find me talking on the phone, she told me that she was ready to collapse because she didn't sleep day or night, and our lack of concern for the child made her angry. I told her that what made me angry was her coming in without permission, and shouted at her to go away and leave me in peace. I was especially cross because I was listening, consumed with jealousy, while a friend told me about a handsome Egyptian singer who was here, and the parties they had in the evenings, and who was chasing him and who was spending a lot of time with him. As she was talking, I pictured her still in her nightdress with no pain, her breasts not swollen as mine were, in spite of my attempts to empty them of milk. Or probably her maid was putting on her make-up for her or taking it off. I could no longer stand the sight of them, when they visited me just to show off their dresses and talk to one another, not to me, indifferent to my gasps of pain.

Saleh was no help to me during this period; he began giving me words of advice, saying that I must pick my daughter up, nurse her myself instead of giving her a bottle, and not smoke when she was in the room. I was at my most annoyed with him when he woke me up every morning as soon as he heard her voice, and brought her to our bed; I don't know why but I began blaming him for everything, even for going to his office. I began to avoid talking to him and acted as if I didn't care whether he was there or not. But instead of being prompted by my coldness to make it up with me, he no longer concerned himself with me either. He began to live his life as he chose, inviting his own friends, and even though some of them came with their wives, I refused to leave my room and sat in front of the video hour after hour. Feelings of depression and resentment towards him seethed inside me and I felt like I did when my cat escaped and hid in some inaccessible place; I'd be angry to the point of tears and stamp my feet, almost choking each time I thought of the pleasure I felt when I had her in my grasp.

When he told me one morning that he was going away I didn't answer; I turned on the video and he snatched the cigarette out of my mouth and repeated, 'I'm going away.' I lit another cigarette. 'Goodbye,' I replied. His going really did make me feel more at ease, for confrontations and displays of stubbornness were no longer daily occurrences and I found myself welcoming phone calls, and if no one come to visit me I went out visiting myself. When I was asked if I had seen Saleh on the television news, I shrugged my shoulders unconcernedly. I didn't go to see his mother as I'd promised to do and when she came to my house, I left her with my child and the nanny. As soon as Saleh came home from his trip I asked him for a letter giving me permission to go abroad with my mother. But I actually travelled with Mother Kaukab.

As usual I erased the traces of the desert as soon as the plane was in the air. I went into the toilet, and from my hand luggage took out a short sleeveless dress. I bundled up my abaya, and untied my hair and let it fall loose. Feeling some embarrassment, I returned to my seat and when Mother Kaukab gasped and reproved me, I told her that my husband didn't mind. More and more I felt that marriage meant freedom, and especially material freedom. For despite the monthly allowance which I'd continued to receive from my father I'd been in debt to a lot of people; to Nahed the Egyptian woman who sold off-the-peg clothes by all the most famous designers and had threatened to complain to my father when my account was approaching a hundred thousand; to the Syrian jewel merchant, although I'd sent Mother Kaukab to him with some jewellery I no longer liked. And I knew that I was being exploited a lot: the Lebanese woman, Madame Sandra, had demanded an exorbitant amount for designing a tree with silk leaves that had a place for a bottle of perfume at the base of each leaf; and so had Jameel who designed my room for me, and Fernando with his paintings; even Ibtisam, who was from the desert herself, had sold me a fake antique claiming that it was truly old and covered with gold leaf.

I lay stretched out, wondering whether my pleasure had reached the floor under me, for the heat of it was almost burning me. In the large hotel room the rock singer was drinking water from a bottle. His face and its features appeared small, and there was nothing handsome in him; his white body was narrow and thin as he tipped his head back, and he was uncircumcised. I pictured Mother Kaukab spitting as she described the ugliness of his thin white body and said he was like an obelisk. All the same, I'd been in a state of eager excitement ever since I'd met him in a disco and he'd danced with me for hours, ignoring the woman he'd come with.

When he reached out his hand under the table to touch me I knew that he'd stay with me that night. It had been ages since I felt this happiness mixed with anticipation, even tension, and it reached a pitch when he followed me up to my room, giving me a few minutes' start so that I could lock the door leading to Mother Kaukab's room. Once I looked like staying abroad for a long time, or rather once I'd gathered up my courage and admitted to myself that my body was the main outlet for my feelings, I'd moved to an hotel, claiming to Saleh, in the course of one of our telephone conversations, that I felt car-sick every time I travelled from our house in the country into central London.

The rock singer picked up my dress from the floor and asked who the designer was. Then he put it on and looked at himself in the mirror and admired the shoulders, which were shaped like aircraft wings; I replied in a whisper, thinking that I must see him again that night. The touch of his lips, thin and unappealing as they were, made me tremble, and his chest felt broad and strong to me, even though I could see his rib cage.

I couldn't help asking him, 'Will I see you at the disco tonight?' He was fiddling with things of mine that lay about in the room, picking up a diamond ear-ring and laying it down again on the table, and he shrugged his shoulders carelessly and said, 'I don't know.'

I brought my hair close around me. He was the first man to take hold of my hair and ask if it was real. Not believing my answer, he tugged on it and said, 'Ding dong,' as if he was ringing a church bell. 'Shall I have it cut?' I asked him.

'Is this what they have instead of crisps where you come from?' he returned, holding up an old manuscript which Saleh had given me for Christies to examine, so that they could tell him if it was authentic. I asked him about my hair again, feeling a sense of loss and trying to devise a way of seeing him that night.

'Yours is the most beautiful hair I've seen in my life,' he said, turning to me. 'When I saw you dancing, I said I want that hair.'

Feeling somehow reassured, I ventured, 'Let's go to another disco tonight.'

He didn't answer and was still holding on to the manuscript which was made of torn, shrivelled vellum. 'What does it say?' he asked. He'd sat down beside me on the bed again but seemed indifferent to my body; I hadn't covered myself up and was deliberately vaunting my naked beauty because my thoughts were all channelled towards seeing him that night, and I wanted to please him at any price. I began trying to remember some of the obscure writing which Saleh had read out to me. Before I began to tell him what I knew he stretched out his hand to me, making me sit down beside him, and rested his hand on my shoulder as if we'd been friends and lovers for a long time. I noticed his amazement growing with every word that I spoke and felt happy; I was sure that it was making me figure more vividly in his thoughts, although I was astonished at his total ignorance of my country, even of its geographical location. He got up to look for a pen and could only find my black eye pencil which he stared at in disappointment and self-mockery: 'And here I was thinking you'd use kohl like Cleopatra!' He began writing letters which looked more complicated than the ones on the manu-script. He crossed them out, rewrote them, asked me to read again, then asked me more questions; I explained, and he wrote and pondered and hummed to himself.

He was so delighted to find this rare and original material for a song that he took my face in his hands and kissed my eyes and nose and lips and chin, the beauty spot on my cheek, the downy hairs on my upper lips, then my hair and my forehead. He was carried away by his enthusiasm and bent over me whispering 'I'll reward you for this,' but I just wanted to make certain of that night. When he got up he said he'd stick a red star on the country I came from, because he had a map of the world at home and he remembered coun-tries by the women he'd met.

He left only when a smell of cardamom began to pervade the air, and Mother Kaukab tried the door. When I didn't respond she must have assumed that I was still asleep and he jumped up, hurriedly pulling on his clothes, and gathering up his papers and blowing me a kiss on the way out. I rushed to the door to ask him about the evening and he answered, 'Come to my house and I'll let you hear the song,' and told me his address. I smiled with joy at him, for my heart had sank hopelessly. When I opened the door separating me from Mother Kaukab, she asked me excitedly, 'What did you have to eat at the princess's?' I couldn't think what she meant then I remembered that I'd told her that I'd been invited to dinner with the English princess, the Queen's daughter. She sat there, asking me eager questions: 'What did you talk about? Did you have fun? What did you have to eat? What did they wear? Your dress must have been nicer than theirs! What did they say about your ear-rings?'

She wanted to know all the details so that when she went

back to the desert she could repeat it to the servants and the other women. Then she poured me a cup of coffee, remarking innocently, 'I said to myself, Nur must have switched on the radio while I was still asleep.'

When I went to his house I prepared myself for kisses, but instead, to my disappointment, he sat me down in his studio and sat at the piano, strumming and singing:

My love is from a tribe in the heart of the desert.
Her forefathers suffered the heat and the thirst.
They buried alive their baby girls
Yet took the women prisoner in battle
Preserving them to bear men-children.
Her blood must not be mixed with strange blood.
And yet my love, she loves me.

5

I returned home and set off on my travels once more. This time, like a cook who can only handle a giant ladle, I spooned out for myself enormous quantities of emotion, parties often lasting most of the night, conversation and laughter. Perhaps the fact that Saleh was always travelling and showed no interest in me also pushed me further in this direction. What I was doing could quite possibly have remained a secret, but it seems that I began to frequent places where many of my fellow countrymen also spent their evenings. I was swept up into a circle of dancers, actors, musicians and men of society from the Arab world, whose fame spread because of their beauty and wit. One of them used his charm and humour to entertain professionally: sometimes he would dress up as a dancing girl and cry, 'Your donations, gentlemen, for the Prophet's sake,' and ten-pound notes would rain down on him; or he would put on a dress, tie his hair back in a scarf and imitate a housewife doing her housework, talking irritably to the saucepans and plates. When he'd done his turn one night and the applause had died down, he announced, 'I want to thank Nur, who realized that I was an artist, not just a clown, and encouraged me to turn professional.'

It was true that I'd become addicted to his wit and thought him worthy to be ranked with the great characters of comedy, and I'd offered money to the cabaret owner to let him up on the stage. This wasn't the first time such a thing had happened, as we'd already made a third-rate dancer famous by applauding wildly and opening bottles of champagne for her until she was promoted and eventually became a top dancer in the oriental clubs of London. I sank down in my seat at the sound of my name, feeling afraid, but forgot the incident by the following day as I became involved in the details of daily life once again. I never thought about the desert except when I smelt cardamom, and then when Mother Kaukab asked me one day about going back. This made me realize that it must be time, and that I'd have to do my best to keep things going here for a bit longer. I claimed appointments with doctors and urgent shopping; and Mother Kaukab commented that she was enjoying herself, although her excursions here were limited to going to the shops with the driver, and she was even happy to go in the car if it was to visit families from our country who were in London. 'They all ask if Saleh is with you,' she told me. 'I don't say no and I don't say yes. I just nod my head.'

6

The doorbell of the flat rang early one morning (I'd moved into my father's flat by this time). Before I could close my eyes again, Mother Kaukab came in to wake me, saying that a man from our country was asking to see me and insisting on waking me up although she'd told him that I was still asleep and that I'd gone to bed late. Many thoughts came to me but I didn't guess the reason until he showed me a piece of headed paper from Saleh's office, signed by Saleh. The letter, written in a dry official tone, said that I must leave for home that morning.

I thought immediately of contacting Saleh, but changed my mind, and wondered about my family. All of them must have heard what was going on by now. I looked at the man and said, 'But I haven't finished doing all I've got to do – I've still got an appointment at the doctor's.' 'I really don't know . . .' The man's voice tailed away and he shrugged politely.

I said nothing more, and went back into my room to pack, but I was overwhelmed by a powerful sensation that I'd only just arrived from the desert and was really unpacking. The long nights of laughter had suddenly vanished, and my heart began to pound, but I shrugged my shoulders, pretending not to mind, and told myself that I was luckier than many. My cousin had opened his eyes one morning to find himself in his house in the desert, when the last thing he remembered was going to bed in a Hong Kong hotel. The papers wrote of the fantastic amounts which he'd lost in a casino in Hong Kong, and the dud cheques he'd signed. And there was a friend of my brother's who'd been put on the first plane to the desert in handcuffs after his family had discovered that he was a drug addict.

Although the man stayed in the hall I felt as if he'd bound my hands and feet and blindfolded me. A car stood waiting at the entrance to the building and he opened the door for me and stood waiting by it while the driver and another man went up to fetch my cases and bags. I didn't feel free of the oppressive weight of his presence until I'd gone aboard Saleh's private plane. Mother Kaukab turned to me and said, 'Saleh must have missed you. Yesterday he phoned three times and I told him you were having dinner with the Queen's daughter. He said hasn't she had dinner with the Queen yet, but I told him Nur's young and she wouldn't have anything to say to old women . . .' Then she went on, 'Saleh's fame and prestige have reached London.'

In circumstances roughly similar to these I'd returned from the private school in Cairo: everyone in the plane could hear my whispering and crying the whole journey and see my blood-red eyes and my abaya flying through the air, followed by shrieks of protest. The man accompanying me on that occasion had been an employee of my father's, and although I was so young I'd promised myself that I would marry with all speed. I remember that the moment my companion went to the toilet I signalled to the foreigner beside me to order me a whisky and pour it into the glass of Pepsi Cola which I already had in front of me.

All through the flight I repeated to myself that Saleh was behind all this, that he must want to divorce me, but why hadn't he said so openly? When we landed, everything seemed normal. Saleh was waiting for me and he didn't confront me then or later. The idea of his doing so was absurd anyway, not just because men had had all the rights since the time of our fathers and grandfathers, but because there was much to be feared from a confrontation: if the sounds of our voices reached beyond the house walls, I would be removed from the family's sphere of influence and denied its protection. Saleh didn't divorce me, although he hinted to me that I could ask for a divorce if I wanted to. He was fearful for his honour and self-respect in the face of my family and society. Then shortly afterwards I found out that I'd lost my passport. It was the one thing that I guarded carefully, holding on to it as if I needed it to live, like oxygen. I'd learnt its shape and colour and number by heart. It was also the one thing which I kept hidden, wrapped in a plastic bag in a metal strong-box, while I forgot about my jewels and left them lying among the lip pencils and nail varnish and creams. It wasn't in Saleh's drawer, nor in his parents' house, not even in his office drawer. I secretly enlisted one of the people who worked for my father to help me in my search, thinking that it must be in Saleh's briefcase which he carried with him from place to place, but my emissary opened the case and didn't find it.

The only way was to make it up with Saleh and get him back. But it appeared that he'd cut me out of his life, and he no longer even visited the house since I'd tried to provoke him to argue with me. Instead he began sending for Ghada to spend a few days with him whenever he returned from abroad. Each time I asked him for my passport, he stalled and said I was still his wife and he wouldn't let me travel, but I didn't give in to him and ask for a divorce. He couldn't marry a second wife because I'd made that a condition of our marriage and the sheikh had repeated it during the formal signing of the contract which Saleh had attended with my father and the rest of the men, while I and my mother and the women had waited in another reception room: 'Nur . . . stipulates that Saleh . . . will not take another wife while he is married to her, as she fears this would result in her being wrongfully treated, and she has no defect or fault which would make living with her difficult; just as the Prophet, blessings and peace be upon him, stipulated that Ali should take no other wife besides Fatima, fearing that she would be wrongfully treated.'

I didn't want a divorce until I'd found another husband, since I was still enjoying the big house, the servants, the money to spend, and my freedom, even though I was barred from the skies and bound to the expanses of the desert. The rich needed money more than the poor, not only to preserve their standard of living but to improve it, for there were a lot of rich people and great rivalry existed between them, the men, the women and even the children. I asked Mother Kaukab and her friends to look around for a suitable husband for a friend of mine. Mother Kaukab guessed what I was up to and didn't comment. In no time she produced names and descriptions of possible suitors; among them was al-Sayrafi, an old man with two front teeth made of diamonds who swore that if I accepted him my dowry would be my weight in sheets of gold, but he was fanatical in his passions and would be jealous even of the breeze; another man wanted a second wife because his first wife had grown old, and he was blessed with plenty of money and wanted to enjoy someone younger and more beautiful. 'He follows where his heart leads,' remarked Mother Kaukab, 'and God created the heart.'

'We all act in accordance with our hearts' desires,' added another woman.

But I knew that this man lived by himself with his family all in separate houses round about him!

Mother Kaukab didn't know what had happened between me and Saleh; not even my family knew, and Mother Kaukab was convinced that he was like the rest of the men here and all that was wrong was that he neglected me and enjoyed himself when he was abroad; she assumed that I wanted someone richer or more generous and made unfavourable comparisons between our house and some of the palaces, or the houses with marble walls, and her lip curled with displeasure. Once I asked her, 'What about the private plane and the yacht?' And she answered, 'I know, but real wealth is on land, not in the skies or on the seas.' In any case she thought Saleh was mean because she'd often heard him telling the servants off for not closing the packet of tea properly, or complaining when he went into the garden to inspect the newly-planted trees and found that the water had overflowed on to the gravel and washed it away. I asked her about Fadl's son who'd been divorced for some time but she said, 'He's not good enough for you. They say there's singing coming from his house and his car night and day, and you know how the sound of drums does queer things to the brain, and you'll find the Devil behind those drums and tambourines.'

With every new day that came I realized that Suha was further from my mind; and one day I found myself thinking that this day was going to go by just like the one before, and I didn't want to spend the evening by myself. I phoned my sister-in-law and she told me that the party that evening wasn't to be missed because my brother had discovered some young man in the Turkish restaurant.

That night I set off after I'd put on a dress that sparkled, and pinned up my hair with shiny pins so that I looked as if I'd come straight from Rio de Janeiro. Perhaps the smell of my perfume was very powerful because Mother Kaukab called to me from her room, 'Wearing perfume, my precious Nur, is a kind of adultery. A man smells it and his spirit is aroused.' 'If only you were right,' I thought of saying to her. I wanted to be the most attractive woman there, as I always used to be. The other women, and their clothes and jewellery and hairstyles, had walked through my imagination, and I was especially conscious of the fact that they would still be going abroad while I was dependent on my mother's taste, and magazines, and whatever the Italian designer chose to send me.

The young Turk was at the party, answering the questions that cascaded down on him from all sides. Everybody, including me, choked with laughter at the plain straightforward way he did it, especially when he told us the story of how his father was put in prison because he loved his cow. 'The moon was rising, the breeze was fresh and cool,' said the father to the judge. 'It wasn't my fault. My heart fluttered, and my cow is beautiful . . .' After a little while I grew restless and began looking at the faces around me. Old familiar faces with nothing in them that aroused my curiosity; even when it was said that the Lebanese comic had finally been granted a visa to come to the desert, I couldn't summon up any enthusiasm. I had to have a different atmosphere, different people. I asked the driver to take me to my parents' house. My mother and father were out for the evening. I sat down on the sofa and leant my head back, and the next thing I knew was my mother shaking me by the shoulders, asking me why I hadn't come that afternoon. Then she called to her maid to fetch her the big suitcase. It was full of clothes, all punk style just like I'd asked her to get me, with the right shoes and accessories and coloured hair spray. I began to try them on and stared at my face in the mirror. Not a single spot or line marred its purity, even though my nights merged into my days and I was assailed by heat and cold and lack of sleep; though pills to put me to sleep and pills to wake me up fought each other down my throat, and my body was on display to both sexes like a shirt on the washing line, in frantic motion or quiet and still, depending on which way the wind blew.

Epilogue – Suha

I marked the sixteenth of June, the date of my departure, with lipstick on the wall calendar. I was so worked up about it I couldn't concentrate on packing my cases. Would I not regret this step when faced with the security situation in Lebanon, living temporarily with my mother, the separation from Basem and the effect of this on Umar? But my tension slipped away from me when I got into the car, and Said took me along the bumpy unmade roads and the broad asphalted streets bound by high walls. I asked myself and the monotonous desert, 'Have I ever been into those houses? Do I know that woman?' Of course. Her house passed through my mind: the brass coffee jugs and those reddish brass ashtrays which had become a trademark of all the houses here. How had I been able to put up with listening to their conversation, thought of inviting them to my house, or remembered engagements with them with some interest and enthusiasm?

One afternoon after I'd decided to leave I'd been obliged to visit Ingrid, since she'd come in person to invite me. When I came out of the house hundreds of migrating birds with blue bellies and orange wings were passing overhead through the desert air then disappearing as if consumed by fire. The grass was dying in Ingrid's garden; the new crop of sunflowers was thrusting its way upwards while the seeds of the old ones were dropping and their yellow petals fading.

Ingrid was crying; she hadn't been able to buy her mother a present for Mother's Day; the prayer times had changed with the sunset and the shops were closed. Myra was sitting sadly waiting for someone to ask her what was wrong so that she could tell them about the man who'd tried to attack her while she was hanging out the washing: '. . . he had a cap embroidered with gold and silver and coloured stones, and a patterned shawl over his shoulders; he was wearing trousers and a loose mauve cotton jacket, and on his feet he wore gold sandals that turned up at the front like the ones the genie wears in *Aladdin*.' She'd struggled with him and got him off her, then rushed in locking the door behind her. He'd tried to force it and she'd dragged sofas across and piled them up against the door. She'd sat on her own refusing to open the door for hours even though she'd been able to hear the voices of her husband and daughter outside. Ingrid interrupted her saying that she'd been hoeing her garden once when she'd caught sight of a man's feet. She'd known from his sandals that he'd come to rape her. She'd reached for the garden shears before standing up to confront him, only to find that the man was Said bringing a dish of tabbouleh from me. Maryam asked if the man who threw acid at the pretty blonde Syrian girl's dress was trying to burn it so that he could see her legs or was making a religious protest.

I was far away from them, and my heart beat with fear at the prospect of staying, when I thought of how mine and Umar's passport had been returned every time Basem had sent it to get an exit visa, because the new stamps weren't ready yet; planes bringing passengers in were making the return journey empty.

The boxes and cases were ready at the door. I went up on to the roof to make sure that Umar hadn't left anything. The pigeons' houses were empty, seed scattering the ground; the dishes of water had changed colour in the air and a thick layer of dust lay on the surface of them. I stood at the roof parapet exactly as I'd always done while Umar was riding his bike. I stretched up to look at the road and Umar said, 'You always do that,' and asked me what I could see.

At that moment as I looked down I seemed to see nothing, and I felt regret building up inside me because I'd lived here for so long. So long, and yet the passing time hadn't left many traces: a few little grey and white hairs buried in the thick mass of my dark hair, a few wrinkles round my eyes and on my forehead. I compared myself to the empty cover of a once full book of cinema tickets: the leaves torn off and handed out through the ticket-office window were the times I had wasted at tea parties and coffee mornings, or bouncing around on the back seat of the car feeling chilled by the air-conditioner, then stifled when Said turned it off and the car grew fetid like a packed and airless railway carriage on a long journey; or the years I had spent revolving in a circle of people who didn't change from one day to the next as if they'd been put in a pot with a tightly-fitting lid and drew life from the steam which rose within the confines of the pot, breathing in only their own heat, while a low fire burnt underneath them.

Umar said to me, 'Your skirt's rustling. You must have some chewing gum or chocolate.'

'If only I had, darling,' and I pulled out a lot of bits of paper with addresses written on them. I tore them up into tiny pieces and dropped them on the floor. 'Why did you tear them up, Mama?'

'We're not going to see anyone from here ever again.'

'I don't understand.'

'They're addresses.'

He asked insistently, and with some heat, 'Do you mean we won't see Sitt Wafa again, or her rooster?' 'Definitely not,' I thought, but I said, smoothing his hair, 'Her family lives in Lebanon so when we go and visit them we might see her.'

Recently Sitt Wafa had begun to take the broom with her whenever she went into the garden and beat the rooster with it so that he was knocked senseless for a few minutes while she put down the seed and water and collected the eggs. At the end of the month I'd gone to settle up with her and heard her talking about the rooster: 'It's got very mean,' she was saying to a friend of hers.

'Slaughter it,' said her friend, 'and stuff it with rice and pine nuts. Bless its heart, it's huge, it might not fit in the oven!'

'No, Sitt Wafa, you mustn't!' shouted Umar.

Sitt Wafa said calmly, 'But you like to raise rabbits and birds, Umar. Why are you so angry?' Her friend responded with a slurping noise: 'Ah, rabbits! How good they are and so tender, especially the little ones. You roast them and smother them in lemon and garlic. It's a meal you won't forget.'

I got up in the morning still tired; I hadn't slept well and hadn't been in the mood for Basem's kisses because I was in a flurry of happiness mixed with tension and apprehension about the journey. I looked down at the bed; in my imagination I saw Nur climbing over the wall of my house. As we went along in the car later I stared long and hard out at the town that I would never see after today; I knew this although I'd actually agreed with Basem that Umar and I would visit him once between his visits to us in Lebanon. As if I had just arrived I noticed the walls: every house had a different wall, made of marble, cement, natural stone like the stone you see in the mountains; tiles, factory-made stones, patterned and plain; there was a wall that took the form of a series of arches, so high that only the water storage tank was visible. New young branches were tied to one wall to give them support; electricity cables and telephone cables dangled down from another: no building, nothing in this place, was ever completely finished. The walls were high; the newer they were, the higher they seemed to be. Some were beautiful colours, as if they belonged to calm and tranquil houses. I remarked to Basem, 'Do you know what annoyed me most here?' 'Nur? Suzanne? Tamr?' 'No. The walls, constricting everybody.'

I saw a few men in the street and a single woman in black; I thought of a certain type of black beetle that makes a tapping noise with her body all day and all night when she feels the need to mate.

I sat down on a seat in the airport lounge. Umar was carrying the canary around in its cage, blithely explaining everything to it. I sighed contentedly, feeling as if I'd left all my thoughts and tensions behind outside the airport building and was a normal person again, no longer split between Suha of the desert and Suha the city dweller. I sat with one leg crossed over the other, watching the people and waiting for the flight announcement. For the first time here I was dressed as I wanted to be, in clashing colours that suited my figure and face and personality. I wore a single long earring and a blouse without a bra under it, and my hair was loose on my shoulders.

Said was the one I was going to miss. Although I'd been on edge and unsmiling that morning, he'd been his normal self, assuring Umar that he'd see him again soon. Umar asked him innocently, 'D'you want to come to Beirut? D'you know Granny's house?' Laughing and adjusting his head cloth, Said said, 'Don't worry, Umar. I'll get off at Beirut airport and sniff you out like a dog. I'll ask for the house where Umar and Madame Suha live and I'll find you.' Then he told us about the time he'd gone to Cairo and tried to find an Egyptian engineer who'd been a customer in the restaurant: 'A very important engineer. A nice man. And he lived somewhere in Cairo.' It was a long story: he'd asked a newspaper seller who'd directed him to the owner of a launderette whose son was working as a teacher in the desert. Said had gone off to the launderette and had eventually met up with the engineer who'd been delighted, unable to believe that he'd made his way through the millions of people in Cairo to find him. Proudly Said ended his tale: 'He took me to the pyramids and the zoo and to see a lady and her sisters who were belly dancers and singers.'

I don't know why I thought suddenly of Maaz's wife, Fatima, and the way she used to smile as she stood holding the coffee jug, waiting to refill her husband's cup and Suzanne's.

I craned my neck, looking down. I could see the high walls around the town protecting it from the horrors of the sand. The desert came into view, looking as it had done the first time I saw it: sand and palm trees, a way of life that revolved around human beings without possessions or skills, who had to rely on their imaginations to contrive a way of making their hearts beat faster or even to keep them at a normal pace; to search unaided for a hidden gleam of light, and to live with two seasons a year instead of four.